Black Religion / Womanist Thought / Social Justice
Series Editors Dwight N. Hopkins and Linda E. Thomas
Published by Palgrave Macmillan

*"How Long This Road": Race, Religion, and the Legacy of C. Eric Lincoln*
Edited by Alton B. Pollard, III and Love Henry Whelchel, Jr.

*African American Humanist Principles: Living and Thinking Like the Children of Nimrod*
By Anthony B. Pinn

*White Theology: Outing Supremacy in Modernity*
By James W. Perkinson

*The Myth of Ham in Nineteenth-Century American Christianity: Race, Heathens, and the People of God*
By Sylvester Johnson

*Loving the Body: Black Religious Studies and the Erotic*
Edited by Anthony B. Pinn and Dwight N. Hopkins

*Transformative Pastoral Leadership in the Black Church*
By Jeffery L. Tribble, Sr.

*Shamanism, Racism, and Hip Hop Culture: Essays on White Supremacy and Black Subversion*
By James W. Perkinson

*Women, Ethics, and Inequality in U.S. Healthcare: "To Count Among the Living"*
By Aana Marie Vigen

*Black Theology in Transatlantic Dialogue: Inside Looking Out, Outside Looking In*
By Anthony G. Reddie

*Womanist Ethics and the Cultural Production of Evil*
By Emilie M. Townes

*Whiteness and Morality: Pursuing Racial Justice through Reparations and Sovereignty*
By Jennifer Harvey

*Black Theology and Pedagogy*
By Noel Leo Erskine

*The Theology of Martin Luther King, Jr. and Desmond Mpilo Tutu*
By Johnny B. Hill

*Conceptions of God, Freedom, and Ethics in African American and Jewish Theology*
By Kurt Buhring

*Black Theology and Pedagogy*
By Noel Leo Erskine

*The Origins of Black Humanism in America: Reverend Ethelred Brown and the Unitarian Church*
By Juan M. Floyd-Thomas

*Black Religion and the Imagination of Matter in the Atlantic World*
By James A. Noel

*Uncovering Womanism: Ethical Themes and Values in Alice Walker's Non-Fiction Work*
By Melanie Harris

*Representations of Homosexuality: Black Liberation Theology and Cultural Criticism*
By Roger A. Sneed

*Bible Witness in Black Churches*
By Garth Kasimu Baker-Fletcher

*The Tragic Vision of African American Religion*
By Matthew V. Johnson

# Bible Witness in Black Churches

*Garth Kasimu Baker-Fletcher*



palgrave
macmillan

BIBLE WITNESS IN BLACK CHURCHES


First published in 2009 by
PALGRAVE MACMILLAN®
in the United States—a division of St. Martin's Press LLC,
175 Fifth Avenue, New York, NY 10010.

Where this book is distributed in the UK, Europe and the rest of the world, this is by Palgrave Macmillan, a division of Macmillan Publishers Limited, registered in England, company number 785998, of Houndmills, Basingstoke, Hampshire RG21 6XS.

Palgrave Macmillan is the global academic imprint of the above companies and has companies and representatives throughout the world.

Palgrave® and Macmillan® are registered trademarks in the United States, the United Kingdom, Europe and other countries.

ISBN: 978–0–230–61771–1

Library of Congress Cataloging-in-Publication Data

Baker-Fletcher, Garth, 1955–
Bible witness in Black churches / Garth Kasimu Baker-Fletcher.
p. cm.—(Black religion, womanist thought, social justice)
Includes bibliographical references and index.
ISBN 0–230–61771–9
1. African Americans—Religion. 2. Black theology. 3. Bible—Evidences, authority, etc. I. Title.

BR563.N4B34 2009
220.089'96073—dc22 2008054698

A catalogue record of the book is available from the British Library.

Design by Newgen Imaging Systems (P) Ltd., Chennai, India.

First edition: August 2009

10 9 8 7 6 5 4 3 2 1

Printed in the United States of America.

# Contents

# Preface

My basic self-naming is that I am a "Christian." That means that I identify myself with those basic and fundamental theological affirmations of following God through the grace and love of Jesus of Nazareth known as Jesus Christ. Jesus is "Christ" for me in: the positive affirmation of believing that Jesus of Nazareth lived a full life in liberating, prophetic witness, and service to Yahweh. I believe that He died in a Crucifixion on a crude instrument of Roman torture known as "the Cross." That "on the third day" He arose from death to eternal life in the uniquely Christian assertion that death itself could not conquer the divine life-force within Jesus. That this same Jesus "ascended to Heaven" and sits on God's "right hand." That Jesus will return in what Christians refer to as "the Second Coming." I believe in the ongoing presence of Jesus Christ through the gift of God known as the Holy Spirit. I believe that Christians witness to all the above in a community known as the Church. Such a belief echoes the basic theological themes of the Nicene Creed, with the evangelical interest in emphasizing the signal importance of a personal loving encounter between the individual soul with Jesus Christ. As such I consider myself to be "orthodox," and in the broad "center" of various Christian affirmations.

I am also a "Black Liberation Theologian." That is to say, as an African/Jamaican American; I write theology from a self-consciously "black" perspective. As a "black" person I cannot help but do my theology from the increasingly complex and conflict-ridden social location that accompany being "black." Yet my perspective of blackness ought be seen as a barrier to understanding, or a hopelessly parochial stance. That is to say, as well, that I am inviting all readers (perhaps especially persons of other ethnicities and cultures) to look at the Bible and theology from the perspective of an African/Jamaican. Such a perspective uplifts the messages of Jesus as consonant with a "liberation" perspective Further, having espoused such a stance, I dare to demand social justice and legal-economic-political action commensurate with liberation for all people—especially those fighting: racism, sexism, homophobia, classism, and able-ism.

Finally, I write from the perspective of being a physically challenged American. Although I can stand and take a few steps, I am profoundly dependent on a wheelchair. Such a dependency compels me to look at the world through the eyes of a "half" person, with most adults being taller than I am taken from the perspective of riding a wheelchair. When I am in a crowd of individuals, I am swallowed up. Further, as I wheel myself around, I find barriers to my access in sidewalks, improperly constructed "handicapped" ramps, and most irritatingly, doors. At the same time I realize that the United States of America is far advanced in its progress toward making accessibility for all those who are handicapped (mentally and physically) in comparison to most other countries. I cannot visit Nigeria, though it has been my fondest desire. My wife informed me, after returning from a conference there that even Korea is not set up to be "handicap-friendly."

Writing a book about the Bible in relationship to any kind of theology is a risky business. It is fraught with the ironies of having a limited knowledge of biblical languages, and yet wanting to make some important points based on those original languages. As a trained ethicist I found myself just wishing that I could write about biblical ethics and be done with it. But the project called me to do more. As it is I find myself still wanting to put some more original language "meat" on the table.

I am not a trained historical-critic; but I am trained in theology and ethics. My approach in *Bible Witness in Black Churches* is based on what has been described by Stephen L. Harris as literary criticism.[1] Such an approach seeks to tease out theological and ethical themes present in the text, not the kind of tracing and analysis of pertinent, prewritten oral traditions, redactions, and pericopes used by historical critics. I try to use some historical-critical insights where appropriate, but my knowledge in that field is limited.

So do I have something to say? Yes. It is a burning desire to see the fires of intense study of the Bible to be inwardly integrated into the theological and ethical task of Black Theology. It is an inward fire that I have come to by having a personal experience of the presence of the Holy Spirit that could be called "the baptism of the Holy Spirit." Such an experience has also been called "Pentecostal." I share that experience with my Pentecostal brothers and sisters, yet I do not share the commonly right-wing political presuppositions of such churches.

Politically I sit in that broad center known as being a "moderate." I agree with the personal and "conservative family values" shared widely in Republican circles, yet shy away from the kind of divisive "single-issue" politics practiced by Republicans. I embrace the wide range of social justice imperatives, environmental and ecological concerns; and liberal attitudes toward gender and cultural differences that Democrats espouse. As a result, I tend to vote Democrat more than Republican, but am not adverse to choosing various individual conservative politicians.

One cannot write a book alone. First I give honor to pastors in my life. Those include the late Emil Brunner, former pastor of Macedonia Baptist Church, Dallas Texas. I learned from Rev. Brunner that one cannot leave an encounter with the Bible as the living Word of God the same as one was before such an encounter. Rev. Tyrone Gordon of St. Luke's "Community" Methodist Church in Dallas helped to provide excellent pastoral and worship leadership in my life. Pastor Gordon's gift as the head leader in worship involves his enormous skills both of singing and preaching. Former pastor of St. Luke, Zan Holmes has served an inspiration to this work. Pastor Holmes' complete commitment to the advancement of the poor, as well as his social justice leadership has pointed me in one of the primary directions taken in this book. Finally, Pastor Gerald Brooks of Grace Outreach Center in Plano invites me to grow every Sunday in his thought-provoking, soul-changing sermons. Always seeking to grow, Pastor Brooks challenges his congregation to grow with him in knowledge of the Bible.

I thank my colleague Theo Walker for his patient early reading of this text. His pointed questions had me refocus and clarify this book's purpose. I also thank Catherine Keller for her extensive and sensitive criticism of the final text, something that helped me to make final adjustments. I thank Dwight Hopkins for his friendship, feedback, and encouragement about this project as being worthy of publication. Dwight's wife Linda Thomas is an important conversation partner and a valued friend.

I thank all of my students whose insights have informed and shaped how I present the text as an aid to teaching. These students include all those taking various Bible courses, including Survey of the Bible, Survey of the New Testament, Survey of the Old Testament, and Biblical Theology.

Finally, and most important, I thank my beloved wife, Karen Baker-Fletcher, for always pushing me to do better and be better. A well-known, and highly respected theologian herself, Karen has never looked at me in a condescending manner. Our mutual love and her belief in me are truly the most outstanding features of our relationship. We have been blessed with three children: Kristen (21); Kenneth (16), and Desiree (13) have been incredibly patient with their father as he dove into long sessions of concentration necessary to write the book.

# Introduction

## Having Church: Black Folks Doing Church

Black theology, like most other theologies, has been produced for students in theological schools and ministerial students as though they are preparing to become future theological scholars. While this might be laudable in an ideal world, in the world of real church folks whose everyday spiritual concerns revolve around questions about whether or not God really hears them, whether their prayers are for naught, and why bad things happen to good people, such theologizing seems rather disconnected from reality. To be more precise, we Black theologians and ethicists tend to write theology for each other. We tend to ask each others' questions, read each others' books, and frame each others' concerns, and act as if those of the wider church audience are of inferior concern. This is puzzling because we have gained our language world from that same church world. Such words as "mystery," "being," "spirit," "love," and "holy" arise from the everyday rhetoric, liturgies, and prayers of church folks. It would not be such an exaggeration to stress that it is that very same quaint church that is the lifeblood, essence, and source of holiness, sacrality, and spiritual authority that inspires theologians to struggle to articulate even as many of us also seek to displace its importance as the center of serious theological enterprise. Why has this happened? Perhaps it is because theologians, Black or otherwise, are torn between two loves—being considered credible as academics in the academy in university-based theological schools, and/or being considered faithful to faith communities. Many books have given detailed analysis of the historical displacement of theological education from denominational seminaries into free-standing and university-based divinity or theological schools. Tracing that historical trajectory is not my task Rather, I hope to outline a pathway to reclaiming theology's high road of both faithfulness and credibility. If we are to really reclaim the vitality, resourcefulness, and truthfulness that ought to be the hallmark of our theologizing, then it seems to me that we need to return to the source of our theological meaning-making. The upshot of this return to the source of our theological meaning-making in Black churches is that regular church folks may find renewed interest in Black theology's radical liberation claims once they know that Black theology is more upfront in its claims to biblically centered theological claims.

For me, the journey of returning to the source of life-giving spiritual meaning has been a rediscovery of the power of the Bible as most authoritative text for Christians. Without becoming a "Bible-thumper" or a fundamentalist, by becoming a Bible teacher in a college, I began a journey of awakening to some very basic facts of church folks existence. Most church folks come to church wanting to learn something more about what the Bible has to say about God. Most church folks use the Bible as their basic textbook to teach them about their faith. For us highly trained, theologically sophisticated, seminary educated individuals, we tend to write theology as if one cannot possibly appreciate theology without including elaborate sections on the Classical Fathers (Augustine, Tertullian, Aquinas, Calvin, Luther, Anselm, etc.); discussion of doctrines; balanced presentation of the "marks of the church;" and various other indications that we are truly "educated." These sections are important indications to us of not only how we think to ourselves and each other, but also as signifiers of our belonging as members in the theological in-group. Unfortunately, when we include such extended indicators, they are signs to regular church folks that they are not members, and that we are probably "showing-off!" Not only that, such *indicators* are also occasions for yawning, mental "time-outs," day-dreaming, and other kinds of psychological escapes for church folk (according to my cousin Karia Bunting). For church folks, the real stuff of a sermon, or a teaching is when the teacher or preacher gets to the biblical information. Thus *Bible Witness in Black Churches*, while recognizing that many biblical scholars have very real concerns about the dangers of biblical literalism and bibliolatry, stands up as a kind of a return to the Bible, and a warning that all theologians ought to pay more attention to interpreting the theological material resident in their Bibles. The challenge is "How do we write credible, rigorous, and faithful theology that includes the Bible in a fundamental way?"

The moment most contemporary theologians hear that church folks want more Bible theology, they panic, and rightfully so. We were not taught to think as biblical theologians in seminaries and theological schools. We were systematically underdeveloped to even consider the *primary text* of Christian historical tradition. Think about that for a moment, and let it burn into your consciousness...We ought to all write heated letters to our alma maters. No theological school or seminary worth its salt (and here I am referring mostly to those called "liberal," "moderate," and "mainstream") should consider its curriculum complete if it has taught its students how to do theology only outside of the parameters of the Bible! This is not to say that the classical theologians—Aquinas, Augustine—or Tillich, Barth, or feminist, liberationists, deconstructionists, or whoever else do not also have a role in the constructive task of theologizing. No. Rather, it means that a complete theological education must include a rigorous incorporation of biblical texts—their historical framework, and complex witness. Theologians do not need to become biblical scholars, just comfortable with doing theology with the Bible. Conservative theologians have always known this, but so-called mainstream and liberal theologians have ceded that territory to Bible scholars, the same scholars, by the way, who often have no training or interest in theology. So the theologians cannot interpret the Bible, and the biblical scholars cannot do theology! The blind leading the blind, and regular church folks either laughing at both, or rightfully ignoring both as what they perceive to be educated fools. We must not rest easy with our educational theological apartheid that has shaped us into stilted creatures whose knowledge is a thousand miles high, and one inch deep. It is up to us, the so-called educated to insist that if we are to educate the next generation of ministers, theologians, and religious scholars, then we must insist upon maintaining rigorous biblical interpretation meaningful to the church as well as contemporary postmodern critical theoretical rhetorical structures that speak to the academy.

*Bible Witness in Black Churches* is necessarily partial and incomplete. Such a church-directed theology is, nevertheless, postmodern in its recognition of the contextual nature of the author, the multidimensional and plurivocality of our daily cultural contacts, and our Western inescapable complicity with oppression even as we attempt to redress its multiple historical legacies. Thus I write from the self-critical perspective of an African American Christian male, one who has experienced life as both oppressed as Black, physically challenged, who has had to work through some mental hardships as well; while at the same time I have had the advantages of being an oppressor as being an American, a male, a person who has exercised sexist behaviors and must continue to monitor himself constantly. I believe myself to be a person that is a sinner saved by grace. To embrace such a biblical understanding of sin and grace is to demarcate a confessional position both theologically and psychologically. It is to embrace the traditional Protestant position set forth by Martin Luther when he cried out that salvation came by faith, grace, and Scripture "only" ("Sola fide, sola gratia, sola Scriptura).[1] Psychologically, the fact that I remain a *sinner* reminds me of my faults, my weaknesses, and those areas in my personality that I recognize are still not examples of what I would want others to take as Jesus Christ's life living inside of me. Thus, to remember that I remain a "sinner" keeps me cognizant of my need for grace, of the unfinished work still yet to done on me.

As the sinner saved by grace that I am I also locate myself in the midst of a modest, ongoing community of faith consisting of African American, Jamaican, and various other Caribbean emigrants who have looked to God through Jesus Christ as their Savior for healthy, life-giving, soul-nurturing faith. My soul has been shaped by the mocha-brown hands, curry-spiced scents, cocoanut sweetness of a Jamaican American immigrant community, mixed with the soul-food grits and cornbread mother-wit virtues that flowed from the matrix of African American folk culture. These two cultures were in active dialogue with the dominant European American apple pie, Uncle Sam, love-it-or-leave-it white, unfortunately, racist and supremacist cultural more. This tricultural stew was radically altered in my lifetime by the profoundly inspirational witness of the civil rights movement under the prophetic leadership of the Reverend Dr. Martin Luther King, Jr., whose life and death served as profound benchmarks to my generation on its march toward opening up the United States of America to greater expressions of its self-understanding as the world's best bastion of freedom. Through Dr. King the United States has begun to more fully realize a more complete possibility of what "American Dream" might actually be for all of its citizens, and of the almost eschatological implications of that Dream.

## Standing on the Shoulders of Those Gone Before

In the African American community we celebrate the achievements of our ancestors, their legacies, and how we are connected to their work with the phrase, "We stand on the shoulders of those who have gone before us." I begin with the typology of Randall Bailey concerning various interpretive stances toward the Bible. To Bailey's typology I add another interpretive stance—that of black evangelicals such as Ronald C. Potter and William Bentley. They provide an evangelical understanding of the role of the Bible in Black theology. Black evangelicals hold to a strictly biblical worldview, starting point, inerrancy, and so forth; while Black theologians *sitz im leben* (situation in life) begins in the Black community.

After expanding upon Bailey's typology I move to explore pioneering Black heologian James Cone, and his students James Evans, Jr., and Dwight Hopkins. They have all written about the important historical role of the Bible from the period of slavery to today. All three write extensively about the intentional misinterpretation of the Bible of white slave masters specifically regarding all Africans being the actual progeny of the biblical "Ham," and therefore "cursed" forever—thus rightly cast in chains and kept as slaves in perpetuity. Cone, Evans, and Hopkins carefully set these ideas in stark contrast to the liberating manner in which the slaves employed the Bible themselves. African American slaves inserted themselves into the biblical narratives, resonating with the Exodus deliverance, Daniel in the lion's den, the symbolism of David and Goliath, and a whole host of other stories. Far from being simple-minded biblical literalists, their interpretations revealed a grasp of the finer details of hermeneutics, as well as a keen sense of applied symbolic understanding. *Bible Witness* believes that we ought to fully appreciate the rich background our ancestors laid out for us.

The first chapter ends with several biblical interpretive points that I have chosen as representative of a kind of "progressive evangelical" biblical stance. It includes such positions as the Bible as an Absolute Norm of all other norms, and even the Wesleyan Quadrilateral.

## Chapter 2: The Word

Chapter 2 examines the African American claims about reading the Bible as "God's Word." My approach notes that if there is a Word contained in the Bible then it is resident in those very same problematic words, thus the biblical theologian must help reveal a pathway between scholar's questions and the hunger for meaning in the church folks.

Chapter 2 explores the Gospel of John as a biblical launching pad for careful analysis of the Bible. Elaborating a Black progressive evangelical theology of Scripture, I provide a preliminary answer to the question of Black Church folks. They want to know "What is God's Word for us?" To ask what God's "Word" is to probe behind those problematic translated words contained in the written text of the Bible that form the basis of our theologies. It is the "Word of God," what in Hebrew is called the "davar"—the living event, the enlivening moment, happening.. The "Word" is never merely just an articulation of syllables, but an embodiment of an event that changes something and everything else that occurs afterward. The "Word" is translated and proclaimed through the witness of the Bible.

## Chapter 3: Translated Witness

Chapters 3,4, and 5 elaborate the primary understanding of Word in *Bible Witness in Black Churches* as being that of "witness." To be a "witness" to something is to give one's testimony, to attest to having seen or having been in the presence of something; whether in the legal sense of courtroom testimony, or merely as a matter of declaring information. .

Fundamentally we must ask the question "In what way is translation the truth?" The Bible was written in a wide variety of ancient languages, primarily Hebrew and Greek, but small sections were also preserved in Aramaic and other dialects. Biblical scholars spend years learning these arcane languages. As a theologian and ethicist I rely on their expertise to sort through what various translations mean. Our job as readers is to carefully tease out possible translations, compare the meanings, and cross-reference their applied meanings. Since we operate with the theological premise that God is acting in these words, we seek out in what ways the Divine is speaking to us. When we ask this question, sometimes various translations shock us with multiple meanings in the very same verse.

## Chapter 4: Proclaimed Witness

Chapter 4 further unfolds the theology of witness in Black churches one step further by calling it a "proclaimed witness." Proclamation is the heart of Black Church practice, and might even be considered one of the most important historic contributions of African American Christians.

In chapter 4 I explore various meanings of the term "Gospel." In what ways was Paul's "Gospel" the same, or different from that of Jesus? Are there anti-Christian "gospels" present in our society?

We shall listen to the humanist "gospel" proclaimed by Professor Anthony Pinn.

Proclamation is the initiation of a process, the first step. This first step is a projection that comes from the preacher moving out to the hearers. Proclamation is the Word carried out on vocal waves from the preacher's inspired voice to the listener's ears, and it is either received, rejected, or temporarily housed but lost after a while because there is no proper follow-through. God expects that the Word will reap more than is sown. This theological principle of abundance becomes the basis for the fifth chapter.

## Chapter 5: Empowered Witness

Chapters 5, as well as 6, and 7 describe how the Bible speaks to regular church folks as the authentic voice of a liberated vision. In chapter 5 the specific aspect of liberation theology in *Bible Witness* may be understood as an "empowered witness." In constructing an African American progressive evangelical theology it is necessary to show how it is also a "liberation" theology. Liberation theology has reminded us that God speaks to us in words and acts that deliver us from social, economic, and political bondage. This deliverance is part of a twofold process of deliverance and empowerment .They are the left and right hands of genuine, biblically based liberation. *Bible Witness in Black Churches* focuses particularly on empowerment.

Empowerment, historically, has included "coming to voice" according to Black feminist Anna Julia Cooper in *A Singing Something* back at the turn of the twentieth century. Then, as even today, this meant affirming the *imago dei* as the concrete basis for African Americans knowing that we are Children of God.

From the starting point of the *imago dei* what may be called the empowering witness moves to uplift the sanctity of marriage and family. Such a view of sanctity is neither "Left" nor "Right" but attempts to provide a mediating position between extremes. The sanctity of family is founded on the presupposition that the members of the family are created in the *imago dei*. It is also a social space for unity. The family as space of unity functions as an occasion for celebrating unity rather than division in biblical Christianity.

An empowering witness in *Bible Witness* means that Black church folks are intentionally taught to reclaim that thick, religious-cultural heritage of resistance nurtured in Black Churches from slavery times.

It is a strategy of Christian resistance and liberation that Gayraud Wilmore articulates in *Black Religion and Radicalism*.[2] This tradition theologically identifies Jesus as a co-sufferer with all those who suffer injustice. It is also a strategy that embraces all instances of the outpouring of the Holy Spirit, including times where physical manifestations of Spirit-possession, dancing, and praise predominate.

## Chapter 6: Proverbs: Mother Wit and Da Streetz

The Book of Proverbs provides a wealth of wisdom resources for all peoples, especially oppressed Black folk. Proverbs, like much of the rest of the Bible, has become a part of the common vernacular of the African American community.

A proverb-filled life is a life lived in *chokmah* (Hebrew for "wisdom") or *Sophia* (Greek for "wisdom"). It is a virtuous life. To be virtuous, in the biblical sense, is to live in righteousness (following the commandments of *Torah*, and thus receiving the blessings of God Almighty). Righteousness, in the fullest Hebrew sense of the term, does not mean self-righteousness or pride, but joyful obedience to God's *Torah*, a walking the paths of uprightness.[3]

In *Bible Witness in Black Churches* I contextualize the claims of *chokmah* to the African American (in particular) and broader contemporary milieu with a metaphor taken from the medical profession. Here I use a rather shocking, or certainly uncomfortable, metaphor. It is my fervent belief that developing an extensive biblical vocabulary taken from Proverbs can act as spiritual maggots cleansing the spiritual gangrene that infects our body politic.

Gangrene is an ages-old miserable experience, often from wounding in battle, and surprisingly enough, the most ancient "cure" is still used—the controlled application of living maggots to literally eat away the dead tissue (!) We postmodern people cringe at the thought of both gangrene and maggots, but both still exist and have a role and place even in our highly technological world.

What do these two ugly terms mean to me in relationship to the Bible, Black theology, and having a *Bible Witness*? They refer to theological-ethical, and political "state of the world" that we inhabit right now, and to how we as Christians must address what is wrong. My family lost a first cousin, Andre Fletcher, in the tragic collapse of the World Trade Center Tower on September 9, 2001. He died because he was a firefighter, turning off gas valves in the subbasement of building number one. Little did we know that President George

W. Bush would use the 9/11 tragedy as a springboard for unleashing policies of militaristic strategies that have led to obvious ploys for American global domination. When your own family has suffered a loss then the "need" for revenge can sometimes make one understand such a need at a national level. Such a national need may become an occasion for irony and paradox.

For African Americans, rappers have described the condition of our communities from the perspective of what they call "Da Streetz." This chapter explores that gritty viewpoint. Another way of putting it is to call their reflections an example of "Mother Wit." Proverbs has contributed to the store of Mother Wit resident in Black communities. In the hip-hop generation, Mother Wit has passed on through the medium of rap music. Church folks do not readily recognize the Mother Wit and scriptural references and allusions in secular rappers. Slowly, in order to reach a new generation, Christians have developed their own version of Gospel Rap that is taking root in Black churches. Gospel rap speaks to what rappers call "Da Streetz." Da streetz informs the lyrics of Cross Movement, or L. G. Wise, T. Bone, Rough Riders, Christsyde, and several other excellent Gospel rappers. Gospel rappers are reaching out to "Da Streetz" in proverbial wisdom.

## Chapter 7: Vision

African Americans, like all Americans, require a new vision that is positive and life- affirming. Chapter 7 of *Bible Witness* is rooted in a biblical, theological hope that springs from an appreciation of what the Bible teaches us about human nature, and God's vision. The book ends with an analysis of the Bible's most systematically theological book, Romans, and an interpretation of some of the visions of the Apocalypse of the Book of Revelation.

In order to keep the focus on a biblical exposition of vision, *Bible Witness* confines its articulation of the Apocalypse of the Revelation to the letters addressed to the seven churches . In these letters that which might be called an *eschatological vision* found in the first three chapters of Revelation are as follows.

When we combine the theological richness of Romans and the eschatological vision of Revelation's letters, we gain something of what each one of the letters end with when they state that believers are meant to be overcomers. As overcomers, African American church folks have been serving God and each other through slavery, Jim Crow, lynching, beatings, good times, hard loving, and low-down dirty blues. Through faithfulness and faithlessness the community still has marched on. Does "the ole ship of Zion" still sail on Sunday morning? My answer is "Yes!" The Bible has provided the still, quiet, yet powerful anointing that transforms us all. Black theology and the Bible need to have an even deeper conversation with each other. In such a time as ours the stakes are high that we may yet envision a new church that surpasses the very solid history of "the ole ship of Zion." I believe that church folks can still rise to new heights.

# 1

# Standing on the Shoulders of Those Gone Before

In the African American community we celebrate the achievements of our ancestors, their legacies, and how we are connected to their work with the phrase, "We stand on the shoulders of those who have gone before us." Like a sculpture that is slowly crafted together, piece by piece, so are the achievements and legacies of our memories, our pasts, of who and what we are. Without waxing philosophical, perhaps it is something of a universal truth to say that none of us can birth an idea alone, nor nurture a school of thought without the support of many others, and so the fact that we "stand on each other's shoulders" is a representation of the ongoing-ness of the generations. *Bible Witness in Black Churches* reveals that Black folks have been about the business of spinning tales, stories, and sermons that relied upon the Bible in unique ways for a long time, and that Black Church intellectuals have long and varied traditions interpreting how the Bible ought to be used.

On one side of that variety are the pioneering Black theologians of James Cone and his students. On the other side of that variety are the Black evangelicals like Ronald Potter and Tom Skinner. For our purposes, standing in front of them are biblical scholars like Cain Hope Felder, Renita Weems, Robert Bennett, and Vincent Wimbush.[1] All of these various theologians and biblical scholars have done the groundwork on the Bible and theology with and for church folks! They are recognized persons to church folks because they are committed to the church, and have not divorced themselves from the life of the church. For them the Bible is not a set of abstract philosophical principles, or lectures, but a living vibrant Text, requiring careful, exacting exegesis. While dedicated to the scholarly task, they are faithful, faith-filled workers, and worthy of admiration.

## African American Biblical Scholars

In a 1995 article, Randall Bailey lamented that there were only 45 persons who held doctorates in biblical fields, a situation that Bailey characterized as a "crisis."[2] While it is clear that there are probably more than 45 persons now, it is also widely discussed by African American religious scholars and professors that patterns of opportunities for advancement, education, and encouragement have not been opening, but closing.[3] This kind of atmosphere is particularly disturbing for those attempting to complete a doctorate in a biblical studies degree in either Old or New Testament because such an advanced degree is probably the most difficult, arduous, and praiseworthy of degrees to attain. Such a doctorate requires facility in (at least) nine languages, including Hebrew, Greek, Aramaic, Ugaritic, Akkadian, Sumerian, Coptic, Arabic, and Latin. It usually takes people at least seven, and sometimes as much as ten, years to complete. It is the piece de resistance, the highest of the highest degrees in the field of religion in the current academic field of religious studies, and African Americans are not typically encouraged or supported to enter or to compete in the rather elite guild. I am not exaggerating when I say that we theologians and ethicists tend to look on with awe and admiration at those biblical scholars!

Bailey helpfully delineates four types of biblical research that he has discerned in African American biblical scholars. These types are

1. African Presence in the Bible;
2. Response to White Supremacist Interpretations;
3. Cultural-Historicist;
4. Ideological Criticism;
5. Upon the recommendation of Karia Bunting I will add a fifth type, Evangelical and Conservative Worldviews.

The African Presence type argues "We were there, Recognize!"[4] It has a range of intensity from conservative advocates who see everyone in the Bible as African, except the Philistines and Graeco-Romans, to more recent moderates who are asking "So what?" Charles B. Copher, Professor Emeritus of Old Testament at the Interdenominational Theological Center, is considered the modern-day parent of this type, according to Randall Bailey.[5] His pioneering research into Black presence "served as a major corrective to heretofore normative views of whites and the Bible," by treating the text as a reliable historical text of African lineage. In Genesis 10:6–8 (the "Table of Nations" the famous sons of Ham, such as Put and Canaan who became Egypt), who being Black secured a Black presence in the Bible.[6] What is fascinating about this kind of exegesis is that it takes the same fundamental historical starting point that racist exegetes always have done in the past. The change is that it turns the starting point upside down and gives it a positive spin, noting that this Table of Nation insures, rather than condemns, African presence in the Bible. Copher also went further, noting that there were Cushites living in Mesopotamia or Asia, as well as in ancient Egypt, thus challenging notions of where Blacks could exist.[7] Robert Bennett of Episcopal Divinity School and Cain Hope Felder have both built upon the foundation that Copher so carefully wrought.[8]

From the viewpoint of biblical interpretation, or hermeneutics, I would call this kind of type a hermeneutics of reappropriation. Bailey finds several problems with the conservative and extreme forms of this type, noting that it is a classist form of argument since it exalts Black people as being the progeny of kings and queens, paying little attention to the Exodus 1–14 account of Pharaonic oppression.[9] This leads us to the modern moderates who are asking the question, "So what?"

Bailey notes that Clarice Martin has broached this question in her work on the Ethiopian Eunuch in Acts 8 in which Eurocentric scholarship has usually focused on the identity of the person as a Jew rather than as an African. Martin reveals that the eunuch's identity as an Ethiopian is important as an African for the fulfillment of the command of the Resurrected Lord to the disciples in Acts 1:8c, where "the gospel is to be preached from Jerusalem to the ends of the earth." Martin interprets the ancient understanding of "ends of the earth" to point to Ethiopia.[10] Abraham Smith dedicates a literary critical analysis to the first 12 chapters of Acts to show that the literary patterns in these chapters would be disrupted if this Ethiopian unit were to be omitted (something that is inferred by some radically Eurocentric biblical scholars!). Smith goes on to cement the importance of the Ethiopic passage as what he termed a validator[11] to sanction the gospel. Randall Bailey considers his own work as part of this corrective, moderating literary critical understanding of African presence in the Bible, looking specifically at the poetic passages in the books of prophets and wisdom. He noted that Eurocentric scholarship tends to "de-Africanize the text by arguing for the elimination of African presence,"[12] but then he also notes that arguing for identification of African presence is only the first part of the task. Bailey wants the reader to pay attention to how the Africans in the textual passage were used, so he developed a fivefold schema of interpretive analysis: (1) the farthest place to the south, (2) strong military political and military might, (3) economic wealth, (4) wisdom, and (5) standard of valuation. Bailey then took these five schema and explored their functions and variables in the Pentateuch and historical books of the Hebrew canon as a way of overturning white supremacist interpretations of "viewing all Africans in the [biblical] narratives as slaves" by providing new interpretations of plot and character development within a scholarly analysis of biblical narratives.[13]

Bailey goes on to cite two important New Testament scholars, Brian Blount of Princeton Theological Seminary, and Boykin Saunders of Virginia Union University who have utilized rhetorical criticism of the gospel pericope concerning Simon the Cyrenian to "explore the ways in which this character functioned as an outsider who filled the role of disciple."[14] Blount pressed forward the notion that through a "literary presentation of the character" of Simon the Cyrenian the reader is intended to gain "an understanding of the true nature of discipleship."[15] Saunders builds on Blount's argument, using historical-critical resources, citing African/ Egyptian early sources that treat these citation of Simon, and finally, examining the import of Simon's character as an African. For Saunders, Simon's "national and ethnic identification was central to the intention of the writer of the unit."[16]

For *Bible Witness in Black Churches* the hard work of biblical scholars in a hermeneutic of reappropriation is welcome because it reclaims a proper balance of true African presence in the Bible. It is important for African Americans to know that Africans really were in the Bible, bearing the Cross of Jesus, suffering with and for Him. It is important to know that Moses, Zipporah, Jesus were Afro-Asiatic-Jews. It is also essential for African Americans to reappropriate the knowledge that the entire so-called area of the "Middle East" as part of a land bridge between the continents of Africa and Asia. Those are facts twisted by racism and long traditions of white supremacy, something we shall continue addressing in the next section. However, like all peoples, we have not been perfect, sinless people. If Africans were in Mesopotamia, as Copher argues, and there are indications that they were,[17] then we were a part of that crowd that both gave birth to Abram and Sarai in Ur, and were the practitioners of all manner of vice and evil in the twin cities of Sodom and Gomorrah. If Africans were Egyptians, then they were part of that crowd that both designed the magnificent Sphinx, and cruelly oppressed Hebrew slaves for hundreds of years. To complicate things even further, if Africans were part of that "mixed multitude" that escaped with the Hebrew slaves during the Exodus, then they choose to be part of the oppressed Hebrews who were on their way toward freedom (Exodus 12:38f.). We, as Africans, had glorious Pharaohs, and oppressive ones, great leaders, and narrow-minded ones; sinful ancestors, and ones that we can learn from. Moses and Zipporah most likely were "Black" by modern standards, but so was the Pharaoh Rameses who oppressed the Hebrew slaves so that Moses and Aaron cried out, "Let my people go!" Jesus, by modern-day standards, might surely have had "dreadlocks" (an African-centric hairstyle certainly), and His coloring may have categorized Him in American standards as "African American," or at least, "colored." One thing is certain, we know that Hollywood representations of Him have yet to present Jesus "colored" the way He probably was, in the mocha-tones still seen in Ashkenazi Jews of Israel right now. So it seems to me that skin color, and what persons since the 1700s have called race, did not mean the same things to the ancient world than they meant to us in our modern terminology. *Bible Witness in Black Churches* can utilize a hermeneutics of reappropriation as a double-edged sword, revealing both the falseness of white supremacist readings of race backwards into the Bible as well as the attempt to rewrite ourselves into a fake, glorious African biblical past tense.

## Responses to White Supremacist Interpretations

This type specifically delineates the long tradition of racism and white supremacy that has suffused Eurocentric biblical interpretations. Charles Copher is again the modern leader of this tradition, according to Randall Bailey, tracing anti-Black rhetoric even in rabbinic exegesis of the Talmud and Midrashim, particularly in their racialized interpretation of the so-called curse of Ham.[18] Copher's research demonstrated how such exegesis was utilized initially by medieval commentators, and then later on by Enlightenment and even post-Enlightenment hermeneutics. Copher's coup de grace to his research is the revelation that modern historical-critical interpretation, even those used in the annotations included in the NRSV, have built upon these same supremacist assumptions.[19]

Two of the foremost proponents of this kind of research according to Bailey are Cain Hope Felder and Clarice Martin. Felder's *Troubling Biblical Waters* is one of the most well-known, and groundbreaking texts in African American biblical research even today.[20] It is at this point, however, that my reading of Felder departs from Bailey's. Bailey interprets Felder as arguing against the white supremacist process of oppressive ideological interpretations he calls "sacralization," where these ideologies are raised into a "sacred premise," and "secularization," which is a concurrent process to "sacralization" wherein "powerful biblical motifs for justice are watered down."[21] I think that Bailey oversimplifies what in Felder is a complex conceptuality. Felder himself describes sacralization as "the transposing of an ideological concept into a tenet of religious faith (or a theological justification) in order to serve the vested interest of a particular ethnic/racial group."[22] Secularization is even more complex. It is not merely a watering down of biblical motifs of justice; but for Felder is the "weakening of a powerful religious concept under the weighty influence of…'secular' (i.e., socio-political and ideological) pressures," wherein Felder sees that "ideas are wrenched from their original religious moorings due to the weighty influence of nationalistic ideologies and cultural understandings."[23] Usage of the adjectives "pressure," "weighty," and the verb "wrenched" imply that there is a tremendously active and I dare say violent ideological process that Felder means when he describes secularization. Thus the twofold dynamic of sacralization-secularization reveals Felder's strong ideological criticism of white supremacist knowledge, and how it denudes the sacred and religious quality of the biblical narrative itself.

Bailey finds that Clarice Martin, in addition to challenging white supremacist readings, challenges African American patriarchal readings. To put it another way, she challenges the ways in which Black Church[24] folks can be open and "progressive" on justice issues concerning race, but not on issues of gender equality.[25] Church folks need to join African American women in finding ways to see the Bible as a text of liberation rather than a text of repression and domination, at least in regard toward women-church folk, which is the way it has been used by some preachers and churches. As this book unfolds we shall be saying a great deal more about this subject, particularly from my viewpoint as a male who is conscious of his victories and struggles in this area.

## Cultural-Historicist

Bailey notes that the cultural-historicist approach to biblical research opens up African American readings of the Bible to ways of integrating questions of how the Bible has been read and interpreted by African Americans throughout our historical struggles here in the so-called New World. Although Bailey mentions several biblical scholars, I will focus on three that he uplifts as representative: Vincent Wimbush, Renita Weems, and Brian Blount.

Bailey turns to Vincent Wimbush, a leading New Testament scholar in the nation who has taught both at Union Theological Seminary and Claremont, and has provided an "interpretative history" of African American readings of the Bible.[26] He notes that each "reading," while representing a period in the history of African Americans, the readings themselves are not strictly chronological, for there is overlap, melding, and integration between one successive period and the next.[27] Wimbush proceeds to outline what he discerns as five readings of the Bible in African American history: (1) First "Reading"—Rejection, Suspicion, and Awe of "Book Religion" (Beginning of African Experience in the New World); (2) Second "Reading"—Transformation of "Book Religion" into Slave Religion (Beginning of Mass Conversions in the Eighteenth Century); (3) Third "Reading"—Establishment of Canon and Hermeneutical Principle (Beginning of Independent Church Movements in the Nineteenth Century); (4) Fourth "Reading"—Esoteric and Elitist Hermeneutical Principles and Texts (Early Twentieth Century to the Present); (5) Fifth "Reading"—Fundamentalism (Late Twentieth Century).[28] Each "reading" is worth a short discussion. Wimbush notes that when Africans came as newly enslaved, conquered human beings to the New World, they encountered the Bible as the Holy Book of their conquerors. The Bible "functioned as an image-reflector, as a road-map to nation-building...provided the Europeans justification to think of themselves as a 'biblical nation,' as God's people called to conquer and convert the New World to God's way as they interpreted it."[29] Needless to say, the Africans rejected both the view of the Europeans, and the Bible itself, holding it with a mixture of suspicion and awe. As people from oral religious cultures, they were fundamentally suspicious of this "Book religion" culture that had conquered them, and yet, on the other hand, "It did not take them long to associate the Book of 'Book religion' with power."[30] Because of their awe for the "Book" soon some found ways to begin to learn how to read it.

In the second "reading" African American slaves were surrounded by the religious ethos of the mass conversion evangelical fervor of eighteenth-century America. In that time both European Americans and African Americans found themselves responding to evangelical preaching, "the emphasis on conversion experience as the sign of God's acceptance of the worth of the individual," and the importance of personal testimony of one's faith.[31] Most importantly for the interpretation of the Bible, African Americans took with utmost seriousness the principle of biblical reading from their European evangelical fellow Christians—that is:

> Each person had the freedom of interpretation of the Bible...Africans learned that that they, too, could read "the Book" freely. They could read certain parts and ignore others. They could and did articulate their interpretations in their own way—in songs, prayers, sermons, testimonies, and addresses.[32]

The underlying hermeneutical principle that guided this "reading" of the Bible for African Americans was the guidance of the Holy Spirit. They believed that everyone had the Holy Spirit, including African Americans, and that the Holy Spirit "guided" them to those parts of the Hebrew Bible that dealt with the ancient Hebrews escaping from bondage, and the eighth-century prophets denouncing injustice and proclaiming social justice, and to those New Testament texts about the compassion, passion, and resurrection of Jesus.[33] Wimbush calls this the "foundation for what can be seen as an emerging 'canon.'"[34] Since most people use the word "canon" only in regard to the strict boundaries of the biblical books, this usage of the word outside of those parameters is probably jarring, but I believe that Wimbush uses it in a functional sense. He means the concrete functional texts that Black Church folks actually used in the Bible over and over again during that time in their common worship. Wimbush himself calls it the "pragmatic" readings that aided the slaves in strategies for survival, liberation, amelioration, and relative accommodation to existence and the limited opportunities they had as enslaved human beings.[35]

This "canon" included spirituals like "Go Down, Moses," "Were You There?" and "Sometimes I Feel Like a Motherless Child." Such spirituals and other songs employed a hermeneutic of "playfulness" and "looseness" toward the Bible that engaged the stories of the Bible, seized the imagination of the slaves, interpreted the stories in light of their situation, often veiling their reinterpreted meanings in light of veiled social criticism. These "veiled social criticisms" enabled the slaves to make indirect social critique in the form of worship, praise, and song—or what has been called by mother wit "Hitting a Straight Lick with a Crooked Stick."[36]

The third "reading" was the establishment of the "Canon" and a Hermeneutical Principle during the beginnings of the Independent

Church Movements in the nineteenth century. In this "reading" we find African Americans beginning to form their own independent denominational bodies. In addition, a corpus of sermonic literature is developing in which certain themes can begin to be traced. What is particularly significant for Wimbush is that Black preachers are also Black freedom fighters, and that they describe the African American social situation in biblical terms and language, thus using the Bible as a language world.[37]

Bailey finds that Wimbush also discerned an important biblical, ethical, and hermeneutical principle that African Americans uplifted as the heart and soul of genuine Christianity. Wimbush uses the Latin term—locus classicus—or "most important place, most important point" to describe this verse, Galatians 3:28: There is neither Jew nor Greek, there is neither bond nor free, there is neither male nor female: for ye are all one in Christ Jesus. Ironically, this verse became the hermeneutical principle, foundation of canon, and ethic, simultaneously with the rise in separatist denominationalism in America!

Galatians 3:28 nevertheless lies at the heart of the third "reading," a reading Wimbush characterizes as prophetic apology. The prophetic apology makes use of the Bible "in order to make self-assertive claims against a racist America that claimed to be a biblical nation…for the realization of the principles of inclusion, equality, and kinship that they understood the Bible to mandate."[38] Thus the mandates of the Bible are seen as coterminus with the ideals of America, ideals that racism eviscerates, undercuts, and has forever held the country back from honoring and fulfilling. Thus African Americans utilize the prophetic apology as a biblical means of calling America to fulfill its biblical calling to oneness; to "the realization of the biblical principles of universalism, equality, and the kinship of all humanity."[39]

What I think is fascinating about Wimbush's understanding of the prophetic apology here is that he interprets it as African American's profound desire to be integrated into American society. While being "critical, polemical, and race- and culture-conscious reading of the Bible" it nevertheless reflected a deeply held longing "to enter the mainstream of American society."[40]

This desire to be integrated into American society directly clashed with the fourth "reading" of the Bible in which there developed exclusivist tendencies in interpreting the Bible; esoteric knowledge of Scriptures wherein one had absolute knowledge and exclusive possession of that knowledge (or of other holy books "or previously apocryphal parts of the Bible").[41] Wimbush even uses a special term for their usage of sacred texts, calling it bibliomancy "the reading of holy books for the purpose of solving personal problems or in order to effect some wonder from which one can benefit."[42] I would equate bibliomancy with a magical usage of the biblical text, although Wimbush is careful to note that he sees this usage in the fourth "reading" only as a "tendency," rather than as the only way the Bible was read.

The groups that are included in this fourth "reading" have usually been pejoratively labeled as "sects" by mainstream church folks. They include Black Muslims, Black Jews, African Orthodox, the Garvey Movement, the Holiness/Pentecostal Movement, reverend Ike's Church, and the Science of Living Institute.[43] Wimbush reminds the reader that all African American churches have been called sects by social-scientific researchers because of their derivative, nondominant, and reactive status in a dominant society. Their "radical psychic stance" toward dominant society have enabled some of these groups, paradoxically, to break down barriers of separation and enabled the creation of new, egalitarian, and cosmopolitan visions of faith-centered communities.[44] Thus, while overtly rejecting the American dream, they have often generated new visions of universalism.

The fifth and final "reading" of the Bible by African Americans is the most troubling for Professor Wimbush—fundamentalism. He views fundamentalism as the encroachment of a white intellectual theological problem into Black Christianity, by un-thinking Black Church folk. The rise of the fundamentalist movement came as an attempt by European Americans to wrest back meaning from the increasingly destructive undermining of authority that had accompanied the rapid advance of historical consciousness in universities, seminaries, and particularly biblical studies. Reading the Bible as "an ancient document" rather than a sacred text undermined its authority for the founders of fundamentalism, so they deemed it necessary "to provide a way for common folk to read the Bible that would keep the old world intact, and at the same time speak to some of the difficulties that the new breed of scholars had pointed out."[45] This led to a reading of Scripture called dispensationalist that secured the "fundamentals" of the faith against the depredations of the "modernists." African American involvement in fundamentalist Bible schools, academies, seminaries, and so forth has occurred only in recent decades. Wimbush believes that it is precisely the attempt to interpret Scripture "without respect for the historical experiences of persons of African descent in this country" that radically demarcates, and separates this "reading" from any other kind of "reading."[46] As a result, Wimbush believes that persons who follow this kind of "reading" set aside African American cultural considerations as secondary, or unnecessary to proper Scriptural interpretation. We shall examine this interpretation from an insiders viewpoint later in this chapter. Needless to say, she will challenge Wimbush's interpretation of fundamentalist/conservative readings of Scripture from an African American perspective.

Bailey then turns to Renita Weems who takes on the fascinating quandary of how Black women have continued to find in reading the Bible throughout our history despite its usage as a tool of oppression.[47] Weems insists that marginalized and oppressed women find in the Bible a credible portrait of themselves, and follow it not out of "a lack of sophistication or a slavish devotion to the Bible" alone that has no basis in the lived reality of their lives.[48] As is true for Wimbush's analysis, Weems applies a thick and richly textured analysis to answer her question.

First she examines the socio-cultural location of African American women in relationship to the larger American history in order to see how the Bible was read as an "authoritative" text (What kind? By whom?). The second part of her analysis looks into the various texts found the Bible that African American women gave voice and value in light of their gender and socio-cultural situation.[49]

The very first point that Weems establishes is that it has only been within the past one hundred years that large numbers of African Americans have been able to read. Illiteracy was the standard because in slavery it was forbidden to read.[50] Since the one "required" piece of literature made available to slaves was the Bible, communicated in public readings and sermons and interpreted by a slave master hermeneutics, slaves learned the content of the Bible. Reems notes that whether we might consider the content to have been distorted by the slave master's justification of his system ("servants, be subject to your masters with all fear: not only to the good and gentle, but also to the forward. For this is thankworthy, if a man for conscience toward God endure grief suffer wrongfully..." 1 Peter 2:18–19), the slaves laid claim to the biblical materials with their own powers of listening and memory.[51] In much the same way as Wimbush's "second reading," Weems speaks about how the slaves began a hermeneutical strategy of interpretation wherein they learned biblical passages in their aural culture, repeating and interpreting them in accordance with their strategic needs for resistance and liberation.[52] Weems thus drew the interesting conclusion that Black women's reading of the biblical text was first dependent upon their pretext, a pretext of enslavement wherein women of color sought to find hope and meaning in a text that was held out as congenial only if it meant that they would remain enslaved.[53] Here for Weems there is a large something Black women did that was unexpected. Black women recognized, first, that their outlook played a central role in the "how," the "why," and the "what" of reading of the Bible. Second, the very experience of oppression forced marginalized and oppressed African American women to retain the right to resist any and every thing within the culture and even within the Bible itself that was "obnoxious or antagonistic to one's innate sense of identity and to one's basic instincts for survival."[54] Thus Weems makes the radical claim that oppression gave African American women a critical lens whereby to interpret everything they heard as "authoritative," including passages of Scripture. Weems notes that they learned to "hear" the "Word of God" with critical ears, and to approach the reading of the Bible with "extreme caution."[55] Such a radical "hearing," and "reading" of the Bible enabled them to do radical biblical exegesis long before the rise of twentieth-century biblical scholarship!

Having said all of the above, Weems nevertheless asserts the historical truth that African American women have found in many portions of the Bible provisions for existential insight into their own dilemmas; and that it reflects the values and advocates the norms that they aspire to live by.[56] Despite all the multiple and complex processes that must be factored into how African American women read the Bible—factors that include whether their voices as women are repressed or not, or whether the Bible is a "male text" in a "male voice,"[57] they continue to read it as their own. They have found "substantial passages" in the Bible where the following world is depicted:

> ...the oppressed are liberated, the last become first, the humbled are exalted, the despised are preferred, those rejected are welcomed, the long-suffering are rewarded, the dis-possessed are re-possessed, and the arrogant are prostrated. And these are the passages, for the oppressed readers, that stand at the center of the biblical message, and thereby, serve as a vital norm for biblical faith.[58]

Weems notes how the complex relationship between the mistress Sarah and the Egyptian slave Hagar have mirrored African American women's experiences with dominant women here in America.[59] Such biblical stories have helped Black women throughout their sojourn here in America to embrace the Bible as a text that made it possible to see themselves and articulate their own stories. African American women even developed reading strategies that enabled them to see in the Bible a partner for resistance to dehumanization, and an active place that enabled self-value and self-worth.

Princeton Theological Seminary's Brian Blount's strategy for reading the Bible, Bailey notes, also involved a turn to the historical basis of a slave hermeneutics.[60] Sounding very much like both Wimbush and Weems, Blount speaks about how African American slaves reconfigured the evidence presented to them in sermons from white preachers taken from the Bible. As they heard about Moses and the Exodus story, the slaves, according to Blount, so identified themselves with the ancient Hebrews, that they reconfigured the reading of the Bible "in light of their space," the space of enslaved people.[61] As white preachers spoke "figuratively" about Moses and the "law of liberty," the slaves took it literally. The slaves politicized the Gospel because, "Their faith in the reality of Israel's story was also the foundation for their hope that their own story would end similarly."[62] In agreement with Jacquelyn Grant, Blount notes that the slave hermeneutic was not merely a rejection of the white preacher's sermon, but "an internal critique of the Bible."[63] The slaves were officially "illiterate," yet this did not mean that their perception of the New Testament (or Old) was not authoritative. Rather, for Blount, this meant that the slave hermeneutic acted as a filter through which they interpreted every biblical passage that they heard, and they reconfigured, incorporated, or if necessary, discarded passages according to their slave experiences and perspectives.[64] Having stated this, Blount praised this kind of biblical reading as being highly participatory, and interactive. The slaves were most assuredly not passive recipients of the biblical words, but actively sifted through the possible meanings and valences of meanings of the words that they heard, and repeated them in their own prayer, praise, and worship meetings away from the oversight of the slave masters.

To further Blount's critical analysis, African American slaves used a lens of liberation when they heard the biblical material, and the central figure they were looking for was the "Jesus event."[65] Their hearing, sifting, and appropriating of the Bible was ethical—based on an "event ethics" that was "structured around the event of Jesus' life, death, and resurrection."[66] Specifically, Blount gives an example of an "event ethics" with Jesus proclaiming the coming Kingdom of God in the Gospel of Mark 1:15:

> The time is fulfilled, and the kingdom of God has come near; repent, and believe in the good news. (NRSV)

What is the "event" that Jesus was proclaiming? According to Blount, the slaves interpreted this, and other passages like this as a revelation of the potent sweeping force of God's power breaking into history, and that just like God did it in Palestine in the first century, God would do it for them.[67]

What can we say then about Wimbush, Weems, and Blount? All three may be said to take very seriously the notion of space. As Dussel notes, one's spatial location does effect "what one sees, or at least how one sees."[68] Space truly is the "communal and/or personal lens that influences how we read through the event lens that provides a sense of constancy for the New Testament's moral reasoning."[69] None of these three authors believes that space determines our reading of the Bible, in the sense that social, cultural, and historical factors are the only factor in determining how we read the Bible. Rather, they present a complex, layered, and textured picture of the ways in which the un-lettered and "primitive" community of African American slaves nevertheless developed an aggressive and interactive manner of reading the Bible. Blount calls it reading "in front of the text," in order to "recognize the text for what it really was: the words first century human writers employed in their attempt to convey the Word of the eternal God."[70] Without ever studying in seminaries, these slaves became "the first biblical critics in North America"[71] because their hunger for the righteousness and power of God was so overwhelming, and their need so strong.

## Ideological Criticism

Randall Bailey's final type of academic biblical research is ideological criticism. This kind of approach to the Bible radically questions the various ideological factors that are played out in the verses without any challenge or criticism. The most vocal challenge has come from womanist scholars such as Renita Weems and Clarice Martin to what they interpret as the unquestioned gender biases in various Haustafeln (Household Codes) in the Pauline Epistles (Colossians 3:18–4:1; Ephesians 5:21–6:9; and I Peter 2:18–3:17). Clarice Martin, for example, takes apart the sexist assumptions behind influential male theologian Charles Ryrie when he insists that the biblical injunction that the subordination of wives to their husbands is not an interim ethic but "constitutes an interminable norm, meant for all times," as part of some kind of eternal "order."[72] Then Martin goes on to note how Jarena Lee, historical AME (African Methodist

Episcopal) preacher in the nineteenth century, noted her equality of calling before God as a preacher because (1) "nothing is impossible with God;" and (2) "the Savior died for the woman as well as the man."[73] For those called women of God in Black Churches there was tremendous ambivalence about their "propriety," even as Black people actively resisted those areas of the Haustafeln that called on slaves to be obedient and submissive slaves.

I believe Bailey would affirm that Martin asks why there was such ambivalence resident in African American church folks. Her answer is twofold. First, African Americans exhibited a dominant attitude of resistance and liberation in their biblical hermeneutics. They took as their paradigm Exodus 14 in which God was the God of Moses, the God who liberates.[74] At the same time, there was a second, countervailing factor that African Americans uncritically had accepted. This second factor, according to Martin, was the patriarchal model of male control and supremacy typical of Eurocentric, Western, Protestant tradition.[75] In other words, because the patriarchal norms of the dominant society were mirrored in African American society, biblical statements about women's "place" were read literally, without question as well. For the womanist ideological biblical critique, this patriarchal kind of reading of the Bible "inhibits the advancement of women in the socio-political and ecclesiastical spheres."[76] within African American communities.

## Evangelical and Conservative Worldviews

Black Evangelicals Ronald C. Potter and William Bentley provide an evangelical understanding of the role of the Bible in Black theology. According to Potter while God has always been the epistemological starting point of theology for white evangelical theology, Black evangelical theology rightly holds that God "uses the human/social context to reveal himself," and thus theology's proper starting point must be dialectical—divine and human. God "reveals himself to his people... it is indeed God, who is doing the revealing and not merely human projections."[77] In order to properly discern the revelation of God, humanity requires a biblical norm, "... grounded primarily in the witness of Holy Scripture"; because without the biblical norm, "all God-talk drops to the level of humanism and anthropology."[78] William Bentley carefully documents the historical reason why Black evangelicals have adhered so closely to a strong biblical norm before and during their radicalization in the Black theology movement. He pointed out that they had been heavily influenced by the Schofield Bible, the Bible School movement, the Dallas Theological Seminary faculty, and most notably "Lewis Sperry Chafer theology." His interpretation of the rigors of this type of biblical theology stated that it regarded both the Black and White mainstream churches as "apostate"[!][79] As leader of the National Black Evangelical Association during the inception of Black theology, Bentley found himself leading the group past their former theological leanings toward an exciting time of developing a "holistic liberation" theology that included elements of traditional evangelical theology with the liberation message. A recent graduate of Dallas Theological Seminary Karia Bunting explains Black evangelical theology as having a separate *sitz im leben*[80] than Black theology since Black evangelicals hold to a strictly biblical worldview, starting point, inerrancy, and so forth; while for Black theologians, their *sitz im leben* begins in the Black community. Nevertheless both theologies are in utter agreement that the Bible can and must be applied to spiritual, economic, social, and political needs of the Black community in an uplifting way. She suggests that it would be advantageous for the two sides to agree to disagree on Black theology. She suggests that it would be advantageous for the two sides to agree to disagree on their starting points since they have "arrived" together anyway.[81]

Of great interest to me was the hermeneutic Bunting and other African American Dallas Seminary students employed to sift through their education. Conservative Black Christians take much more seriously the biblical *Sitz im Leben* in seeking to maintain the Bible's pristine integrity as the "bottom-line" for reading the Bible. They also eagerly learned the ancient biblical languages of Hebrew and Greek; but radically parted company with their fellow European American students about the possibilities of the Bible's social justice valences. Often European American students drew a strict wall of separation between so-called political matters, and matters they considered "spiritual" or pertaining to the "Word" in the Bible. For evangelical and conservative African American students, the Bible spoke to both the spiritual and social-political matters. Further, for Bunting the biblical worldview stands on its own as a witness for justice, (Amos 4–5; Micah 5; Matthew 25:31–46) without need for a liberationist hermeneutic or clarification. In other words, the biblical call for "liberation" arises from a thorough, faithful, and competent reading of various biblical texts particularly in the *Torah* (the Hebrew Law); the *Nevi'im* (the Prophets); and the Gospel (Luke 4, Matthew 25, etc.). There is a real trust in such a hermeneutic that the Bible calls us to acts of compassion, social responsibility, justice, and love within our communities without labeling ourselves "liberationists." What is most valuable in such a reading is that we read the Bible as curious, spiritually and intellectually hungry Christians who humbly urge themselves to remember the challenge to be led by the Holy Spirit.

Having lived on "both sides of the track," hermeneutically speaking, as an avowed liberationist *and* an evangelical/charismatic Christian, valid criticisms can arise against such a hermeneutic as Bunting's. To the liberationist who employs a "hermeneutic of suspicion"—deeply questioning the socio-political, gender, and class interests of the authors of the biblical texts—the kind of "faith" offered by those like Bunting seems naive or even cliché. Conservative readers concerned with issues of liberation, however, have every duty to raise concerns about what could be considered the corrosive effects of the "hermeneutic of suspicion" on reading the Bible as the central document of Christian faith! Such a suspicious hermeneutic is "corrosive" because it, while intending to be academically rigorous, actually degrades faith by belittling its necessity for a so-called true reading of the Bible. The challenge that an evangelical hermeneutic presents is in what ways is it possible to read the Bible as a book in which God is actually "speaking" to us if we have already prejudged it to be "untrustworthy" or "suspicious" because of the "interests" and "motivations" of the human authors God used? I do not believe that radical liberals or radical liberationist biblical scholars have ever answered the above challenge with answers that make any faithful, credible, and Spirit-inspired sense to regular church folks!

## James Cone and His Students

Pioneering Black Theologian James Cone, and his students James Evans, Jr., and Dwight Hopkins have all explored the important historical role of the Bible from slavery times until the contemporary context in their theologies. James Cone stresses the importance of the Bible as a unique and fundamental text of liberation,[82] while Evans speaks of the Bible in a somewhat broader sense as a text for "Outsiders."[83] Hopkins, developing an argument that resonates with postmodern sensibilities about the constitution of power, uplifts the liberating power of the written word in reconstituting dismembered African selves.[84] All three write extensively about the intentional misinterpretation of the Bible of white slave masters specifically regarding all Africans being the actual progeny of the biblical "Ham," and therefore "cursed" forever—thus rightly cast in chains and kept as slaves in perpetuity. Cone, Evans, and Hopkins carefully set these ideas in stark contrast to the liberating manner in which the slaves employed the Bible themselves. African American slaves insert themselves into the biblical narratives, resonating with the Exodus deliverance, Daniel in the lion's den, the symbolism of David and Goliath, and a whole host of other stories. Far from being simple-minded biblical literalists, their interpretations revealed a grasp of the finer details of hermeneutics, as well as a keen sense of applied symbolic understanding. *Bible Witness in Black Churches* believes that we ought to fully appreciate the rich background our ancestors laid out for us.

James Cone, from the very beginning of his systematic presentation of Black theology in *A Black Theology of Liberation*, stated that "Black theology is a biblical theology."[85] Cone, in true Barthian fashion, makes sure that he differentiates the Bible as a witness and source from Jesus Christ, stating

> the Bible is not the revelation of God; only Jesus is. But it is an indispensable witness to God's revelation and is thus a primary source for Christian thinking about God.[86]

When Cone moves on to articulate his view of revelation, he again turns to the biblical view as being the liberation view. He notes that within a biblical view of revelation history is the arena in which God acts, and through which God's will (which for Cone is "political emancipation") is enacted.[87]

Cone even defines Christian love in biblical terms, noting that the "divine-human fellowship" is to be understood by "what God does for humankind and not what humankind does for itself or for God."[88] To the surprise of many unfamiliar with Cone's writings, he even approvingly quotes the entire Scripture of John 3:16!

Nevertheless, while Cone's theological writings are shot through with biblical references, his theological interpretation of the Bible bends toward a liberationist reading. He states, on the one hand, that the "love of God is the heart of the Christian gospel," and quotes I John 4:6, 16 "God is love."[89] On the other hand, Cone works to make connections between the historical Jewish Jesus, and the proclaimed Christ Cone calls the Oppressed One. A tantalizing section reveals how radically Cone makes the connection between the historical Jesus and the Oppressed One:

> Unless the contemporary oppressed know that the kerygmatic Christ is the real Jesus . . . , to the extent that he was completely identified with

> the oppressed of his earthly ministry, they cannot know that their liberation is a continuation of his work.[90]

The above sentence is of paramount importance to understanding Cone's biblical theology of liberation. For Cone, however, the point of reading the Bible is to understand God, and in understanding God through the revelation of Jesus Christ is to act as liberators in the world. One cannot say that one is a Christian without acting as a liberator.

For James Evans the Bible is the "primary conduit," but not the "exclusive" one, of how the community can understand the "being and acts" of God.[91] Evans, like the Cultural-Historicist Model, develops a rich and historically informed analysis of how African Americans have read the Bible from slavery to the present. In particular, Evans notes that African Americans had to wrest their own meaning from the cultural imperialism of that presented to them by their white slave masters. The slaves "constructed their own scriptural world on three pillars of biblical interpretation":[92] (1) The Exodus Model (Exodus 1:12; 2:1–3:22ff.; 14–15:1ff.) in which the Exodus experience was "the archetypal myth" and "the lens through which the Bible was read";[93] (2) Hebrew Model—a variant of the Exodus Model prevalent with the slaves of the South "most clearly seen in the sacred music of the African slaves" like "Go Down, Moses," and "On Mary, Don't You Weep."[94] Evans sees in the Hebrew people and the slaves parallel stories so that the African American people put themselves into the biblical narrative with complete identification;[95] (3) Ethiopic Model (Psalms 68:31; I Kings 10:1–10, 13; Song of Solomon 1:5) in which African Americans identified with the Ethiopians, Egyptians, and Cushites mentioned in the Bible; and that sometimes even fanned nationalistic yearnings, and desires for cultural integrity.[96]

Of unique interest in Evans' interpretation of African Americans' reading of the Bible is his incorporation of Robert Alter's proposal to read the Bible as a "paradoxical activity of deception and unmasking."[97] This paradoxical activity creates in the text a positive kind of indeterminacy of meaning, so that no one can grasp onto the "right meaning" for themselves, and control it for themselves, or their group.

In the real world social groups use biblical interpretation in another kind of power dialectic, according to Frank Kermode—that of proclamation and concealment.[98] This kind of reading creates a "bivocality of the text";[99] one, for the "insiders," and one for the "outsiders." One voice conveys a "secret sense of the text" that is "conventional" and an institutionally acceptable interpretation. Evans states that this voice "seeks to destroy or banish all indeterminacy within the text."[100] Meanwhile, the other voice is the outsider's voice, and sees the indeterminacy of the text as evidence of its divine origin in the experience of the holy."[101] The "outsiders" are those whose "station" and place in life make their interpretation of the Bible illegitimate according to the "insiders"; and yet it is precisely for this reason that they are ideal candidates to be explorers of the actual "secret sense of the text" in all of its exciting, divine indeterminacy.[102] Evans has no trouble reveling in the language of indeterminacy, seeing in it the kind of Divine openness, and rediscovery of meaning key to vitality for an oppressed people.

African Americans were, and are the ultimate "Outsiders," according to Evans. He posits four points for the Bible in Black systematic theology. First, "social location conditions biblical location."[103] African American status as "outsiders" in the United States has positioned us to be uniquely sensitive to "misuses of Scripture," and "more open to its critical dimension."[104] Second. "what the Bible means takes priority over what the Bible meant." By this Evans does not put down historical-critical scholarship, or the "reconstruction of the Sitz im Leben."[105] Rather, he places the priority of Black theology on the "living community of faith." Third, "Story takes priority over text." This is a rather awkward way of saying that since slavery times the oral culture of African Americans has based our faith heritage on the telling and retelling of stories rather than on the criticism of a written text. For African Americans "text serves story and not the other way around."[106] Fourth, African American theologians must grant canonical authority to a liberating hermeneutic of Scripture in the experience of African American people. The point is that the liberating hermeneutic is what enabled Black Christians to discern what they would receive and transmit to one another as Gospel. It was this liberating hermeneutic that enabled African American Christians to decide what was true or false, alien or meaningful, life-giving or death-dealing.[107]

## Dwight Hopkins

Hopkins has dedicated much of his academic career to recovering and building upon key theological themes and insights in slave narratives. In his recent constructive theological monograph, *Down, Up, and Over: Slave Religion and Black Theology*, Hopkins uncovers fertile details of the ways in which slaves utilized the Bible as a power to create new selves. For example, Hopkins interprets the reading of the

Bible as "a miraculous resurrection of the Black intellect from the hell of whiteness and ignorance" for runaway slave Henry Bibb.[108] Hopkins interprets Frederick Douglass as seeing in the Bible "an enabler of the constitution of the new Black person" because of "the transformative power of the written text."[109] Douglass learned about the Bible's power to be a transforming capacity in the following from his slave-master's words: "If he learns to read the Bible, exclaimed Douglass' master, it will forever unfit him to be a slave." For Douglass this was a "new and special revelation," because it revealed to him, "the white man's power to perpetuate the enslavement of the black man…And from that moment I understood the direct pathway from slavery to freedom."[110] This is God's will for macro-social liberation.

Hopkins sees in the Song of Songs 7:1–3; 6–8; 10–12) God's will for the micro-social relationship of love and liberation. Here we find the profoundly erotic and beautiful love poetry that many church folks (and squeamish preachers!) have overly spiritualized. Hopkins, on the other hand, does not spiritualize the sexual imagery at all, but states that God desires for man and woman to be in a relationship of "divinely sanctioned intent, thus locating a site of knowledge about God…appreciating the natural beauty of the other."[111] Such a reading of the Bible is not only radical, but I suggest that it is necessary and refreshing for church folks.

Finally, Hopkins, like Cone before him, places the Bible as a primary source in the systematic construction of Black theology.[112] Also like Cone he speaks about the preeminence of the Exodus biblical motif,[113] and of Jesus Christ's prophetic calling taken from Isaiah 61:1–2 found in Luke 4:18–19.[114] Hopkins also finds particularly striking the "sheep and goats" biblical reference in the Gospel of Matthew 25:31–46.[115] Quoting a former slave turned preacher, James Pennington, Hopkins notes how the themes of judgment and accountability to victims arises:

> [Those who are the victims] will all meet You at the bar….What excuse could you offer at the bar of God, favored as you have been with the benefits of a fine education, and through a long life with the gospel of love, should you, when arraigned there, find that you have, all your life long, laboured under a great mistake in regard to slavery…I can only say then dear sir, farewell, till I meet you at the bar of God, where Jesus, who died for us, will judge between us.[116]

For Hopkins Jesus represents the "Spirit of liberation," and is the one who "goes to work on the inside to render a sense of full self and full voice to the downtrodden."[117] In fact, for Hopkins, the slave conversion experience was the site of a "fierce contestation between who will possess and rule the physical nature of the oppressed."[118] As a slave woman, Sister Sally put it "It seem like the voice of Jesus was inside of me," activating her physical senses in a fierce "battle" with a seeming "legion of demons."[119] Hopkins identifies the evil to be overcome as the "legion" of "psychological, emotional, and visceral demons" that oppressed slaves every day. The Apostle Paul spoke of a symbolic "journey of conversion" in Romans 6:8–13, which Hopkins quotes in full, and through which he reinterprets as "Paul narrates a similar notion of down and up, dying and rising with Christ in the baptismal ritual for the oppressed and in the crucifixion-resurrection ritual with Jesus."[120]

When taken together *Down, Up, and Over* is a richly biblical liberation theology. It interweaves a liberation hermeneutic of the Bible into its constructive theological agenda with cogent urgency.

## J. Deotis Roberts

There are other views, or positions in Black theology. J. Deotis Roberts, for example, specifically repudiates biblical infallibility (as well as that of the pope, patriarchs, councils, or any earthly form of church-based organizational structure or authority). Instead he aligns himself with Karl Barth and uplifts God as the One who "indulges in self-disclosure," thereby focusing on the singular importance of the doctrine of "revelation."[121] As a practicing Baptist Roberts frequently supports his theological points with Scriptural references throughout the text, yet with him this is more a matter of churchman's style than theological dogma.

## Bible Witness in Black Churches Concluding Points

When I first started writing this chapter I mistakenly believed myself to be writing in a vacuum, standing almost alone. Surely no one was as interested in the Bible in the world of Black theology as myself! It did not take me long, however, to realize that African Americans, no matter what their persuasion, from the most liberationist to the most fundamentalist, from the most liberal to the most conservative, are biblically concerned theologians. Black folk love their Bibles! They sing, praise, preach, speak, argue, love, and write from the Good

Book. The Bible, without a doubt, is the preeminent source of Black theology.

So what, then, is the purpose of writing *Bible Witness in Black Churches* if I have decided that we are such a biblical people? Have I answered all my questions in one chapter? No. *Bible Witness in Black Churches* is about establishing the primacy of what is already practiced in most Black Churches—the Bible as a source, a norm, and the center of Black theological reflection in Black Churches for Black Church folk. It should come as no surprise that the Bible is the source, norm, and center of theological reflection in White, Red, Yellow, Tan, and Brown churches; or any multicultural admixture thereof.

So then the reader may fairly ask the question, Are you a liberationist, a conservative, a moderate in relationship to the Bible? Without affixing a label, it would seem more appropriate to elaborate specific details of biblical belief in relationship to theology. The following are good starting base points:

- Absolute Norm—The Bible is the Absolute Norm in the sense that it is the repository of Divine Truth. It is the site of revealed Truth, and as such is uniquely trustworthy as a source of revelation of that Divine Truth. There is a profound mystery in affirming the Absolute Norm of the Bible because it is written with fallible human words, words that have been translated by fallible human beings. Nevertheless, the Divine Truth that is resident in the Bible is revealed to believers through the Holy Spirit, and indeed, it is only through the Holy Spirit, operating in the illumined mind of a believer that the Normative Truth of the Divine Word of God in the Bible can be revealed.
- Word of God is written in words of human beings—God has used the fragile, changeable tent of human language to reveal the drama of Divine history to humanity. This is a cosmic risk, but one that God has chosen for our benefit. It is our task to "Study to shew thyself approved unto God, a worker that needeth not to be ashamed, rightly dividing the word of truth" (2 Timothy 2:15). Such "study" is rigorous, disciplined, intellectually informed by a variety of biblical scholars, and their host of interpretations and their historical-critical/redaction/literary-critical Bible perspectives.
- Spiritually Discerned—The Bible can be studied and understood on several different levels, but they are by no means equal. While many scholars spend a lifetime helping us understand as close as possible what might be the "original" meaning of a text in its historical setting, for church folks (and believers in general) it is very important to find ways to bridge the gap between that original meaning and possible meanings in everyday, contemporary life. Such things often may seem of secondary importance to biblical scholars, but to church folks they are all that matters. Luther, quoting Romans 8:16, used to speak about the "witness of the Spirit in our hearts" as we read the Scriptures. This witness of the Holy Spirit is a kind of Holy

"Yes," a cosmic Nod of agreement that we understand to be the meaning of the Word of God for us by the Spirit of God. That Witness of the Spirit is what we need to cultivate as we read the Bible, so that we can discern the Word of God for us, today.

• Authoritative Witness—I use the term "authoritative" rather than "inerrant" because of the charged atmosphere that surrounds that word. That word is an "in-group/out-group" word. If you embrace it either you are accepted by the right wing of the Christian divide, or ostracized by the left wing. Either way, both sides of the divide have already decided what it means, and have closed their minds about discussing the terms of the conversation. On the other hand, the Bible is a singularly unique, primary, and irreplaceably authoritative witness to various testimonies about the ongoing historical revelation of God. Over and over again we find in its pages narrative, poems, parables, and other kinds of literature that bear witness to vital, interesting encounters with the God of the Universe. Without this Book we would not have a trustworthy account by which we could continually reference with the certitude and confidence that is the hallmark of the Western civilization that has developed around the Bible.

• Wesleyan Quadrilateral—Scripture, Reason, Tradition, and Experience are the norms by which the Church can discern "the spirits" (I Corinthians: 12:10). Scripture is the highest, and most important norm of the four; and it is the "objective" guidepost of the four in the sense that it rules over them. Nevertheless we need the other three in order to achieve balance lest we make of the Bible an idol, and worship it, rather than God.

• Prophetic Intent/Liberationist Ideal—From the Deuteronomistic History (the Former Prophets—Joshua, Judges, 1 and 2 Samuel, and 1 and 2 Kings) through the Latter Prophets—Isaiah, Jeremiah, Haggai, Zechariah, Joel, Amos, Zephaniah, Hosea, Jonah, and Malachi ) we find the Hebrew spokespersons for Yahweh. Their fervent zeal for revealing Yahweh's message to the Hebrew people was always a message of return to righteousness, social justice, and repentance in order to fulfill the commandments of Torah. Torah righteousness resonates with contemporary liberation theology in its zeal for the liberation of the poor from all bondage.

• New Creation—2 Corinthians 5:17: Therefore if any man be in Christ, he is a new creature: old things are passed away; behold, all things are become new. Revelation 21:5–6: And he that sat upon the throne, Behold, I make all things new. And he said unto me, Write: for these words are true and faithful. And he said unto me, it is done. I am Alpha and Omega, the Beginning and the End. I will give unto him that is athirst of the fountain of the water of life freely. What these two biblical passages represent in *Bible Witness in Black Churches* is the ongoing purpose of Jesus' will for humanity—to make all things new. Transformation, recreation, and a new start are the hallmarks of the Reign of God, or what in an older parlance has been called the "Kingdom of God." We do not have to wait for it to come, for it is already here, living in our transformed, recreated hearts as Christians.

All of the above "positions" are pretty standard Christian, mainstream statements. They would not rattle anyone, anywhere who was a regular church-going person. Yet after facing the hard realities of tragedy in both my family's loss in September 11, 2001, and the permanent loss of personal mobility in January 2003, one comes to recognize that sometimes our lives must dip deeply into an ancient spiritual wellspring. That ancient wellspring for me was a closer walk with Jesus Christ mediated by daily meditation in the Scriptures. After being humbled by the recognition of my sinfulness, arrogance, and need for repentance, I have turned away from the prideful pathways and haughtiness that characterized my writings and theological position of a decade ago. One cannot go through such life-shattering, soul-transforming experiences without either becoming a more wise person, or a dead person—there are no facile third ways to stumble upon.

I find myself called out of the cynical lyricism of tragedy and humiliation to a wiser walk with God. One cannot forever regret mistakes, nor recount losses or wish that one had taken the other fork on a road long gone. One day you wake up and God has blessed you with not just a second chance, but a fourth or fifth, and life stretches out in front of you with endless possibilities once again. I know what it is like to believe that all our promise is lost, and, thank God, I have been blessed to know that God can put us back together again.

I am far more concerned to follow a biblically mandated life than I used to be earlier in my life, and my values as the father of three growing children are far more conservative in my fifties than they were in my thirties and twenties. I am not ashamed to admit that I belong to a church that believes in folk standing up and giving testimonies about how good God has been to them this week. The verses in the Bible mean something very "real" to me, right now. My embrace of an enthusiastic evangelicalism on the one hand has not dampened my zeal for the political fires of liberationist activism. In fact as I have deepened my appreciation of the Divine Truth of the Bible, so the Bible seems to have deepened its call on my life to change unjust social situations. So the easy "labels" do not fit me. What *Bible Witness in Black Churches* challenges me to do is to find ways to bring that calling of the Bible on my life to the wider congregation of folks worshipping God next to me every week. Tragedy will never have the last word, the God who changes the lost and the left behind reaches out and remembers.

# 2

# The Word

As a child I was taught that the Bible was God's "Word." This "Word" was unique in that it was utterly trustworthy because it belonged in some unique way to God. Biblical scholars spend a good deal of time demonstrating the "problems" associated with the words contained in the various translations of the Bible, rightfully so. If there is a Word contained in the Bible then it is resident in those very same problematic words, thus the biblical theologian must help reveal a pathway between scholar's questions and the hunger for meaning in the Church folks.

In Black Churches preachers often exhort their congregations to challenge the preacher with the phrase "We need a Word today." The congregation and the preacher respond to each other's response to the powerful stimulus of that living Word acting on their hearts, minds, mouths, arms, legs, and other bodily parts. The living Word is an enlivening Word for "church folks." It is that which persuasively insists, and thereby quietly and yet overwhelmingly commands, indeed demands their performance of praise. For some persons, even some African American persons, this performance of praise has been a source of either embarrassment, censure, explanation, or even dismissal. W.E.B. DuBois called it "the frenzy" in The Souls of Black Folk at the turn of the twentieth century.[1] Preston Williams of Harvard Divinity School spent many sessions with me during my pastoral education there carefully parsing the various historical trajectories of various Black Christianities. He wanted to make sure that I never made an overly easy generalization about Black worship styles! For him there were and continue to be many kinds of African American church folks. He was particularly proud of his Black Presbyterian heritage of restrained, intellectually reflective, and quiet worship. I respect the empirical truth of his claims.[2] It is also empirically verifiable that the vast majority of African Americans (over 90 percent), belong to denominations, or churches that practice a style of praise that Dale Andrews would call performative. In the performative style the preacher uses storytelling, poetry, call-and-response, exhortation, shout, humming, moaning, and even dancing from the altar into the aisles as part of the process of interpreting the Word in the words of the Bible.[3]

Black theology needs to answer the church folks who want to know "What is God's Word for us?" To ask what God's "Word" is is to probe behind those problematic translated words contained in the written text of the Bible that form the basis of our theologies. It is the "Word of God" that is the genuine articulation of the living God of the Universe that we seek. This is what in Hebrew is called the "davar"—the living event, the enlivening moment, the happening. The "Word" is never merely just an articulation of syllables, but the embodiment of an event; an event that brings out change and that changes everything else that occurs afterward. When we build our theology from the starting point of the "Davar," the living event of the living God moving among, within, and through the believing community—the "church folks," then we can begin to peal back some of the overly fussy, abstract, and complex theologizing that academics sometimes do. Church folks want the Word in their lives. They want it breathing in them, moving in their hearts, transforming the cold, lifeless places into warm tenderness and turning what was lost into something found. Often this desire for new life cannot be articulated in eloquent words, but it comes out in tears, in sighs, in the shouts and moans of mothers who are worried about sons languishing in jail cells; or grandmothers who are mourning the deaths of their grandbabies in a war overseas (or as often drive-by shooting down the street, if the truth be told). African American church folks, like most American church folks, are a people under terror-alert, stressed-out, and in need of God's tender touch. The Word, in such a time as ours, will not be a liberating Word if it does not fulfill its most radical (and here I am speaking of the word "radical" in its etymological sense "at the root") and original meaning. For Bible Witness, Black theology has been, and must remain a theology of the Word. Such a theology of the Word is built, for most African American churches, on a firm appropriation of the Gospel of John and its particular understanding of God and Jesus Christ as the Word of God. Therefore Black theology ought to look at the theological resources of the Gospel of John, particularly its first chapter, in order to provide both priestly counsel and a prophetic voice.

## In the Beginning Was the Word

The cosmic introduction of the Gospel of John that the King James Version[4] has forever translated into a poetic paean of praise to God's Word reads as follows:

> In the beginning was the Word, and the Word was with God
> And the Word was God.
> The same was in the beginning with God.

God, in the words of Warren Stewart, Sr., is the "point of departure."[5] To faithfully craft a theology of the Word is to begin the theological task with the basic question, Who Is God? The first two verses of the Gospel of John provide two preeminent theological issues, that of eternity, and transcendence. "In the beginning" relates God both toward the continuum of time and beyond its barriers. Black sermons and popular gospel songs are filled with references to God being an "on-time God." In fact the phrase "He may not be there when you want Him, but He'll be there right on time" is part of the recognized lexicon of traditional African American sermonic rhetoric.[6] Cecile Coquet notes that Mircea Eliade's understanding of sacred time, *hierophantic* duration, or what in Latin he called in *illo tempore* is that "superior time dimension which flows directly from the times of the sacred 'beginning,' when God or revelation was closer to the earth."[7] Theologically, "In the beginning…" is a phrase that connotes both God's eternity and transcendence. There are certain valences when one attempts to speak of God in relationship to time, be it sacred or mythic time, or chronological, so that then we tend to use the category of eternity. Yet we recognize that God exists beyond time, in the "beginning…" whenever, wherever, and however that event, time, or happening may have been. God has always been, exists in the present, and shall always be in a state of everlastingness, and we assign this ultimate category the name eternity. Furthermore, this realm of being that God lives in is not effected by our perception of time: no birth, death, aging, decay, or mortality.

Throughout Christian theological tradition when speaking of God, on the other hand, whenever we are speaking in ultimate relationships of space, breadth, and depth, then we tend to use another category, and that is the word transcendence. Twentieth-century philosophical theologian Paul Tillich was helpful by reminding us of two of Augustine's favored categories, finite and infinite. That which is finite is limited: bound by mortality and thus the certain realities of birth and death, sickness, weakness, faults, senses, feelings, space, and all the categories of ordering known to our understanding of existence. On the other hand, the infinite is unlimited: unbounded, immortal, timeless, beyond the categories of spatiality, temporality, sensuality, and so forth. Transcendence is coterminus with the notion of infinity. It connotes the boundlessness of divinity. God, as the Word, is an Event not limited by the categories, and thus able to connect into that hierophantic duration "when the word was sacred enough to change the face of things by its sheer spirit-power."[8] God is thus named as the transcendent Word, or the God living above the normal time, beyond, and outside of mortal existence and the finite constraints of everyday ordinary beings.

### Discussion Question

Make a list of all the "God is beyond..." things that you can imagine. Do not limit yourself but let yourself go! That is what transcendence is like—the utterly beyond-ness/above-ness /un-limitedness of the Divine.

## God the Creator, Life, Light of the World

The Gospel of John chapter one verses three through five articulate the most important function and character of God as Word—to be Creator and Light:

> All things were made by Him; and without Him was not anything made that was made. In Him was life; and the life was the light of men
> And the light shineth in darkness; and the darkness comprehended it not.

Before we talk about this passage as referring to the preexistence of Jesus as the living Logos, or the Second person of the Trinity, all important theological developments to Christian tradition, I believe that the core biblical theological claim that needs to be uplifted in a theology for church folks is that God as the Word is a Creator. We are pointed back to the opening words of the Hebrew Scriptures in Genesis 1:1: "In the beginning God created the heaven and the earth."

In the Hebrew tradition Yahweh is presented first as Creator, the One who speaks the cosmos into existence by the creativity of His creative Words—the 28 letters of the Hebrew alphabet that are considered to be sacred partners with God, commissioned by God's holy, creative command.[9] The specific exegesis of John 1:3 refers to the Greek idea of the Logos, the rational, germinating Word that orders the cosmos, applied to Christian metaphysics in such a way that undeniably links the Greek Logos with Jesus Christ. Therefore Jesus Christ is uplifted, literally *deified* in this passage in a way that is much bolder than in any of the Synoptic Gospels. This deification brings together powerful sacred ideals that must be noted because of their close proximity to each other in these two verses. In the implied deification of Jesus as the Christ, naming Him as the Word, he is given the attributes of

- Creator of all things (verse 3a);
- Agent without which all things could not have been made (verse 3b);
- Bearer of Divine life—the light of humanity (verse 4a);
- Is the light shining in darkness which darkness cannot overcome (verse 4b).

This Word, or Logos in Greek, is a creating force in the universe. According to this verse in the Bible, everything that is has been made by this creation-making Word. It is the active ingredient, the Maker. It is the agent, or the one who chooses to act. This is important for Black theology because it reveals that creation is always and ever the choice of God's will. God always chooses to create whoever and whatever is created. So often we grouse and complain about what is already in the created order. That is not our responsibility. Our responsibility is to deal with what already is here. It has already been chosen to be here. Now it is our creative responsibility to pray for guidance for how to best deal with its presence. This leads to another important aspect of what kinds of things God creates.

God, as *Logos*, creates Life, and brings Light. *Logos* is the primordial Light, Light from primeval time when life was just beginning. God is Life and is the Light-bearer. As Life-bringer, and Light-bearer, we can begin to discern what kinds of activities are righteous, and what kinds of activities are sinful. Yet the Life-bringer and Light-bearer was a specific Divine person, not an abstract person, or a theological symbol taught in seminaries or written about in scrolls and books. The Gospel of John makes it clear that this Life and Light bringer has actually walked on the earth, and came to the earth. Verse 4b records the stunning, and yet not surprising result that Divine life and Light encountering the symbolic, unenlightened darkness of humanity resulted in misunderstanding, and a lack of comprehension, and a determined resistance radiating from within that Light to never be overcome by the ploys of darkness.

## And the Word Was Made Flesh...

John 1:14 proclaims the mystery that typifies the uniquely Christian theological symbol—the focus of the Word becoming human flesh, or the Incarnation:

> And the Word was made flesh, and dwelt among us (and we beheld His glory, The glory as of the only begotten of the Father,), full of grace and truth.

Jesus Christ is the Life-bringer and the Light-bearer we spoke of in the previous passage, the Incarnate One. He is the one spoken of as the "true Light" that had come into the world that was rejected by his own people (John 1:9–11):

> That was the true Light, which lighteth every man that cometh into the world. He was in the world, and the world knew Him not. He came unto His own, and His own received Him not.

The Gospel of John provides Black theology with the rich fullness of contrasts that is the Incarnation, for in that mysterious theological symbol we proclaim that the Word of God became human flesh, came down to His own people, and was rejected by them because they could not understand who He really was! In this mystery we find the mystery of both divinity and humanity, because God's life somehow always eludes description, even when it is given to us in the clearest terms—like it was in the life, miracles, parables, and teachings of Yehoshua of Nazareth, and His death on a Roman instrument of torture, a cross. Likewise, we African Americans recognize what it means to struggle for Light in the darkness in our ongoing struggles against the evils of dehumanizing forces in the United States of America. Look what a difficult time Martin Luther King, Jr. had rallying Black folks outside of the South while he was alive (not since he has been dead and martyred)! King strove for more than civil rights: he struggled for human rights, for world peace, and what he called the "brotherhood of man." While the peacemaker King used nonviolent means to sue for greater access to civil rights, he was assassinated brutally, and his murder set off a week of social unrest in urban neighborhoods throughout the land. For Black people, their "prince of peace" had been crucified by hate-mongers. A Black theology of the Word can deeply appreciate the work of Martin Luther King without mistaking him as Christ, yet he did incarnate something of God's loving justice for African Americans, and for all people because he helped us to continue to move forward the agenda of justice that is the social realization of love in society.

My father-in-law, retired Superior Court Judge in Indianapolis Taylor Baker, Jr., notes "The Civil Rights Movement is an ongoing movement. It is still going on. What happened when King and the 1960s was involved, it was a moment in time, and more importantly, when whites and others went South and became involved, then their involvement was deemed as important." He also noted: "Most of the Black folk involved in the Movement have not been recognized, and now they've already passed, they're dead."[10] What my father-in-law reminds me, theologically, is that the Word that was made flesh in the Freedom Struggle of the mid-twentieth century is merely part of what ought to be an ongoing Incarnation for a Black theology of the Word. Without carrying on the Freedom Struggle of those who marched, sang, staged pray-ins at lunch counters, and resisted virulent injustice with disciplined nonviolent action then our current generation will allow the gains of the past to slowly dribble away with each regressive piece of legislation passed by national, state, and local officials whose neoconservative agenda is to rollback and erase those gains. For African Americans and all those who joined us in the Freedom Struggle something akin to the in-breaking of God's love was beginning to happen in the United States of America in the 1960s and 1970s. But with the onslaught of Reaganomics and the dual Bush Dynasty it has become clear that the dominant population of this country (with a meager 30 percent exception) wants to rollback the gains of that time with a vengeance. Black theology cannot answer such a time with an abstract recounting of the biblical coming of Jesus to Palestine in the first century without application to the current situation. It requires a hermeneutics of socio-political action, taking the Bible off the shelf and into the streets. If the maxim is true that it is in the nature of oppressed people to continue their oppressed mores until their oppression is really over, and even then, as the Exodus story reveals, the effects of the oppression may linger for generations.

Even so, the Word must bring the Light even when the Light expects to be rejected but that is not all.

## But As Many As Received Him... Sons/ Daughters of God

The telos or end of the theology of the Word is the creation of Sons and Daughters of God:

> But as many as received Him, to them gave He power to become the Sons [Daughters] of God, even to them that believe on His name: which were born, not of blood, nor of the will of the flesh, nor of the will of man, but of God.

Throughout my life I always remember hearing that God was a "Gentleman." By this, the preacher always explained that he, or she, meant that God never forced or coerced one to believe, join, or come into the Kingdom of God by fear of Hell-fire or eternal damnation. In other words, you cannot become a believer in God because you want to avoid burning in Hell forever. A theology of the Word does not stress becoming a child of God because you choose to avoid Hell. Black preachers need to stop trying to preach church folk into their churches by scaring the Hell out of them. God is the original "Gentleman," because a true Gentleman escorts, is courteous, knows how to speak at the proper time, in the proper and appropriately modulated tone of voice, is always dressed for the occasion, and most importantly, is always right on time! As was stated earlier, we know that if God is anything, God is always, right on time. So what does a preacher do if he or she cannot preach the Hell out of their church folks? Other alternatives are possible, like trusting in God.

It appears that the Gospel of John emphasizes, and I repeat emphasizes that Jesus brought life and Light and then gave the folk a choice. Bring the church folks life and Light and then let God do the rest, leave them alone and let them make the choice for God. God does the work, not us. The word does the inside choosing work, not the preacher. There is a mysteriously open, and unfinished quality about the phrase "as many as believed..." It implies the same kind of unfinished and open type of universality that is found in the famous Sunday School verse John 3:16b: "...that whosoever believeth in Him should not perish, but have everlasting life." Even in the Dake Bible, to John 3:15: That whosoever believeth in Him should not perish, but have eternal life, the annotator, Dispensationalist Finis Jennings Dake remarked, "There is no exception—all can be saved."[11] While preachers, scholars, and regular church folks can debate with one another until the cows come in about the word "can," the simple fact of the matter is that God is the one who is working in us, according to the John 1:13, God's will, not ours. Preacher's wills need to get out of the way.

So the preacher becomes the vessel bearing the Word of life and Light to the church folks, and God's will acts within them, enabling them to become the Sons and the Daughters of God. This action of the will of God the Gospel of John vividly describes in the Greek word *gennao* or "bringing forth, born." This process of being brought forth or being born as a Son or Daughter of God is called in John 3:3: "Except a man be born again [*gennethe anothen*], he shall not see the kingdom of God." The *gennethe anothen*, or to be begotten from above, what contemporary church folks call being "born again" is the act of God's will moving in the hearts of men and women here on earth. It is the transformation of women and men wherein we are adopted into Sons and Daughters of the Living God through believing in Jesus as the Christ.

So where does belief enter the picture? Belief is the cognitive aspect. It is the information side of the package. It is all the information about Jesus and God—Who God is, and How God has acted in history. To believe in God we need to know and understand all of the biblical information, traditions, and so on. Yet information requires more than information. It also requires the spark of God's Holy Spirit, and the unction of God's will acting within our will, enabling us to choose. God's "Yes" aids and guides our "Yes!" In the following passage Jesus answers Nicodemus' uncomprehending question as to how a grown man can enter his mother's womb and be born a second time: in John 3:5–6:

> Jesus answered, "Verily, verily, I say unto thee, Except a man be born of water and of the Spirit, he cannot enter the kingdom of God. That which is born of the flesh is flesh; and that which is born of the Spirit is spirit. Marvel not that I said unto thee, Ye must be born again."

Nicodemus, like most of us, was concerned with matters of the "flesh"—or on the surface of things, and not of the spirit, or connected to God's Holy Spirit. The question of receiving Jesus' words as the Word of Life and Light is a question of receiving Him by the Spirit, and being born again as Sons and Daughters of God. This outward sign of this inward transformation of our spirit is baptism, or the washing of being "born of water" indicated in verse 3.

What do Sons and Daughters of God do? Here is where a Black theology of the Word has tremendous responsibility, for the Gospel of John announces in John 1:12 something very important about our standing. It states: "That as many as received Him, to them gave them power" (*exousia*—delegated power; the liberty and right to use power.)[12] What is "delegated authority" or *exousia*? *Exousia* is the power that has been officially delegated to another party or parties; in other words, it is the power to act as the representative, voice, or in the place of a higher authority. The police act in the exousia of the community to enforce the laws, keep the peace, and punish evildoers. When one is known to possess *exousia*, others look up to that person to act in accordance to their proper expectations of the office and authority of that *exousia*. For example, a pastor of a church has the *exousia* of the Church Universal, and not just that local church, and so both church-goers and non–church folk expect that pastor to live up to the office of a pastor. Nothing damages the cause of Jesus Christ more than a scandalous pastor! Police are expected to uphold the law-abiding *exousia* of their office, so that when it is found that there is corruption in their ranks, the reputation of the entire department is put at risk.

For church folks, the Daughters and Sons of God, *exousia* ought to be understood in at least three ways: (1) in the spiritual realm; (2) in the socio-political realm; and (3) in the economic realm. African American churches have historically acted in all three of these realms of human activity, but often have not necessarily applied their theologies to their politics or to their economics. Thus we have the interesting and true paradox of Black Americans being predominantly religious conservatives, while adhering to political views that lean from the center to liberal. It is not my concern here to put forward the political agenda of either the conservative Republican party or the liberal Democrats, but rather to say that church folks ought to be able to justify their spiritual, socio-political, and economic viewpoints from an informed, consistently biblical point of view. Such a viewpoint, informed and consistent, means that it is rooted in "the Word." This means that church folks recognize themselves to be "born again," having received the transformation of "bringing forth" wrought from God, from "above." Such a transformation is spiritual, yet its effects on the person radiate outward throughout the entire personality—transforming their understanding of how things ought to be there: faith communities; political involvements; job opportunities for themselves and those in their local communities; young people and their educational opportunities; local streets involvement with criminal elements (be they drug-trafficking, gangs, drive-by shootings, white-collar crime, or "DWB"—"Driving While Black"); evangelical outreach organizations; and local, state, or even national social justice movements that deal with the plethora of social issues that plague our global community—including the various injustices on ecology, gender, ethnicity, sexuality, and disability among others. A Black theology of the Word need not confine itself to issues of "Blackness" by any stretch of the imagination. To be a Son or Daughter of God is a tremendous obligation to the universe. It is a calling to rise above the petty confines of the "flesh," exercising the exousia of God, and thus moving outward into risky realms of Spirit-directed ministry that one could never dream or imagine without the unction of Divinity acting within.

### Discussion Question

With the advent of Prosperity Gospel messages infiltrating all churches, any political message outside of anti-abortion, antigay rights, or proschool prayer is condemned as "liberal," or ignored as not being the Church's proper business. What issues do you believe that your church must begin to examine in light of the exousia that the Bible conveys when it is read as the living, creative word?

## Ye Shall Know the Truth, and the Truth Shall Make You Free

John 8:31–32 proclaims a remarkable promise to the Sons and Daughters of God, yet it is a conditional promise. It is a conditional promise based on the continuing study of the Word—meaning the biblical sayings concerning the teachings, life, miracles, healings, life, death, and resurrection of Jesus Christ:

> Then said Jesus to those Jews which believed on Him. If ye continue in my word, then are ye my disciples indeed: and ye shall know the truth, and the truth shall set you free.

To "continue" in Jesus' "word" is to immerse yourself in studying the Bible. It is not casual, Sunday School-only, Sunday-only Bible reading. Only 18 percent of contemporary Christian Americans read their Bibles regularly; and only 43 percent of so-called born-again Christians read their Bibles more than on Sunday morning.[13] We tend not to immerse ourselves in studying, but to play-study; doing all kinds of almost magical things with the Bible like Scripture-popping. Scripture-popping is when you just open up the Bible and point to a Scripture, assuming that God has "led" you to that particular Scripture! My high school choir director at Interlochen Arts Academy, Dr. Kenneth Jewell, told me the story of Scripture-popping gone awry that went this way. Once a man opened up to the verse that said, "Judas went and killed himself." He was, of course, horrified. So the man thought to himself, "I'd better ask the Lord to show me another Scripture quick!" He opened up the Bible again, and pointed down at the words. "Go, and do thou likewise (!)" Such manipulation of the Scriptures is not studying the Word, it is magic, and dangerous. Pastor Michael Jones notes that one needs to have (1) a planned time to study the Bible, (2) a clearly defined book, books, or theme to study; and (3) concentration on God.[14] Study requires a concentrated time, place, and mind. One cannot discern the Word of God in the words of the Bible where there are the distracting voices of loud chatter, a blaring stereo, your children's favorite television show, or any other kind of mental clutter. Throughout all of the Gospels one finds Jesus taking "time-outs" to get away from the hum-drum of everyday life to go up on a mountain, or go out into a "deserted place" in order to pray, and get back "in touch" with His Father. I would add one more item to Pastor Jones' excellent list. Bible study time can double as prayer-time, or even spiritual refreshment time. If we allow ourselves the luxury of aromatherapy, or massages in order to relax after busy days, and many are beginning to try at least to find time to do these things for themselves, then we should try to slip in some Divine refreshment time too.

What makes *Bible Witness in Black Churches* a slightly different kind of enterprise than many self-help books is that it brings together the two notions of spiritual refreshment and intensive study. Many times regular folks in the church pews are subtly convinced that they cannot understand difficult and complex biblical and theological issues. This is accomplished under such down-home rubrics like "I'm a country preacher, y'all," or "Make it plain." While such phrases are a part of African American church culture, what they imply is that Black folks cannot understand anything that is not "country" or "plain!" Such a thing is insulting to the vast stores of mother wit, coping skills, as well as various intellectual resources of criticism and curiosity that inform all types of people. The "truth" of Jesus Christ is that He was, and is (John.1ff.) the Logos (Word) of God of whom preexisted from before the beginning of time; creator of all things (John.1:9, 8:12); the Light of the world (John.4:10–15); the giver of living water (John.6:35); the bread of life (John.10:9); the door to abundant life (John.10:11); the good shepherd (John.10:36); the Son of God (John.1:51; 13:31); the Son of Man (John.11:25); resurrection and life (John.10: 9,14:6); the way, truth, and life (John.15:1) and the true vine. All 12 of these titles tell us something about the nature of Jesus Christ as described in the Gospel of John in particular. We cannot say that we understand the "good news" of Jesus Christ without knowing all of these various titles. Furthermore, we cannot attain the maturity and richness of our status as Sons and Daughters of God without discerning the direction and leading of the Holy Spirit that is indicated in each one of these offices. Although complete books and monographs have been written on each one of these titles, a short discussion of each will have to suffice in this space.

We are mining from the Gospel of John the formative elements of a Johannine Christology, or a theology about Jesus Christ according to the faith community around which arose the Gospel and letters of John. Such a Christology is, in many ways, more complex than that of the earlier Gospels, especially that of the first Gospel of Mark. While the Gospel of Mark does indicate Jesus as the "Son of God" in an inspired outburst by Peter (Mark 8:29), Mark kept this title as a messianic secret until it was time for Jesus to be revealed after His resurrection.[15] Mark's Christology is considered a low Christology, emphasizing Jesus' humanity, and the title "Son of Man," spending more time on that aspect of Jesus than on His divinity. A high Christology, by contrast, emphasizes Jesus' divinity—His pre-existence, foreordained recognition, knowing and doing—while spending less time on His human aspects. Biblical scholars have agreed that while the Gospel of John probably came from a marginal community of specific late first century (or even later) Christians with radically complex and meditative theological reflections on the meaning of Jesus' life, teachings, miracles, death, and resurrection, and distinctively high Christology slowly became accepted into the main body of Christians known as proto-orthodox who would later become the orthodox community in the third and fourth centuries.[16] What made the Johannine community so different from other early Christians was their insistence on Jesus' "near-equality to God."[17]

## Logos

Under this simple Greek word lay a world of rich philosophical and theological traditions in the Hellenistic world. For the Johannine community it was a way for them to express beyond the shadow of a doubt just how "high" their view of Jesus was. Jesus had existed with God before time at the very primordial beginning of beginnings, and thus, He was God. In Greek philosophical tradition, the Logos was the principle of divine, or cosmic Reason, giving "order and coherence to an otherwise chaotic world, making it accessible to human intellect."[18] Greek philosophers had been using the term since Heraclitus (born in 540 BCE); and in John's own time in Stoic philosophers the Logos had become a popular term for how the divine intelligence created and sustained the universe. John combined this Greek understanding of the term with the Hebraic understanding of chokmah in Proverbs 8:22–31, where Wisdom is envisioned as the divine female Companion to Yahweh as He creates the universe. By John's time the Hebrew tradition viewed Wisdom as "both Yahweh's agent of creation and the being who reveals the divine mind to the faithful (Ecclesiasticus 24; Wisdom of Solomon 6:12–9:18)."[19] So the genius of the Gospel of John for the theology of the Word is that the Logos brings together the Greek philosophical understanding of religious origins with that of the Hebrews.

## Creator of All things

The title of Creator of all things indicates both the most fundamental way that we recognize who the Godhead is and what the Godhead does. God is the One who created everything. As the early Christians began to develop an increasingly "higher" Christology, they began to see Jesus as not only as being "like God," but actually "being God." There is nothing that is that has not been created by God and the same theological insight was attributed to Jesus. By "created things" these early verses of the Gospel of John can be elaborated more fully in the epistle to the Colossians 1:16, where it is shown that "created things" refer to the visible and invisible realms of being:

> For by Him were all things created, that are in heaven, and that are in earth, visible and invisible, whether they be thrones, or dominions, or principalities, or powers: all things were created by Him, and for Him.

While such a claim may be easily stated and viewed biblically, it is more difficult to spin the web of theological meaning for church folks.

Why is it important for the folks in the pews to know, believe, and receive Jesus as the Creator of all things? The singular answer offered by the Gospel of John is its focus on the divinity of Jesus Christ. Jesus' divinity is the connection that Jesus of Nazareth had with the ultimate Creative power of the universe. To say that Jesus is a "creator" is to recognize the first relationship title of spiritual importance to us church folks, because Jesus is the one we believe has created all things: our selves, our bodies, our churches, our world, and life itself. For the child of God Jesus is everything, the very Alpha and Omega spoken of in the book of Revelation 22:13:

> I am Alpha and Omega, the beginning and the end, the first and the last.

## True Light/Light of the World

The theology of the Gospel of John is shot through with the ongoing contrast between light and darkness, with light always representing the reception and/or recognition of God's presence, God's illumination, God's will, and God's glory acting in the life and actions of Jesus Christ. Darkness functions as a symbol of the stubborn resistance and ongoing refusal to recognize, receive, praise, or to be illuminated by God through Jesus Christ. As John 1:5 states, the "light shineth in the darkness" but the "darkness" did not have the capacity, nor the power during that time period, nor does it have the power even now to "comprehend" in King James English—or what in contemporary English we would say overcome, or conquer the light.

Jesus' nature, according to the Gospel of John, is Light. He not only was the Creator with the Parent or "Father" aspect of God, but He is the Light. He is the one who illuminates the universe, that is, He transmits the glory, the will, the love, the grace, the truth, the justice, the healing, the mercy, the righteousness, and the joy of God .

Light is an all-encompassing metaphor. It can have a variety of meanings. In John 1:4 it says "In Him was life; and the life was the light of men." In this case "light" means "life," and not merely the physical, mortal kind of existence in one's body, but the spiritual, eternal kind of life. John 1:6–8 speaks of John the Baptist:

> There was a man sent from God, whose name was John. The same came for a a witness, to bear of the Light, that all men through Him might believe. He was not the true Light, but was sent to bear witness of that Light.

Notice here that the Scripture differentiates the word "Light" from any word "light." It is clear that John, while clearly given the prophetic status of "witness," was not to be confused with the greater status of being "the Light." He was the one to precede the Light.

Of interest to a theology of the Word in John 1:8b is the qualifier, "true" before the word "Light." Jesus is the True Light. It helps elaborate the type of life that Jesus brings in His light of the life in John 8:12:

> Then spake Jesus again unto them, saying, I am the light of the world: he that followeth me shall not walk in darkness, but shall have the light of life.

This is the first "I am" saying we are considering, although John 6:25 "I am the bread of life" is the first to appear in the Gospel of John. There are seven in all, and we shall consider all of them. "I am" is John's way of providing a biblical echo to the ancient Hebrew resonance of Yahweh's Holy Name in Exodus 3:14: "I am That I am" in answering Moses question about who he should tell the Hebrew slaves had sent him to deliver them. In Hebrew the translation is mystical, and difficult. It can mean many things, including "I am what I was, what I am now, and what I will be," or "I am whatever you need me to be," or "I am the everlasting eternal living one."[20] Obviously it is meant in the Gospel of John to cement the claim that Jesus and the Father are One and the same. Jesus' office is the "Light of the World," and as such He brings the "Light of life" to humankind. This kind of "light" is the spiritual illumination that blossoms within believers as eternal life.

As any regular churchgoing Christian person knows about John 3:16, "God so loved the world, that God sent His only begotten Son, that whosoever believeth in Him should not perish but have everlasting life." The issue of "everlasting life," eternal life, unending life with God through Jesus Christ is one of the most important theological points of the entire Gospel of John. To receive Jesus as the True Light, as the Light of the World, is the same thing as to receive Jesus' eternal life as one's own.

## Giver of Living Waters

The fourth chapter of the Gospel of John contains one of the most intriguing conversations between Jesus and a woman. The woman is a Samaritan, and a notorious sinner, but after her conversation with Jesus, becomes an enthusiastic disciple (verses 29–30), bringing the entire city to hear Jesus' message! In the midst of their exchange Jesus tells the woman that he is related to the ancient prophetic title of God "the fountain of living waters" (Jeremiah 2:13; 17:13; and Zechariah 14:8) in John 4:10:

> Jesus answered and said unto her, "If thou knewest the gift of God, and who it is that saith to thee, Give me to drink: thou wouldest have asked of him, and he would have given thee living water."

The biblical ties of the "fountain of living waters" to Jesus' claim to being the Giver of Living Water is significant in that both prophets Jeremiah and Zechariah spoke to the people of Israel during times when repentance was necessary in order for the blessings of Yahweh-God to be fully experienced. "Living waters" is a symbol of God's "unfailing and eternal water."[21] We need to ask ourselves, however, what kind of "water" are we speaking of? In the Gospel of John water is usually written in conjunction with the word "Spirit," and is associated with baptism, repentance, action of washing, and most importantly, eternal life.

It is clear that in John 4:10, the living water that Jesus is offering the Samaritan woman is eternal life from the verses that follow. He says to her that whoever drinks of Jacob's Well (the well from which they are currently near) will surely be thirsty again, because such water can only slake the demands of physical thirst. Jesus goes on in verse 14 to state the following:

> But whosoever drinketh of the water that I shall give him shall never thirst: but the water that I shall give him shall be in him a well of water springing up into everlasting life.
>
> 15. The woman saith unto Him, Sir, give me this water, that I thirst not, neither come hither to draw.

This part of the conversation is intriguing, and puzzling if it were taken at face value. After all, in verse 7 Jesus had asked the woman "Give me to drink." He had been the one who had been thirsty! So how was it that now He was the one talking about giving away some kind of spectacular kind of supernatural Living Water so special that one could overcome thirstiness entirely? Unless one approaches this text with "spiritual eyes," one cannot possible see what is going on.

Apparently the Gospel of John saw Jesus as the consummate Rabbi who used every occasion, even when thirsty, as one to teach about God. So while Jesus asked this Samaritan woman for a drink of water, He used the occasion to draw her closer to God, finding in her an eager, willing, and teachable spirit. She was one who was thirsty for the everlasting life that was symbolized in the phrase "living water," that eternal life that could only be given by her relationship with Jesus.

The context of Jesus speaking of providing His living water in John 4 is in a prophetic conversation with a woman who is moving from a sinful state (being a Samaritan, having five husbands and living with a man, not knowing how to worship). Jesus, in a brief and terse exchange, deals with each of these issues in such a way that the Samaritan woman (and it is one of the great ironies of biblical history that we do not ever know what her name is!) leaves her encounter with Jesus convicted, excited, and a disciple. Her proof of discipleship is the following (John 4:29–30):

> The woman then left her waterpot, and went her way into the city, and saith to the men, Come, see a man, which told me all things that ever I did; is this not the Christ? Then they went out of the city and came unto Him.

Churches of every stripe, complexion, and creed are suffering from the slime and sewage of brackish spiritual waters. We have allowed spiritual pollution to weekly pass for preaching, and horrid poison to pass for prayers. We wonder why even large congregations seem cold and unfriendly, and why we cannot find genuine "fellowship?" We all need to open ourselves once again to the Giver of Living Waters, to receive genuine eternal Life. Death can be replaced by Life, and dryness with excitement and energy.

## Bread of Life

> *And Jesus said unto them, I am the bread of life: he who cometh to me shall never hunger; and he who believeth on me shall never thirst.*
>
> *(John 6:35)*

Beyond all of the times when this Scripture is heard during Communion, we need to rehear this verse as one of the seven "I Am" Christological titles of Jesus in the Gospel of John. Jesus not only reminds us again of His divinity, but also of His nature as One who nurtures. Jesus Is

Nurture. His nature is to feed, take care of, and completely satisfy the deepest of our needs within us. Our needs are fundamental—we need that which sustains our bodies. For so long Christians have spiritualized the Gospel and talked incessantly about our "spiritual needs" as being most fundamental. In a metaphysical, abstract, and religious sense this is "correct," but it is a cold and unfeeling analysis. Within these physical bodies God recognizes that we have physical as well as spiritual needs.

In the sixth chapter of the Gospel of John we find this Gospel's version of the miracle of the Feeding of the Five Thousand with five barley loaves and two small fishes (Jn.6:1–13). The I am the bread of life saying arises as part of the climax of Jesus' explanation of what really happened in that miracle. He wanted the disciples to understand that the real miracle was deeper than physical food, more longer lasting than that which bread and fish can temporarily satisfy. Jesus in the Gospel of John is God, and as God meets our spiritual hunger. The spiritual hunger, the spiritual thirst that all human beings experience can only be met by what Jesus calls Himself in a later verse (John 6:51):

> I am the living bread which came down from heaven: if any man eat of this bread, he shall live for ever: and the bread that I will give is my flesh, which I will give for the life of the world.

This is mystical theology at its best, and it is difficult to understand if you are a literalist. Jesus was not saying that His body was bread to be literally eaten. Of course not! Historical critical biblical analysis notes the intense antagonism between the early Christian Jews and non-Christian Jews becomes apparent in the next verse when John says, "The Jews . . . were puzzled and did not understand what Jesus meant by eating His flesh."[22] Yet Jesus is speaking here of the mystical union of the believer with the spiritual body of Jesus, a union that brings eternal life into one's body, and into the world. This mystical union is ritually celebrated every time we have Communion service (the Eucharist liturgy, Mass, etc.) in our various churches throughout the Christian world. Unfortunately Christians have divided themselves into various camps concerning what happens during the Communion—whether it is transubstantiation, consubstantiation, or a simple memorial.[23] A theology of the Word deeply informed by John recognizes that our everlasting life is dependent on our mystical communion, our counited, everyday walk with Jesus Christ. He is the bread of life, feeding our inward spirits, providing the nurturance that cannot be satisfied anywhere else.

## Door of the Sheep

> *Then said Jesus unto them again, Verily, verily I say unto you, I am the door of the sheep. All that ever came before me are thieve and robbers: but the sheep did not hear them. I am the door: by me if any man enter in, he shall be saved, and he shall go in and out, and find pasture. The thief cometh not, but for to steal, and to kill, and to destroy: I am come that they might have life, and that they might have it more abundantly.*
>
> *(John 10:7–10)*

I confess, this is one of my personal Scriptural favorites. I liked it as a young child because I had a wonderful Sunday School teacher who taught us that we were like lost sheep who needed a good strong Door to close us in to keep the big, bad robber out, because they were trying to rob us, and eat us! We acted out the scene, and we ran around the room, squealing away, with our "Baah-Baah's" and so forth. There were other children playing the devils wolves, robbers, and thieves. They were chasing us, and we were afraid. We were little lost sheep looking for a safe Door because we were afraid. Suddenly the Jesus Door appeared, and we ran for Him. The Jesus Door was one of the great big Deacons of the church, and he opened his big arms, and we scrambled under them, and then he symbolically "locked us up!" We were safe. I remember the meaning of this verse in the very muscles, tissues, and sweat of my body from my childhood. It is important to remember that good church folks can put deep impressions on their children, and truly teach their children well.

Theologically we need to look at two Christological points: (1) Jesus is the access point to all forms of salvation; and (2) Jesus is the access way to abundance of life. Notice that the word access is featured in both points. Oppressed persons, the outcast, the marginalized and downtrodden, disabled people, people who look for hope when there seems to be no hope at all, see in Jesus the unmistakable quality of His accessibility. He is the one who provides Access. Like a Door opens up a closed room, so Jesus opens up the closed blessings of eternity, the hidden treasures of miraculous living, the secret pastures of peace that only the only begotten Son of God could do. The kind of salvation that Jesus provides is not limited, it is unlimited. We cannot limit, must not limit God's salvation to any preconceived ideals of what we perceive is "spiritual," "material," "liberational," "political," or any other particular thing perceived in the human mind as wondrous, high, awesome, and godly.

There are awesome implications in this Scripture for the disabled/handicapped/differently abled community who have historically needed real, concrete, social-political economic access to opportunities in their lives, and still continue to need them right now. In many ways this community is the living embodiment of a "neglected oppressed community," in the sense that disabled/handicapped differently abled persons are the dishonored "sheep" living in the midst of able-bodied Sheep, looking for our own safe Door in which to enter a grand Pasture. In recent years the ADA (Americans with Disabilities Act) and other progressive laws have begun to raise some hopes, but we need the "Jesus Door" who brings "abundant life," and no other; authentic transformation, and not hallow victories. Access, for those with limited abilities to move around, and have been too often never to look outside the window at vistas of glorious opportunity, is a most precious and wonderful gift.

## Good Shepherd

*I am the good shepherd: the good shepherd giveth his life for the sheep. But he that is an hireling, and not the shepherd, whose own the sheep are not, seeth the wolf coming, and leaveth the sheep, and fleeth: and the wolf catcheth them, and scattereth the sheep. The hireling fleeth, because he is an hireling, and careth not for the sheep. I am the good shepherd, and know my sheep, and am known of mine. As the Father knoweth me, even so know I the Father: and I lay down my life for the sheep.*

*(John 10:11–15)*

The fourth "I Am" Christological statement comes quickly in John 10 after the third. While the third "I Am" reveals Jesus as the Divine access point, this "I Am" reveals the extent of divine care. Divine care will go to any extent for the sake of the "sheep," even to the point of sacrificial death. This is the "I Am" has the shadow of the Cross upon it, and the bloody, vicious sting of the scourging, and betrayal are already rising from its symbolism.

Jesus is not just any kind of leader or "shepherd," He is a "good shepherd," one willing to go toe for toe with the "wolf"; and if necessary give his life for the sake of preserving the life of his sheep. The "good shepherd" is differentiated from a "hireling" by being the one who owns the sheep; the one willing to lay down his life (in order to defend) the sheep; the one who cares for the sheep; the one known by the sheep; and the one known by the Father.

The Good Shepherd demonstrates to us Sons and Daughters how to be true leaders. We are called to be shepherds, not hirelings; to care and not flee when danger arises. When the sheep under our charge are in danger we are called by God in Heaven to stand our ground, knowing that God is empowering us, and that in due time everything will work out all right. Most often we take the hireling route first, fleeing from danger, perceiving any threat as life-threatening. But where would our people be if Dr. King had not stood his ground, with Fannie Lou Hamer? Where would we be without Harriet Tubman and Frederick Douglass? They stood their ground. Good shepherds trust in God, knowing that God will fight the battle and win it.

## Son of Man

> *Verily, verily, I say unto you, Hereafter ye shall see heaven open, and the angels of God ascending and descending upon the Son of Man.*
>
> *(John 1:51b)*

> *For as the Father hath life in Himself: so hath He given to the Son to have life in Himself; and hath given to Him authority to execute judgment also, because He is the Son of man.*
>
> *(John 5:26–27)*

> *Therefore, when he [Judas] was gone out, Jesus said, Now is the Son of man glorified, and God is glorified in him. If God if glorified in him, God shall also glorify him in Himself, and shall straightway glorify Him.*
>
> *(John 13:31–32)*

Jesus refers to Himself this way throughout the New Testament some 88 times, and it appears 13 times in the Gospel of John.[24] It is Jesus' preferred way of speaking about Himself. Oscar Cullman states that "Son of Man" is the most comprehensive Christological title of Jesus because "It embraces the total work of Jesus as does almost no other idea."[25] Raymond Brown notes that in the Synoptic Gospels the "Son of Man" sayings have three meanings: "(1) those that refer to the earthly activity of the Son of Man (eating, dwelling, saving the lost); (2) those that refer to the suffering of the Son of Man; (3) those that refer to the future glory and Parousia of the Son of Man in judgment."[26] What makes the Gospel of John so different from the Synoptic Gospel usage of the Son of Man is that "they lack strong apocalyptic trappings," and stress, instead, what scholars call "realized eschatology" or the Reign of God is now.[27] As is the case in

John 1:51, the Son of Man descends as well as ascends, something not mentioned at all in the Synoptic Gospels.

Jesus is God's redeeming Human for humanity. As Sons and Daughters of God, following our Elder Brother Jesus, we are called to be redeeming human beings for others. Being redemptive beings. Beings for others is following in Christ's footsteps, following in the realized humanity of the Son of Man. This title is an invitation into the fellowship of discipleship, a fellowship of being for others following Jesus.

## Son of God

In a very real sense, the entire Gospel of John is a sustained argument developing the theological conception of Jesus as the creative Word, the Son of God. From the magnificent first chapter until the last words of the twenty-first, Jesus Christ is revealed as the only begotten Son of the living God of the Universe.

Nevertheless, John 10:34–38 has a fascinating argument about Jesus' divinity in which Jesus quotes Psalms 82:6; "I have said, 'Ye are gods: and all of you are children of the most High.'" Notice how Jesus affirms this Psalm as having the binding force of "law":

> Jesus answered them, Is it not written in your law, I said, Ye are gods? If He called them gods, unto whom the word of God came, and the Scripture cannot be broken; Say ye of him, of who the Father hath sanctified, and sent into the world, Thou blasphemest; because I said, I am the Son of God? If I do not the works of my Father, believe me not. But if I do, though ye believe not me, believe the works: that ye may know, and believe, that the Father is in me, and I in Him.

These verses reveal the same kind of "here-and-now" realized eschatology that the Son of Man title demonstrated in the Gospel of John. This is significant because we can begin to draw some tentative conclusions, one of which is that while the Gospel of John is an incredibly meditative, and overtly theological Gospel, we ought to never mistake its wordiness for a sign of abstraction. It was and is a summons to action as well as prayerful reflection. Jesus Himself wanted to be judged by His deeds, and called His detractors to see past His words to the God acting through His deeds. We must do the same. We can do no less in the face of a multireligious, pluralist religious scene that often undermines the credibility of Christian witness in the face of the hostile and hypocritical historical witness that Christianity is compelled to defend as its own.

## Resurrection and the Life

> *Jesus saith unto her, Thy brother shall rise again. Martha saith unto him, I know that he shall rise again in the resurrection at the last day. Jesus said unto her, I am the resurrection and the life: he that believeth in me, though he we dead yet shall he live: and whosoever liveth and believeth in me shall never die. Believest thou this? She saith unto him. Yea, Lord: I believe that thou art the Christ, the Son of God, which should come into the world.*
>
> *(John 11:23–27)*

The fifth "I Am" saying in the Gospel of John is tied both to the raising of Lazarus from the dead, and Martha's confession of Jesus as the "Son of God." Mary and Martha are disappointed that Jesus had not come to heal Lazarus before he had died, noting that he would not have died, yet in verses 21–22 Martha expressed her belief that even after his death Jesus could ask God to do whatever He asked God to do:

> Then said Martha unto Jesus, Lord, if thou hadst been here, my brother had not died. But I know, that even now, whatsoever thou wilt ask of God, God will give it thee.

It is to this supreme declaration of faith that Jesus responds with His fifth "I Am" Christological title. What makes "I am the resurrection and the life" unique from the other self-appellations is that it focuses our attention on what has become known throughout Christian history as the Christian distinctive, resurrection. Christians believe in the bodily resurrection of Jesus Christ. Other mystery religions throughout the Mediterranean held to dying and rising saviors during this time, including the famous duo of Osiris and Horus in Egypt, but none held the centrality of cultus as did Christianity. In the marginalized Christian community from which sprung the Gospel of John a uniquely high vision of the divinity of Christ arose that focused on Jesus' resurrection being part and parcel of God's will and plan from the very start. The Johannine community interpreted Jesus' life as moving toward the direction of "resurrection and life," that is to say, eternal life. So resurrection, bodily resurrection, is the sign of God's power over physical death, and the establishment of everlasting life.

A theology of the Word is a Christocentric theology. This means that it is Christ-centered. In a theological world that often sacrifices adherence to the symbol of Christ for fear of offending of religious sensibilities in the name of "ecumenism," "religious pluralism," "multiculturalism," or other so-called politically correct terms in the liberal academy, the moderate-to-conservative Christian theology of most African American (and most other Christians of whatever ethnicities) is Christocentric. This Christocentric is also a high Christology. Such a Christology draws a lot from what was, at its time, radical and not mainstream or orthodox; yet from the Johannine community in this Gospel of John. That is what is quite extraordinary about this "I Am" statement, "I am the resurrection and the life." We, in the African American churches, need to emphasize this fact to our church folks, because often we take for granted that this truly radical theology of John's is straightforward stuff, when, in point of fact, it is not. John 3:15–16, even though it is used as bumper-sticker material, and this "I Am" title—"I am the resurrection and the life" is the heart of the gospel.

Without it Jesus' life, death, and resurrection would mean nothing, and our preaching would be meaningless.

## Way, Truth, and Life

*Thomas saith unto Him, Lord, we know not whither thou goest; and how can we know the way? Jesus saith unto him, I am the way, the truth, and the life: no man cometh to the Father, but by me. If ye had known me, ye should have known my Father also: and from henceforth ye know Him, and have seen Him.*

*(John 14:6–7)*

The sixth "I Am" statement is a threefold celebration of Christ's mission and atoning working. The work of atonement or at-one-ment, making humanity one with God again, is the important action area of Christology that has been separated into what many theologians called "Soteriology" or the study of salvation. Soteriology in the Gospel of John is most adequately understood as an aspect of Christology. In John one finds salvation through one's relationship with Jesus as Christ. This simple formula has become the sharp bone of contention and the bane of any theocentric Christian who wants Christianity to move away from its Christocentric basis, for John's Christocentric claims—such as those found in John 3:15–16; 14:6–7—imply that Christianity is an exclusivist religion. Exclusive religions believe salvation, truth, and eternal life are revealed only in one "true" way. An exclusive religion sets up strict and hard boundaries, "us" and "them" categories of the "saved" and the "damned," insiders and outsiders that are particularly offensive to contemporary sensibilities of how any religion ought to be. Theocentric Christians—Christians who focus on God rather than on Christ, like H, Richard Niebuhr, his contemporary disciples, and many others, believe that Christianity ought to be reenvisioned as an inclusive religion that desires to recognize the validity of salvation, truth, beauty, meaning, and power in other religions as well as in Christianity.[28]

As a questioning teenager in my Sunday School class I gave my associate pastor fits by asking him when we read this very verse one Sunday what would happen to all of my Moslem, Jewish, and Buddhist friends because they didn't believe in Jesus. His answer that they were doomed to an eternity burning in Hell-fire displeased me very much! We had a fight right then and there, much to the delight of my fellow Sunday School classmates, who found my rebellion the stuff of church legend, especially after I "got religion" a few years later and came back "on fire" for Jesus, preaching and teaching with conviction. I just could never get it clear in my mind how a loving Jesus could be so condemning of all of the rest of humanity. How could my "sweet Jesus" wipe out 98 percent of the world with such callousness in this "I Am" statement? It just seemed like such a cold and callous statement in my teenaged mind. For many adult and mature minds the same question remains.

When I got to Harvard Divinity School as a seminary student, Professor Krister Stendahl provided me with a phenomenally satisfying answer in one of his Bible lectures. Apparently he had had the same questions as a young man when he had been listening in Sunday School! When he became a renowned New Testament scholar, and did historical research into the Greek language and syntax, he discovered something magnificent. According to his interpretation, John 14:6–7 was a bold statement reflecting the love language of Christian believers of the relationship toward their Savior. He said, "Just like a young lover declares to the world, 'You are the only one for me, so these Johannine Christians were telling the rest of the Christians and Pagans of their time that in order to truly be a Christian, Jesus Christ was The way, The truth, and The Life. It was the exclusive love language of lovers, enraptured, caught up with one another.' " I will never forget Dr. Stendahl describing this passage with his thickly accented English for as long as I live, on that snowy New England day. He had provided a way for me to look with new "eyes and ears" at a nettlesome Scripture with appreciation instead of anger, and I was grateful.

Now, perhaps for you this "answer" is not satisfying. That is alright. It may not escape the inherent exclusivism of the passage far enough for you. Or, on the other hand, you may feel perfectly comfortable that the exclusivism in this Scripture is all right, and you have no problem with words coming from Jesus' mouth condemning 98 percent of the world to Hellfire. I needed to understand the rhetorical argument of the Gospel of John—how it was written in order to persuade. The Gospel of John was written in the most uncompromisingly potent, straightforward terms, it gives no quarter. It pulls the reader and listener to decision, there is no shade of turning in its poetic flow, and one can easily see why such a Gospel is still the favorite of preachers. The Jesus Christ of John is the Word for a theology of the Word, the eternal, living, true way into everlasting Life.

Of interest to further biblical study of this passage comes from the Dake's Bible concerning the words "truth" and "life." Apparently the Gospel of John intensified the usage of both of these words more than all of the other Gospels combined. John took great pains to describe Jesus as the truth some 24 times, while that same word was used only 5 times in the other Gospels.[29] Likewise with the word life, a word that any Johannine theologian recognizes rings throughout this Gospel with the certitude of eternity. Dake notes that life appears 43 times in the Gospel of John, while only appearing some 38 times elsewhere in the other Gospels.[30] We can rest assured that as Jesus is the truth that sets us free (John 8:32–36); He is also everlasting life (John 3:15–16) in every way. The Gospel of John is the Gospel of everlasting life. God, through Jesus Christ, is portrayed as the living God; the God who is the source: everlasting life (3:15–16); living waters (4:10); the light of life (8:12); the Bread of life (6:35); abundant life (10:10); resurrection and the life (11:25); and the way, the truth, and the life (14:6–7). A theology based on the Word, grounded, settled, and richly informed by the creative Word must proclaim God's life.

## True Vine

*I am the true vine, and my Father is the husbandman. Every branch in me that beareth not fruit He taketh away: and every branch that beareth fruit he purgeth it, that it may bring forth more fruit.*

*(John 15:1–2)*

This last "I Am" statement combines Christology with Ecclesiology, or the study of Christ with the study of the Church. The vine image is not only an image of Jesus, but also an image of how believers are to exist as a community-acting-as Christ-in-the-world. Throughout Christian history biblical scholars have rightly contrasted the two organic metaphors of John and Paul, the vine (John 15) and the body (I Corinthians 12–14; Ephesians 3; Acts 13:1ff.). While it is clear the Pauline church had the differentiated structure of apostles, teachers, prophets, and so on, the Johannine church apparently focused much more on a unified hierarchy, with the apostles (13:6) transmitting and interpreting their vision of the Holy Spirit, or *Paraclete* in Greek (15:26–27):

> But when the Comforter is come, who I will send unto you from the Father, even the Spirit of truth, which proceeded from the Father, he shall testify of Me:
>
> And ye also shall bear witness, because ye have been with me from the beginning.

Thus Jesus, for John is the True Vine, meaning a genuine representation of the prophetic Israel as portrayed in Isaiah 5:1–7.[31] As Brown states, the vine is a corporeal image of the church in Christ that emphasizes one-ness over differentiation.[32] The point of the emphasis on unity is to stress how individual conversions form a singular collective in Christ. Again we move into a notion of a spiritual communion that we discussed above in relationship to the title "bread of life," and the symbolic phrase of "eating the Body of Christ." The symbolic phrase used in the fifteenth chapter of John is abide, which means to dwell, or to live within something or some place. Jesus invites believers to abide in Him:

> Abide in me, and I in you. As the branch cannot bear fruit of itself, except it abide in the vine; no more can ye, except ye abide in Me. I am the vine, ye are the branches: He that abideth in me, and I in him, the same bringeth forth much fruit: for without me ye can do nothing. (John 15:4–5)

The relationship of the believer in Christ to Christ is analogous to a branch to a vine. The branch is dependent on the vine for its life-giving connection. God is seen as a "husbandman," pruning the branches in order to "purge" the branches in order to make them more "fruitful." Such a view of God, I would submit, is surely agonistic, for it is a rhetoric that clearly implicates God in the act of inflicting pain in order to make us better Christians. I have always chafed at such a view of God, and yet this is what this Scripture is clearly suggesting. If this chapter were to stop at these verses, then God would be a grand Cosmic Bully, and the Christian Story would be a Lie. But thanks be to God that John 15 moves on to elaborate what it means to abide in the vine, and how abiding in Jesus brings love and joy:

> If ye abide in me, and my words abide in you, ye shall ask what ye will, and it shall be done unto you. Herein is my Father glorified, that ye bear much fruit; so shall ye be my disciples. As the Father hath loved me, so have I loved you: continue ye in my love. If ye keep my commandments, ye shall abide in my love; even as I have kept my Fathers commandments, and abide in His love. These things have I spoken unto you, that my joy might remain in you, and that your joy might be full. This is my commandment, That ye love one another, as I have loved you. Greater love hath no man than this, that a man lay down his life for his friends. Ye are my friends, if ye do whatsoever I command you. (John 15:7–14)

Neither the momentum, nor the intention, or the direction of these verses is to go toward tyranny, domination, or hatred. God does not want to overwhelm the believer with pain or fear, but to move us into a higher, wider, and more complete relationship. In verse 15 Jesus states that He no longer wishes them to be called "servants," but "friends" because they have heard everything that God has told Jesus to tell them; been chosen and ordained by Jesus Himself to bear fruit (verse 16); their fruit will remain on the earth (verse 16); that they will be hated because of their relationship to God just like Jesus (verses 18–25); that they will be empowered and instructed by the Comforter and Spirit of truth (verses 26–27) ; and so empowered they will become witnesses to testify about Jesus. To dwell in the Vine that is Jesus is to learn how to love as Jesus loved, not because you are so wonderful or so great, but because the Jesus in you is teaching you how to love in such a magnificent way. To bear the spiritual fruits of serving others, of being a Daughter or a Son of God is possible only by abiding in the true Vine, by being one of the myriad branches on a Vine that has existed for over two Millennia. The Vine image draws on Space-Time as well as on our agricultural background. It stretches back into the primal nether regions of Christian origins, to a place that historians cannot ever accurately confirm or deny with scientific certitude. Such a region is clouded with the mists of pure faith, the atmosphere that true church folks thrive on and relish, because they know that in such a place they can be known as they truly are, and loved anyway by a loving and forgiving Jesus.

## Final Discussion Questions

1. The mystery of Divine Love has captivated great Christian mystics and saints down through the ages. Read and discuss how the Apostle Paul writes about its wonderful and incomparable attributes in I Corinthians 13. Notice how I John 3:11–22 and 4:7–21 discuss the divine nature of love (I John 4:7–8), as well as our human obligation to act in obedience and imitation to that Divine Love.
2. What does it mean to you when someone is said to be "filled with God's love?" Can we really know that they are actually experiencing divine union, or just pretending, or is it an act of faith?
3. What does the Bible state that we human beings need the most?

# 3

# Translated Witness

Chapters 3, 4, and 5 elaborate the primary understanding of Word in *Bible Witness in Black Churches*, as "witness." To witness to something is to give one's testimony, to attest to having seen or having been in the presence of something. The Bible may be described as many things—literature, poetry, symbols, and so on; however, one of the most important theological functions of the Bible is that it provides a witness of God's historical dealing with those human beings chosen for God's purpose. I choose the overarching theme of witness because giving testimony is a transcultural practice that crosses the boundaries of different racial, ethnic, and historical practices. Throughout the history of the Church Universal witness has given rise to the proclamation, reception, conversion, and the spread of the salvation that comes in the name of Jesus Christ. There is a profound connection between the proclamation of the message of Jesus, the reception of Jesus' teaching, and the spreading of Jesus' message to others. This connection is celebrated in a noted tradition of eloquence in African American preaching women and men, gospel music, glorious choirs, call-and-response singing, an enlivening worship experience in most traditional Black Church contexts, and so forth. The Bible itself points to this phenomena in Romans 10:14:

> How, then, can they call on the one they have not believed in? And how can they believe in the one in whom they have not heard? And how can they hear without someone preaching to them? (NIV)

## Translated Witness

This chapter takes on one of the major biblical problems presented in witness—that of translation. Witness cannot refer to Yahweh, Jesus

Christ, of experiences of the Holy Spirit except through the inevitable means of being a "translated witness." One of the most shocking things for my students to realize in the first few weeks of the Survey of the Bible course is that God did not dictate the Bible to one person in English! This is devastating for many because they have been raised with such an intimate feeling for the ancient English words found in the King James Bible. They utterly trust every vowel, syllable, comma, period, and empty space as being placed there by Divine Design. Such theological freight and meaning has been placed on the very tone, cadence, and mystery encased in the verbal musicality of King James' English in many traditional, conservative, and biblically centered churches. In many Black Churches church folks believe that God cannot hear them unless "He" is addressed in the "holy" King James English, "Thou!" This is not a theological "problem" for them, and often students have told me that they thought that I was the person with the problem. I surely must be lying to them! Perhaps I was being either manipulated by the Devil, demonically inspired, or at least deluded. Such are the intensely dislocating feelings they were experiencing during this part of the course after finding out that the Bible is translated. Thus, while this moment of bringing students to a realization of the richness of translation may be most important for understanding the "truth," it is also shocking, and must be handled with a level of sensitivity, and care when we are speaking about "witness" in the context of Church folk.

After months of meditation I have further "scandalized" my biblical survey courses by revealing why the translation challenge must be faced by Christians. To many Christians living in the secured, and culturally cloistered existence of the United States of America there is a great deal of ignorance about the rites, requirements, and customs of other religions. At the point that I help students to recognize the translated nature of the witness of the Bible, I also inform them about the amazing gap between a typical Christian's knowledge of the original languages of the Bible, and that of a Moslem, and a Jew. A Jew, for instance, will have been initiated into the glorious mysteries and riches of Hebrew by the time they have reached the age of maturity (about 12). During the ceremony of *Bar Mitzvah* for young males, or *Bat Mitzvah* for the females, one is required to demonstrate both mastery of Hebrew language and the beautiful musical chants that accompany the reading. Similarly, all Moslems throughout the world spend a great deal of time learning to read the *Koran* in the original language of Arabic. When asked to explain the tenets of his or her faith, a Moslem will recite the *sura* or verse of the *Koran* first in what is considered the holy language of Arabic, and then translate it i.. the vernacular—be it English, French, or whatever. Both Jews and Moslems can discuss, debate, and argue the theological fine points of their Scriptures because of their intimate familiarity with the original language of their Scriptures.

After making this point I always ask whether anyone has ever heard of a preacher demanding that after someone has joined a church that they attend a Greek and Hebrew class. Is it the common practice of Christian evangelists to follow up their standard questions: "Do you believe in the Lord Jesus Christ?" "Do you accept Him as your personal Lord and Savior?" and "Do you repent of your sins and promise to live as Jesus commands?" with the question, "Are you willing to learn biblical Hebrew and Greek to read God's Holy Word?" The answer, not surprisingly, is a resounding , "NO!" No one, from the most erudite, suburban WASP Episcopalian to African American or Latino inner-city Pentecostal church/prophecy-oriented church would even begin to imagine requiring of its members that they gain mastery of the original languages of the Bible. Yet we consider the Bible to be the "Holy Bible." We hold it to contain the "sacred truths of God Almighty." Why do we not, as a people of God, insist that Christians take personal translation of the Scriptures to be as important as our fellow monotheist brothers and sisters? Why should we depend on somebody else to "tell us what it says?" What does that say about us as Christians?

Since the Christian Church has not, as a general rule, insisted upon its regular members becoming full-fledged original language readers, the vast majority of Christians are translation-dependents. Our spiritual education has literally "constructed" us, raised us to be dependent upon the interpretive skills of those who "know better" than us! This is as true for Protestants as Catholics, Orthodox as for Charismatics, High Church or Low Church. Scholars may call this a hermeneutical dilemma,[1] but from our perspective as church folks, we ought to feel quite uncomfortable with the widespread acceptance of this aspect of the Christian tradition. Fundamentally, the accepted culture of Church members acts as if God wants over 90 percent of Christians to accept a second-class status in regard to their ability to read, interpret, and discuss the depths, riches, and complexities of the words in God's Word. So I ask the reader the question point blank,

"Does the God you serve want you to be ignorant?"

I follow this with another question that follows from this hermeneutical dilemma, which goes into a bit of critical social analysis.

"Whose interests are being served by keeping us church folks ignorant of what the original languages may be saying?"

Am I sowing a "seed of doubt" about the Bible? No, but I am trying to stir the pot up about many of the raw power dynamics that pastors, preachers, and teachers of the Bible use over and against regular Christians in their hunger to "know" what the Word is saying to them. In a famous Bob Marley song there is a line that states " 'A hungry mon' is a dangerous mon." Many of those who "translate" the words of the Bible into the Word for the people of God are "hungry mon," very hungry for power, control, and domination of others minds, pocketbooks, and regretfully, bodies. Second-class status always means that there is a first class. Who is the first class in the Church because we have turned over the task of reading the Word to "them" rather than "us?" We shall discuss the implications of the subtle theological justifications that have made such second-class status seem normal, acceptable, and even spiritually "right" later on.

For the student of biblical studies, therefore, knowledge of how translation is a fundamental aspect of reading the Bible opens up a wider and more spacious world of appreciation for the meaning of biblical texts. This, then, is more than a methodological starting point, but a key theological point. It is how I gently but firmly work to bring students away from the possibility of feelings of defensiveness or disillusionment, anger, and sometimes even betrayal. Ultimately it does not matter what our "feelings" are about this matter. Translation of the Bible has gone on way before we ever existed and had the audacity to weigh in our opinions about the "whys" and "wherefores" of hermeneutical difficulties. Translation of the Bible will continue until Jesus returns, perhaps long after we "sleep" (as the Apostle Paul refers to death I Thessalonians 4:13).

The Bible was written in a wide variety of ancient languages, primarily Hebrew and Greek, but small sections were also preserved in Aramaic and other dialects. Biblical scholars spend years learning these arcane languages. While I have spent years learning Hebrew, and am a beginner at Greek, I am a trained theologian and ethicist; therefore I am compelled to rely on their expertise to sort through what various translations mean. Our job as readers is to carefully tease out all the possible translations that have appeared in biblical manuscripts throughout Christian history, compare the meanings, and cross-reference their applied meanings. Our task is much like that of being a Verbal Detective—hunting down all the clues, nuances, and possible avenues of understanding that are revealed as we translate ancient languages into something comprehensible to the contemporary reader/hearer/doer of biblical Truth. This leads inevitably into a theological discussion of translation of human words as it relates to Divine Truth.

## Witness and Truth-in-Translation

Translation reveals the truth, the message that God is delivering to us. It is the Doorway through which the various shades of meaning, possible nuances of understanding, and proper application of the text can be conveyed. Translation provides access to meaning, and it is through fervent and prayerful searching of Scriptures that Christians move toward the Truth that is God.

How can God's Truth be found in translated words? Christians tend to operate with the theological premise that God is acting in and through the words of the Bible—however incomplete, imperfect, and sometimes flawed those words may be. Therefore we seek out in what ways the Divine is speaking to us. When we ask, "How is God acting in these words?" we are asking a theological question of the Bible. Theological questions ask in what way is God, the Church, Christ, and the Holy Spirit involved in the subject matter.

In seminaries and divinity schools such terms as theological premise and theological question are not puzzling. For undergraduates in a college, or interested church folk, however, we are wandering into that realm of complicated academic language that is coded to let certain people "in," and leave others "out!" I know this now because it is at this point that I tend to lose many of my students. So let's spend a little time elaborating on the meaning of what a theological premise is; a theological question is; and how these theological premises and questions can be intimately related to how one reads the Bible. After all, most Americans live in a media-driven culture that is saturated with the televangelist message that loudly proclaims the following dangerously simplistic formulas: "The Bible says what it means, and means what it says," or "The Bible says it, I believe it, that settles it." What these slogans imprint on the hearer is the Bible does not require any translation, interpretation, or careful thinking to be understood because it clearly says what it means. The unspoken message is, "Only a devil-inspired 'liberal' who really does not believe that the Bible is God's 'Word'; and who is trying to confuse you by twisting the Word, calling it 'interpreting the Bible' thereby diminishing and negating the power inherent in the Word of God is now speaking!" Thus terms like theological premises and theological questions, in this kind of slogan-driven view of the Bible, are seen as a kind of smoke-screen for those who "Twist the true interpretation of the living Word of God, which anybody with two eyes and two ears can see for themselves." Do not misunderstand me, I agree that the Bible is a text meant to be understood by the masses of folk, and not the highly educated elite few who deign to dole out bits and pieces of spiritual wisdom only when they feel it suits their manipulative purposes. Yet church folk have been mislead in a fundamental way if they continue to hold the belief that the Bible is so simple that it virtually interprets itself, or that God's Spirit magically whispers the meaning of each verse in believer's ears. The Bible, when theologically understood as God's Word, is far too rich in its meaning, and too complex to be put down and insulted with such phrases as "it means what it says!" Why? Simply stated, because the language in which English readers read the Bible is a translation of ancient Hebrew and Greek words that often have at least two, and often three or four different, interesting, and often applicable meanings. If, in fact the Bible "says what it means, and means what it says," then the question arises, Which meaning is the preacher/reader/translator choosing to determine as the right one? Invariably, the one meaning that the "says what it means, means what it says" kind of preacher chooses as the "clear meaning" of the biblical text, is the one meaning that conforms to his (usually male, but not always) theological preference—whether he recognizes this, is conscious of this, or not. This is the reason why one must be aware of theological preferences, and how theological preference affects one's reading of the Bible, or to put it another way, we always interpret and translate the Scriptures through a theological lens.

Does this mean that there is no "objective" or "right" way of reading the Bible? Am I claiming that only a person who has studied the eight or nine esoteric, and ancient languages of biblical times has the right to interpret the Bible, since only they can truly translate it? Not at all. I do not agree with what may be called the "radical left wing" of biblical scholarship that attempts to strip away all vestiges of theological belief in order to get at the "true meaning" of the Bible.[2] This type of scholarship invokes what Marcus Borg has typified as a reductionist hermeneutic.[3]

While there are many ways to proceed with study of the Bible, when we start with the premise that the Bible is a translated witness using human words to convey the Word of God, we are dealing with reading the Bible from the vantage point of a theological reader. The theological reader of the Bible attempts to be a Godly or Spiritual Detective—discerning where God appears in the plot lines, the narration, the assumptions, hopes, fears, details, and outcomes. There is a profoundly theological reason for this opening premise, and that reason is that Christians' belief that the Holy Spirit, in Greek- the Paraclete—counsels, guides, and leads us into the truth of what we are reading in the words of the Bible. This is particularly true in the theology of the Gospel of John, in Chapter 14, 15, and 16:

> If you love me, obey my commandments, And I will ask the Father, and he will give you another Counselor [Greek: *Paraclete*, Advocate, Comforter, Encourager], who will never leave you. He is the Holy Spirit, who leads into all truth...(John 14:16–17a);
>
> I am telling you these things now while I am still with you. But when the Father send the Counselor as my representative—and by the Counselor I mean the Holy Spirit—he will teach you everything and remind you of everything I myself have told you. (John 14:25–26);
>
> But I will send you the Counselor—the Spirit of truth. He will come to you from the Father and will tell you all about me. (John 15:26) (NLTV);
>
> I have still many things to say to you, but you are not able to bear them or to take them upon you or to grasp them now. But when He, the Spirit of Truth (the Truth-giving Spirit) comes, He will guide you into all the Truth (the whole, full Truth). For He will not speak His own message [on His own authority]; but He will tell whatever he hears [from the Father; He will give the message that has been given to Him], and he will announce and declare to you the things that are to come [that will happen in the future]. (John 16:13) Amplified Bible.

The consistent witness of these four sections (or what Bible scholars call pericopes) of the Bible is a startlingly simple theological lesson—God aids us in reading the words attributed to God. To be more precise, through the living and active presence, power, and agency of the Holy Spirit, God enables us to read the words of the Bible with understanding. In other words, the Bible is not sacred because it is "the Bible." That would make us worship it rather than God, and thus commit the sin of Bibliolatry, something, many liberal Bible scholars imply, that conservative Christians appear to be committing. On the other hand, the Bible apparently is not to be read as merely a collection of words that have no relation whatsoever to God at all.

This is what conservative Bible scholars charge liberals with doing, and it seems that many liberals gladly would agree! Rather, it seems that a sensibly moderate, orthodox Christian approach to the Bible recognizes that the translated witness of the words within the Bible contain the will, plan, and directions of the eternal God, as human beings have variously interpreted it throughout biblical history. How are we to discern this? We cannot agree to such a proposition if we do not recognize the truth-value of the words contained in the Gospel of John as it directs our attention to the work of the Paraclete. Those words suggest that we, as human beings—whether highly trained scholars or the most humble church persons—need the assistance of the Holy Spirit to adequately translate and interpret how God speaks, where God is speaking, and especially what God is saying.

**Study Question**

1. How does the Dictionary define the word "witness?" How do we apply that meaning to the biblical witness?
2. Do you think that translation might alter the meaning of God's word?

## The "Spirit Teaches Us" Can Have Demonic Consequences

Having established that the Holy Spirit does indeed have a central role in clarifying, interpreting, and imprinting the Word into the words of the Bible, it is also important to speak forcefully about how Christian tradition has abused these very same Scriptures. I believe that the very same Scriptures I quoted above—John 14:16–17a; 25–26; 15:26; and 16:13 have been used improperly to limit the interpretive capacity of regular church folks, stifle regular Christians' ability to translate for themselves, and thus create the grounds for more centralized power in the clergy and ecclesiastical hierarchy. Since control of the written text was a way of maintaining political, military, and economic power through the upsurge of illegitimacy, violence, and barbarism that became known as the "Dark Ages," it is not surprising that the monks, priests, and bishops centralized their worldly power through control of the written text during those centuries when the Church stood as the sole remaining institution of sanity, civilization, and the faded imperial majesty of what had been the glorious Roman Empire. What is fascinating to me is how even after the so-called opening of the Text to the "vernacular"[4] of various nations that accompanied the Protestant Reformation in the early sixteenth century, those "divines"[5] who had charge of the Reformation held on to exclusive knowledge about the ancient languages of the Bible. So while they wanted the masses to be able to have direct access to "the Word," on the one hand, they really did not actually allow them to have direct access to those words, since the masses were not entrusted with learning the original languages! One could probably research and do entire volumes on the complex of reasons that justify why Martin Luther, John Calvin, and the others did not insist upon the masses learning the Word as it had been originally written. Such a task is beyond the purpose of this book, but a few points ought to be uplifted: (1) both Calvin and Luther were highly educated and trained in the Classics, and had a strong view of opening up the complexity of ancient languages to the directness and simplicity of what was the vernacular language of the regular folk; (2) Calvin, in particular, did not trust the masses to lead themselves, as reading the words of the Bible in its own original languages would have implied, and held to very strict doctrinal codes of interpreting biblical teachings;[6] and (3) both Luther and Calvin were more committed to establishing their followers with a clear catechism of Christian doctrine than to direct reading of Christian Scriptures. In the twenty-first century it is time for church folks to grow up. We can and must find the spiritual courage to begin the lifelong process of learning the complexities of ancient languages to read the words of the Word for ourselves, so that our translation can become fuller and richer.

## Which Translation Is the Best?

Theological-biblical study stirs our minds and spirits to interpret the Bible's words as having the possibility of many "translations." Hence we have the welcome proliferation of kinds and types of Bibles in the contemporary American scene today—from those accepted by so-called "liberal" and mainstream churches like the New Revised Standard Version, to those more widely received by traditional and conservative churches like the New International Version, or the New American Standard Bible.

I suggest that each and all of these translations is capable of interpreting God's Truth with integrity. The Truth of God's Word cannot be found by simply reciting Sunday School Scripture verses that someone else—usually a trusted elder in our parent's church—has already interpreted for us. But when we take such a critical step of thoughtful and *informed* reading of God's Word, sometimes the various possible translations available may shock us with multiple meanings arising in the very same verse. Thus the "Word" that we affirm theologically to be God's Word can indeed appear in multiple valences, surprising, and perhaps even shocking voices. In Deuteronomy 6:4–9, it must be remembered, we find the famous declaration of Hebrew faith, otherwise known as the *Shema*.

## Hear, O Israel: The LORD Our God, the LORD Is One

In the *Shema* God is declared to be "one." As an example of translated witness we need to look right at the first word. The verse begins with the Hebrew word *Shema*, which in English has traditionally been translated simply as "Hear." The word *Shema*, however, could be its own series of translated sentences alone. It means "give your undivided attention, obey, and give heed..."[7] This simple declaration is a magnificent statement of monotheism,[8] showing how the Hebrews radically departed from and differentiated themselves from the prevalent polytheism[9] of the ancient Near Eastern geographical and cultural context. But it would not be a simple declaration if Bible translators included the entire possible range of meanings in the first word of the verse. If the *Shema* were more fully translated it would be spoken in churches this way:

> "Listen up! Give your undivided attention in order that you might take care to heed and obey, o Israel—Chosen people of God. YAHWEH, God Almighty is our God. YAHWEH, God Almighty is One—the certain and First One.

## The Process

Looking at the Bible as a translated witness is viewing the phenomenon of "translation" from a broad perspective. "Translation," according to the *Encarta Webster's Dictionary of the English Language* (Second Edition) is usually taken in its first sense of meaning, "a word, phrase, or text in another language that has a meaning equivalent to that of the original."[10] The second sense of the term adds a bit of nuance to the first, "the rendering of something written or spoken in one language in words of a different language, i.e., It loses a little in translation."[11] I certainly could argue that reading the Bible in English is a loss of something after one learns Hebrew and Greek, since both of these ancient languages contain subtleties and nuances of expression that modern English lacks. Furthermore, it is clear that the translators of the Bible, from the King James through the New Revised Standard Version, have made definite choices of what certain words "mean," to the exclusion of other possible meanings. In other words, biblical translators have always limited the possible meaning of words to what seemed like the proper context of their appearance. Limiting possible meanings, however, can limit the multilayered fabric of spiritual possibility, challenge, and transformation resident in ancient Hebrew and Greek words. In addition, the theological perspectives of various groups of biblical translators has invariably affected which possible meaning has been chosen. Hence the New Revised Standard Version stood under the condemnation of many conservative and evangelical quarters of the Church because of certain choices made by the largely liberal group of translators. Choices like translating the traditional idea of "Behold a virgin shall conceive, and bear a son..." (Isaiah 7:14) as being changed to "A young woman shall conceive." Such a change created enormous conflict between the two opposing theological positions—liberal versus conservative. The Hebrew term *'almah* used in Isaiah 7:14 is translated *parthenos* in Greek in Matthew 1:22–23.[12]

NRSV translators made the choice of replacing the traditionally accepted church doctrine of the Virgin Birth of Jesus with what they believed to be a more appropriate understanding of "virginity" (the state of being a young, unmarried woman or girl) in ancient Israel. Conservative churches and biblical scholars, consequently, have rejected outright the NRSV's claim of being an authentic, valid, and credible translation of ancient Hebrew and Greek on what they consider to be its improper embrace of a deconstructive view of an important Christian dogma—the belief in a Virgin Birth as part and parcel of Jesus' claim to being "the Son of God." Instead, such conservative churches have overwhelmingly chosen the New International Version as the acceptable modern translation in accordance with their theological and doctrinal views. For the liberal NRSV scholars, the matter of emphasizing Mary's virginity is not as important as what they believed to be a more accurate literal translation of the words involved. Yet one would be hard-pressed not to detect in their choice of the phrase "a young woman" instead of the traditional "virgin" at least some aspect of the liberal theological concern to demythologize out-of-date references to supernaturalism in the Bible. As biblical students we need not condemn either side as much as we recognize the following two principles:

1. Our theological choices color our translation decisions. This refers both to specific words (such as *almah* and *parthenos*) as well as different versions of the Bible. Thus our inherited theological beliefs and worldviews predetermine which version/translation of the Bible we hold to be authoritative;
2. Thus, Bible translators cannot claim any true "objectivity" in their renderings of ancient biblical texts, because every translated word carries a theological Word. As we read a particular version of the Bible we need to be conscious of the theological presuppositions that the translators are carrying in order to discern how certain words have been translated.

While much biblical scholarship elaborates the first two senses of the term "translation," it seems to me that much fruitful discussion could be had if we were to open up what can be listed as a third sense of the word—"a change in form or state, or transference to a different place, office, or sphere."[13] If it is true indeed that the GOD of the universe is communicating to human beings by means of the fragile human words contained in the Bible, as every person of faith claims (in some way, shape, or argument), then some kind of transference, or change of state, must occur in order for these words to become GOD's Word. Thus the phenomenon of transference itself becomes part of the *Davar*—that Hebrew word usually translated simply as "word" (particularly in Exodus 20 "the word of the Lord") means the event, happening, command, saying, active speech..."[14] In particular, the Bible utilizes a multiplicity of verbs, nouns, and adjectives that describe both sound and vision when dealing with encounters with God.

## Ineffability of Language

The *Davar*, the event of divine encounter, is translated as "the word of the LORD" over 1,400 times in the Hebrew Bible.[15] These divine encounters are so ineffable, so beyond the descriptive power of human language, that they animate the imagination of the original biblical writers to push human language in its fullest sense. The prophetic "word of the LORD" has translated a veritable rainbow of meaning to those persons called by God to represent the intentions, commands, promises, warnings, blessings, as well as curses that God wanted to convey to the people of God. Whether it is the potent denunciation proclaimed in Isaiah's first Speech-Event to Judah where Yahweh condemns His own people as "rulers of Sodom…" and "people of Gomorrah" (Isaiah 1:7ff.); or the clear predestined intent of Yahweh to use Jeremiah as the appointed "prophet to the nations" (Jer.1:5), calling Jeremiah even in his mother's womb.

Despite the beyond-ness of the *Davar*, the prophets recognized that at the heart of their Speech-Event experience was the God they believed who is able to communicate to human beings in an understandable fashion. Yet how can we understand that which pushes the limited containers of human languages? The prophetic answer, the answer of church folk is clear even as it may be pooh-poohed by the academic community—we must approach the *Davar* with eyes, heart, and mind engaged in faith.

So interwoven is the prophetic/church folk faith in Yahweh's ability to communicate God's words to us with an often tacit recognition of language's ineffability—its incapacity to really say in the clearest possible terms—that we need to recognize the great mystery that is present. Church folk are right to read these *Davar* narratives as a mystery that ought to be respected even as it is carefully analyzed and subjected to the rigors of engaged human intellect. Perhaps this is why there is such a variety of languages, visions, dreams, and other spiritual encounters used to convey the ineffable always present when one experiences God. So our task is to appreciate that 66 book library that is the Bible.

We, looking back over the panoply of languages contained in the library that is the Bible, are challenged to tease out the various possible strands of meaning. Layers upon layers of meaning lie hidden underneath quick and easy translations, and treasures of spiritual blessing remain locked away behind nuances of meaning left unexplored. Let us look at the ways in which GOD has "spoken" in the Bible to those representative human beings known as patriarchs and matriarchs in the book of Genesis.

## Abraham

In a profound way we cannot speak about discerning the miracle of God's "Word" being translated out of the rough tissue of human words unless we begin with the "father" of all monotheistic faiths—Abraham. Judaism, Christianity, and Islam all claim Abraham as their first "father of the faith" who was able to discern God's voice speaking to him In Genesis 12:1–3 we find the famous "call of Abram":

> Now the LORD said to Abram,
> "Go forth from your country, and from your relatives
> And from your father's house, to the land which I will show you.
> And I will make you a great nation,
> And I will bless you, and make your name great.
> And so you shall be a blessing;
> And I will bless those who bless you,
> And the one who curses you will I curse.
> And in you all the families of the earth will be blessed." (NASB)

We are not given a clear meaning of how God speaks to Abram. There are no exact words that clarify what medium or means God uses to communicate to Abram. We have only the simple translation that "the LORD said..." something to Abram so promising, so soul-stirring, and life-changing that he acted upon it. A sustained look at several divine visitations, visions, voices—could readily be called *theophany*, or divine appearances, that Abraham experienced between Genesis 12 and 25. All of these various divine encounters, taken together, apparently served as a kind of spiritual confirmation of the veracity of that first experience. What is both fascinating and inspiring about this calling of Abram passage in Genesis 12:1–3 is that the wealthy Abram apparently acted on this first experience. Based on this first Divine experience he packed up everything, left his native hometown of Ur in what was known at that time as "the Chaldees,"[16] and began the long journey toward Canaan.

We are never told in what sense God "spoke" to Abram. We are only told that God did speak in a manner that Abram could understand—whether audibly, within his thoughts, or in some other intangible fashion outside of the descriptive power of language. The reason why we are compelled to give sufficient pause to this first "calling" experience is its very un-translatability. In some unique and ineffable way the Creator of the "heavens and the earth," the One who made the cosmos so great that we cannot imagine its vastness as well as the subatomic particles and minutiae so infinitesimal that we cannot fathom them either—that God chooses to communicate with us in an understandable fashion. The only human words that approximate such an experience seem to relate the encounter in the flat words, "The LORD spoke..." We need to find both the time and the inner spiritual wisdom to recognize how polydimensional and glorious this numinous encounter was, reported in human words that are both too one-dimensional and too weak to adequately express what they translate them to mean.

A few verses later, 12:6–7, the LORD (which in Hebrew is "Yahweh") appears to Abram in Canaan:

> Abram passed through the land as far as the site of Shechem, to the oak of Moreh. Now the Canaanite was then in the land. The LORD appeared to Abram and said, "To your descendents will give this land." So he built an altar there to the LORD who had appeared to him. (NASB)

This appearance narrative is based on the Hebrew word *ra'ah*. According to the *Key Word Study Bible*, *ra'ah* is a complex word to translate because it can mean several different things. Primarily the word means "to see" as found in Genesis 29:10; 32:2, 30. It can also mean "to understand," or "perceive" (Isaiah 52:15; Jeremiah 23:13, 14). It is also translated as "ascertain" (Genesis 16:4, 5); "verify" (Genesis 26:28); "examine, investigate" (Genesis 11:5); "to supervise" (Genesis 29:23); "to attend to" (2 Samuel 13:5); "to select" (Genesis 41:33); "to imitate" (Judges 7:17); "to discover" (Judges 16:5); and "to experience" (Jeremiah 5:12).[17] Again, the usage of the word ra'ah indicates an "appearance" of Yahweh to Abram, but it is uncertain exactly what kind of "appearance" it is.

Is the "appearance" of Yahweh in Genesis 12:6–7 a full-fledged theophany, "an appearance of a god in visible form to a human being?"[18] If it is, then it is one of the least dramatic of theophanies to be listed in the Bible. More likely this particular usage of the word *ra'ah* suggests that the "appearance" of the Lord to Abram (at this point) was one of mental or intellectual revelation. Looking at the list of 12 possible ways that *ra'ah* can be understood in modern English, it seems that the "appearance" of Yahweh that occurred here referred to an understanding, perception, discovery, ascertaining, and experience of the LORD addressing Abram's mind. It actually did enable Abram to "see" God's will, plan, and promise more clearly, as well as to ascertain, and to verify with greater certainty that he had indeed "heard" God back in verses 1–3.

When one looks back at the previous paragraph with a critical and appreciative eye it is quite apparent that our contemporary, everyday usage of the term "appear," and the manner in which ra'ah is translated as "appeared" have noticeably distant meanings. There is historical or temporal distance in their application. There is cultural distance—the difference in application of how contemporary society understands "sight" and "vision," versus a premodern, agricultural, nomadic culture.

## Further Study

Use *Strong's Concordance* and a *Key Word Study Bible* of whatever translation to complete your intensive word study of the following figures:

1. Hagar—Genesis 16:7–16 (Theophany "God Who is Seen"); 21:8–21 (Opening Hagar's eyes);
2. Moses—Exodus 3:1–4:17 (*theophany*—burning bush); Exodus 13:20–22 (Pillar of Cloud and Fire); 19:9–20 (Thick Cloud, Fire, Smoke, and a Voice); 33:12–23 (Theophany—God's kabod, His "back");
3. Elijah—I Kings 19:1–18 ("gentle whisper" verse 12);
4. Isaiah—1:1 (vision); 6:1–13 (commissioning vision); 13:1 (*oracle*[19]).

From these four foundational figures we can see a pattern that repeats itself throughout the entire Bible. We find it ringing down through the ages into the experience of Jews in the early Christian era. The pattern continues with Saul, the virulent persecutor of the early Christian church, who has a profound visionary experience of the resurrected Jesus in Acts 9:1–19. In verse 3 the Divine appears as a blinding, flashing light; or in Greek, the *phos*—"daylight, firelight,"[20] and "what gives forth light."[21] The experience knocks Saul to the ground, and from that position he hears the voice, sound, or tone[22] of the resurrected Jesus who presents this query to Saul:

> "Saul, Saul, why do you persecute me?"

This is the "calling" experience that translates into the initial point of Saul's conversion to the most influential early Christian apostle known as Paul. For the first 30 verses of Acts 9 we witness the transformation of Saul from persecutor of the church:

1. Saul is blinded and speechless, a man in need of a miracle (verses 7–9);
2. The disciple Ananias receives a vision from God instructing him to heal Saul (verses 10–16);
3. Ananias obeys the vision and Saul regaining both vision and health (verses 17–19a);
4. Saul becomes a disciple himself, and begins to preach that Jesus is the Son of God to the astonishment of those who remembered that he had persecuted those who had preached the very same message (verses 19b–22).

### Discussion Question

What is the connection between "seeing God," or having some type of vision and calling experience of God—and the translated witness of the Word of God in your view?

## Postmodern Theological Musings—The Tower of Babel

We live in a time of great social, political, ethical, and cultural upheaval that most liberals have embraced and conservatives have loudly decried. It is a period that both sides have more or less agreed to call "postmodern," and it seems to be a time period fraught with the renewed fires of contradictory revivals of fundamentalist religious movements (Christian and Moslem in particular); and a virulent non-theistic/atheistic intellectualism. One of the most popular, seemingly anti-religious movements of postmodernity has been deconstruction; and yet its founder—Jacques Derrida—spent the past decade of his life fervently working out the religious implications of the corpus of his works![23] Derrida has some profoundly important points to make about the translated witness of the Word.

The first, and most important, postmodern theological point about translation is that God is the primary Mover, Causal Agent, and Instigator of Translation.[24] One way of understanding God in this way is to take a second look at an unlikely scene in Genesis 1, in the infamous story of the Tower of Babel narrative.

The very first thing we are told about the pre-Babel people is that they were of one unified language: "And the whole earth was of one language, and of one speech" (Genesis 11:1). This linguistic unity becomes the basis for their grand desires and hubris to be like God in the tower "whose top may reach unto heaven"; as well as secure for themselves a permanent name and place "and let us make us a name, lest we be scattered abroad upon the face of the whole earth" (Genesis 11:4b). God comes down and "confuses" the languages of the people, in order to stop the building of the offending tower (verse 7).

Why does God choose to disrupt this linguistic unity? Could it be because under the solidarity and unifying power of one language human beings could muster almost godlike powers? Perhaps linguistic unity fueled the primal desires for dynasty, or empire, of which this city and tower was the architectural symbol? In other words, is the Genesis 11 story a parable about God's response to the first people who revealed that they had a "God-complex?" After all, they did say that they wanted a "name." In the Hebrew Bible the word "Ha Shem" is "The Name." It is sacred, and related only to God's Holy Name, the unutterable Name, *Yahweh*. In Hebrew sacred traditions, the four sacred letters eventually were considered so holy that they were not even pronounced aloud, so that whenever one came across the word Yahweh in the Bible, the word *Adonay* was said aloud instead. Could it be possible that these early mighty people's desire for a "name" was their greatest sin, and that their Tower was a manifestation of a deep, underlying spiritual desire to have their "name" be like "Ha Shem?" Perhaps this is what God discerned in Genesis 11:5–6:

> And the Lord came down to see the city and the tower, which the children of men built. And the Lord said, Behold, the people is one, and they have all one language: and this they begin to do: and now nothing will be restrained from them, which they have imagined to do. (King James Version)[25]

For Derrida, Babel is the place wherein translation becomes the form, style, prescription, and mandate wherein human beings think God's thoughts after God.[26]

Thus translation is not for communication, but is the ongoing modification of "the formal law of the immanence of the original text"—that "original text" being whatever God has thought and spoken. Derrida has no problem with translation being slippery and always in the process of modification and transformation because for him the actual "event" of translation is "sacred" in and of itself—a movement of "holy growth," "revelation," and "prophecy."[27]

While I have simplified some of Derrida's most complicated and convoluted philosophical mind-games, I think that he has something positive to say to church folk who worry about all this fuss over translation. As a Christian I would simply say that the moments that we translate the original Hebrew and Greek texts into their various English meanings we are engaging the Word as Holy. At that moment of translation we are not merely exercising our intellect to discover "what it means," but our inner spiritual ears are listening to "what it says to our lives." As such, translation moves from the mundane realm of thought to the exalted heights of prophecy.

## Discussion Questions

1. Has your mind been changed about the importance of the Bible as a "translated witness?"
2. What points in this chapter do you remember the most?

# 4

# Proclaimed Witness

Chapter four further unfolds the analysis of witness within a theology of the Word in Black Churches one step further by looking at the Bible as a "proclaimed witness." There would never have been a religious, social, cultural movement that rocked the very foundations of the Roman Empire were it not for the publicly declared witness of the Good News—the proclamation of a crucified Jew named *Yehoshua* as the Risen Christ.

Proclamation stands at the heart of Black Church practice, and might even be considered one of the most important historic contributions African American Christians have made. The very out-flowing nature of proclamation pulsates in all three Greek words that the New Testament uses in describing the term. The first and most recognizable Greek word is *evangelizo*—which means "to announce good news, to declare, evangelize, proclaim." The Apostle Paul often used this verb with the noun *evangelion* ("the gospel, good news") as in I Corinthians 15:1:

> Now I would remind you, brothers and sisters, of the good news that
> I proclaimed to you, which you in turn received, in which also you stand,
> Through which also you are being saved, if you hold firmly to the message that I
> proclaimed to you—unless you have come to believe in vain. (NRSV)

Kerusso is another Greek word—"to act as a herald," or "to call out with power" with one's voice is the second Greek term used specifically in reference to preaching. Calling out with power, from the soles of one's feet to the crown of one's head is traditional Black preaching at its best. Black preachers, from slavery times even into these present days, have never been afraid to raise their voices with emotional strength and verbal eloquence. Proclamation as *kerusso* is the opposite of lecturing. It is not providing a calm, boring, un-inspiring stream of words that are meant to provide intellectual understanding with little or no emotional succor or support. Proclamation is supposed to integrate emotion and understanding, spirit and flesh, sweat and blood, fire and water, life and guts! One is supposed to be moved![1]

The third Greek word is the noun *kerygma* meaning "proclamation, sermon, message, that which is cried out, and communicated by the herald."[2] Paul made sure that the *kerygma* of Jesus Christ he preached was perfectly clear and easily understood:

> My speech and my *proclamation* were not with plausible words of wisdom, But with a demonstration of the Spirit and of power so that your faith might rest not on human wisdom but on the power of God. (I Corinthians 2:4–5) (NRSV)

The Apostle Paul taught and preached the *kerygma* as the Basic Building Blocks of the Gospel—Jesus 101.

- All human beings have sinned (*hamartia*—fallen short of the mark), and cannot do anything to save themselves (Romans 1–3);
- The cross of Christ—His Crucifixion and eventual resurrection—conveys the inherent power (*dunamis*) and wisdom (*Sophia*) of God that enables human beings in the process of being saved (*sozo* —"saved, delivered, made whole, preserved from danger"[3] (I Corinthians 1:12–25);
- Jesus was sent by the Father to die for our sins so that we could be reconciled back to God (2 Corinthians 5:19);
- This gospel (good news) is to be strongly and openly declared and proclaimed (*katangello*) as the true testimony (*martyrion*—"a witness, proof, the declaration that makes something known"[4]) of God. As such, it is proclaimed most effectively in "demonstrations" of the power of the Holy Spirit, rather than relying exclusively on the eloquence and persuasion of words, taking the form of faith (*pistis*) in the hearts of believers. (I Corinthians 2:1–5);
- By his resurrection Jesus Christ demonstrates that he is the Son of God, and adopts us to be the children of God with Him. (I Corinthians 15:1–19; Galatians 1:1; 4:1–7);
- When we receive Jesus within we become part of his "New Creation" (2 Corinthians 5: 16–18). Christians are Christ's ambassadors, representing Him, acting with the Holy Spirit's gifts, power, authority, and love (2 Corinthians 5:20–21; I Corinthians 12:1–26; 13; and 14);

- The Church is Christ's Body (*Soma*) on earth (I Corinthians 12:27–31);
- Jesus Christ will return (*Parousia*), the final mystery of His coming back again in victory to establish His Kingdom on earth (I Corinthians 15:20–58).

## Discussion

Take the time to read all of the above verses; particularly I Corinthians 12–15. In the first 19 verses of Chapter 15 Paul gives a brief overview of the importance of resurrection to the "gospel" or *evangelion*. Apparently Paul believed in the centrality of Jesus' bodily resurrection from the dead, something that is very difficult for modern believers to accept on face value. Do you believe that Jesus "rose from the dead?" What difference does it make to a Christian's faith if one believes in a "spiritual" resurrection, or a "physical" one?

Church folks experience the *kerygma* as "the gospel." Sometimes it is wrapped up in the soaring melodies, earthy rhythms, and embracing harmonies of a gospel, hymn, or praise song. Sometimes "the gospel" is felt most strongly in these artistic "proclamations" of the *kerygma*, especially in historically African American churches. Yet, beyond the stereotype, behind the ethnic-racial classification, all church folk from every background experience "the gospel" in many varied and fascinating forms.

Tradition-bound individuals have frozen certain forms of worship, praise, and music to the states of being the only, proper way that one experiences Jesus Christ. In some local congregations decisions have been made that exclude contemporary gospel music, or praise-dancing as "too worldly," for example. We find Baptist, African Methodist Episcopal, Congregational, Presbyterian, Lutheran, and even Roman Catholic Churches that hold fervently to such views. At the same time there are many churches in these very same denominations that are daring to experiment with bold audacity—developing praise-dancers, step-praise teams, Gospel Rappers, and many other "cutting-edge" types of praise and worship formats. No one can stand in judgment of whether one church is being more *kerygmatic* or not, because the *kerygma* of Jesus Christ seems able to manifest itself in a multitude of forms—as is appropriate to the needs, choices, and tastes of the people. The *kerygma* are those basic doctrinal teachings about the life, death, resurrection, mission, and meaning of Jesus as the Christ. It is above and beyond the confines of any one, particular type of preacher, hymn, praise-song, praise-dance, or Gospel rap. The *kerygma*, while free of being confined to any one form, is ironically able to take on myriad cultural, artistic, and literary forms in order for it to become manifest (what the Greek language calls *apocalypto*—unveiling that which has been hidden cf. I Corinthians 2:6–10). For the Apostle Paul, in the book of I Corinthians, the important thing to remember is that God reveals the *kerygma* to us by the activity, operation, and demonstration (the *dunamis*) of the Holy Spirit. Thus the Holy Spirit—the *Pneuma*—that invisible Breath of God—is able to secretly infuse itself into anything that it chooses. The place that we need to focus our judgment and sense of discernment, therefore, is on properly "seeing" where and when the Holy Spirit is active in our presence—no matter who or what is going on at the time.

A personal example is in order. I remember going to a small church to preach several years ago and finding a surprising blessing. The blessing was in the form of a very old lady singing the perennial Gospel favorite, "His Eye is on the Sparrow." The truth of Jesus being closer to me than any human being, and able to "watch over me" came through despite the fact that she had a terrific wobble in her voice that sometimes obscured the different pitches of the melody. She was also somewhat illiterate, so her interpretation of the refrain included this phrase "...His eyes is on der Sparrows, and I knows him watches me." Now Garth, the son of a perfect-speech school teacher was upset with her lack of proper grammar, and I was distracted at first, I admit! Yet I felt the Holy Spirit flowing through her voice, using her as the instrument of blessing that morning, and it humbled me. I experienced the "demonstration of power in the Holy Spirit" that Paul wrote about in verses I Corinthians 2:4–5. That morning the *kerygma* came to life beyond the pale of merely interesting sounding words.

## Did Jesus Preach the Same "Gospel" as that of Paul?

The book of Luke 4:18–19 reveal that Jesus understood his ministry to be one of proclaiming the "good news":

> The Spirit of the LORD is on me, because he has anointed me to
> *preach good news* [*evangelizo* in Greek] to the poor.
> He has sent me to proclaim freedom for the prisoners

> And recovery of sight for the blind, to release the oppressed, and to proclaim
> The year of the LORD's favor. (NIV)

What was this "good news," this *evangelion* of Jesus of Nazareth? In a few verses later in Luke 4:42—after being rejected in his hometown Nazareth (verses 28–30); driving out an evil spirit in Capernaum (verses 31–35); and demonstrating the power of the Spirit by healing the sick and demon possessed (verses 38–39)—Jesus reiterates his primary calling to those who want to keep Him and his miraculous powers for themselves alone and in their town alone:

> But he said to them, "I must proclaim the good news of the *kingdom of God* to the other cities also; for I was sent for this purpose." (Luke 4:43)

It is in the phrase "kingdom of God" that we find an important distinction between the Gospel of Paul concerning Jesus, and what Jesus himself called the "Gospel of the Kingdom of God." Paul focused on the death and resurrection of Jesus, and the effects of those events on our human salvation. Jesus did not focus on himself. Jesus proclaimed the *kingdom of God*, or what in Greek is the *basileia tou Theou*. The word *basileia* means "royal dominion, kingdom, realm of rule, rule,"[5] or reign. Thus Jesus saw himself as proclaiming the Reign of God—God's divine rule and royal dominion—here on the earth. This Gospel focuses us on what God has done, is doing, and will do in and through the people of God—the church.

Jesus taught extensively about the Kingdom of God during his three-year ministry. In a way one could say that everything Jesus did and spoke uplifted the presence of the Reign of God. Thus what we might choose to call the Kingdom Gospel of Jesus as having a radically different setting than the Gospel of Jesus is proclaimed by Paul. The Kingdom Gospel includes the following:

> The Sermon on the Mount and the Lukan Sermon on the Plain (Matthew 5–7; Luke 6:17–49). Both versions include the famous Beatitudes (Matthew 5:3–12; Luke 6:20–26). In these sermons Jesus reinterprets what we normally consider to be a negative (i.e., being poor and/or poor in spirit, or being persecuted) from the perspective of God's Kingdom. He also reorients the disciples toward a distinctive way of being human in the world—the way of perfect maturity. He recommends a new standard for fulfilling *Torah*

that includes being the "salt of the earth" that preserves the world (Matthew 5:130); the "light of the world" (Matthew 5:14); pure in one's dealing with sexual issues (Matthew 5:27–30); truly committed to lifelong marriage (Matthew 5:31–32); simple and direct about one's oaths (Matthew 5:37); willing to go far beyond typical human reactions like revenge and resentfulness because of oppression; and finally, able to overcome enmity by "loving your enemies" (Matthew 5:43–48). Jesus demands that we "Be perfect, therefore, as your heavenly Father is perfect." The Greek word that we choose to translate "perfect" here is *teleios*—meaning "finished, consummated, complete, perfected, proficient, full-grown, and mature."[6]

## Discussion

Reread the last verse of Matthew 5 (verse 48) using all the possible words provided above. For example, "Be complete even as your heavenly Father is complete." By using these different verses, what do you see is Jesus' way of speaking about "perfection?" Do you now believe that it is possible to be biblically "perfect?"

Reread the Sermon on the Mount in Matthew and Luke.

- Golden Rule—"Do to others as you would have them do to you" (Luke 6:31) (NRSV). In the Sermon on the Mount Jesus expands upon this "Golden Rule," noting that we are to fulfill this rule by loving our enemies *and* by forsaking judgmental ways (Luke 6:36–37; Matthew 7:1–6). Matthew expands this new orientation toward life by noting that we ought to give to the needy without fanfare and self-adulation; ought to pray with our relationship to God foremost, and not how it appears to others, ought to perform spiritual disciplines like fasting in secret; ought to value eternal treasures rather than allowing the pursuit of earthly wealth. (Matthew 6:1–34).
- The Kingdom is Like...Jesus proclaimed the Kingdom of heaven/kingdom of God by using parables—*parabole* in Greek. The word *parabole* means "to compare," thereby making parables "a comparison, a similitude" using narrative, maxims, and proverbial form.[7] Thus, by using the *parabole*, the Gospel writers were able to show Jesus as the teacher and proclaimed of God's rule that is like so-and-so. In Mark 4 Jesus uses two parables about seeds to demonstrate how the Kingdom of God, though it begins as something very tiny, blossoms, and flourishes into something much greater. In the parable of the Growing Seed Jesus declares:

> This is what the Kingdom of God is like. A man scatters seed on the ground. Night and day, whether he sleeps or gets up, the seed sprouts and grows, though he does not know how. All by itself the soil produces grain—first, the stalk, then the head, then the full kernel in the

head. As soon as the grain is ripe, he puts the sickle to it, because the harvest has come. (Mark 4:26–29) (NIV)

The genius of this parable is that it uses comparisons with a farmer's world to teach its lesson. The "man" who scatters the seed can be interpreted as God or God's agent. The "seed" is the radical core teachings of the Word. The "ground" is us, regular church and nonchurch folk. Within the "soil" the "seed" of God's kingdom eventually sprouts and grows—although it does so secretly—beyond easy observation. Nevertheless, the seeds follow a pathway of growth that leads to their natural maturation—from seed to stalk, stalk to head, and head to a full kernel. The Reign of God ripens within us like that seed, growing whether we are aware of its growth or not. Then, as is true for many of Jesus' parables, there is an *eschatological* point, a point about the End of Time, Judgment Day. In this case, the ripened seed is harvested by the "Sickle"—the cutting edge of God's Word—at the end of time. We church folk are growing seed, moving toward the time when we shall become what God has intended for us to become, the "full grain" harvest that is useful for others.

The Parable of the Mustard Seed uses the seed-imagery in a slightly different casting:

> Again he said, What shall we say the kingdom of God is like, or what parable shall we use to describe it? It is like a mustard seed, which is the smallest seed you plant in the ground. Yet when planted, it grows and becomes the largest of all garden plants, with such big branches that the birds of the air perch in its shade. (Mark 4:30–32) (NIV)

In the Mustard Seed parable the Reign of God begins in the smallest, almost invisible ways—personally and publicly. Here the "yet" is, perhaps, the most important disjuncture because even though the presence of the Kingdom can begin in such a small way, it has the potential of growing into the largest, most protective, and impressive of qualities. What starts as a simple confession of faith grows into the most outstanding feature, the most potent example of faith and faithfulness in one's life.

In order to demonstrate the energizing effects of the Kingdom of God as an ongoing and pervasive presence, Jesus told the Parable of the Leavened Bread:

> Again he [Jesus] asked, "What shall I compare the kingdom of God? It is like yeast that a woman took and mixed into a large amount of flour until it *worked* all through the dough. (Luke 13:20–21) (NIV)

The Greek verb for "worked," *zymoo*, can be translated as "leavened, something mixed with yeast, and ferment."[8] The Reign of God ferments the "flour"—the people of God, transforming them from the scattered spiritual material of our lives into a rich, wholesome spiritual food capable of feeding others. Without "yeast," without that leavening agent, flour cannot be transformed into bread. Without yeast the flour remains an element of potential-not-realized. Without the Reign of God ordinary people cannot be the People of God—they cannot attain the status of being "church folk."

The Parable of the Great Banquet describes the Reign of God. When Jesus replied to the claim of someone eating dinner with him, the claim that stated, "Blessed is the man who will eat in the feast of the kingdom of God," he told the following parable:

> A certain man was preparing a great banquet and invited many guests. At the time of the banquet he sent his servant to tell those who had been invited, "Come, for everything is now ready." (Luke 14:16–17)

God prepares a wonderful feast for His guests, and He invites us to partake of that feast and one would expect that any and every person invited to such an occasion would find a way to attend, but that is not the response:

> But they all alike began to make excuses. (Luke 14:18a)

Jesus notes the excuses that each one has:

> The first said, "I have just bought a field, and I must go and see it. Please excuse me." Another said, "I have just bought five yoke of oxen, and I'm on my way to try them out. "Please, excuse me." Still another said, "I just got married so I can't come." (Luke 14: 17b–20)

All of the invited guests were taken up with other concerns that they considered to be more important than coming to the Great Banquet. These excuses may be interpreted in the following way: (1) the first guest was preoccupied with his schedule—he could not fit in a wondrous banquet into his plans; (2) the second guest was so tied to his responsibilities and all of the management skills they require that he could not take the time out for fellowship;[9] and (3) the third guest valued the pleasures of self and family more than responding to the call of the Great Feast-Maker.[10] Of course the one giving the invitation, the "certain man," is none other than God Almighty calling the people of God to come to the Great Feast that He has prepared just for our edification, recreation, and benefit. Yet we, the called people of God, often choose to be world-centered, rather than God-centered.

Notice how the master responds, and how the invitation is broadened:

> So the slave returned and reported this to his master. Then the owner of the house became angry and said to his slave, "Go out at once into the streets and lanes of the town and bring in the poor, the crippled, the blind and the lame." And the slave said "Sir, what you have ordered has been done, and there is still room." Then the master said to the slave, "Go out into the roads and the lanes, and compel people to come in, so that my house may be filled. For I tell you, none of those who were invited will taste my dinner." (Luke 14:21–24) (NRSV)

Since the original guests have spurned their invitations, the master reveals that those who are outcast, downtrodden, ostracized, ignored, and oppressed in one or other way are to become the "replacements" on an ever-widening circle of welcome. Welcome is not confined to the wealthy and privileged, nor limited according to one's sense of entitlement and "chosen-ness." The Reign of God is welcome for all people, it calls everyone. So even after all of the oppressed have positively responded, "there is still room" at the Banquet. Using very striking and intense language, Jesus notes that the call of the Kingdom of God compels everyone to come in. Church folk stand quietly amazed at such overwhelming, assertive, aggressive welcome. Often church folks recognize that within the sanctified security of our private churches we feel all cozy knowing who is coming, and how much they offer to our church in prestige and honor. But Jesus requires aggressive, uncompromising welcome to all people, especially to those who are usually never invited to anything special and wonderful. This parable pinches the greedy and small-hearted, reminding them of the immensity of God's call. God's calling to come into church is bigger than our little churches, no matter how large or small they may be. The severe warning at the end of the parable reminds us that we cannot play loose and fast with God's calling, for we may condemn our very souls if we cannot widen the outreach of love in our hearts.

• The Kingdom Gospel rooted in the *Torah*—uplifting personal and social salvation together. Perhaps the greatest challenge of the Kingdom Gospel is that it demands a larger view of "being saved" than the personal gratification of individual salvation. Perhaps one of the greatest downfalls of many evangelical and conservative church folk—whether in Black Church or not—is that we tend to get excited about our own salvation to the exclusion of how God wants to save the public realm from social injustices as well. On the other hand, many of our more liberal sisters and brothers proclaim a gospel that is so oriented to God's intent for social justice and the ending of oppression that individual relationship with God is severely downplayed, or ignored altogether. Both sides of the church are correct in their perspective strengths—the conservative emphasis on personal relationship individually with God, and the liberal emphasis on eliminating social justice in the name of God—yet lacking completeness. The Kingdom Gospel insists that we fulfill Jesus' interpretation of *Torah*, as represented in the following scripture:

> Just then a lawyer stood up to test Jesus. "Teacher," he said, "what must I do to inherit eternal life?" He said to him, "What is written in the Law [*Torah*]? What do you read there?" He answered, "You shall love the LORD your God with all your heart, and with all your soul, and with all your strength, and with all your mind; and your neighbor as yourself." And Jesus said to him, "You have given the right answer; do this, and you will live." But wanting to justify himself, he asked Jesus, "And who is my neighbor?" (Luke 10:25–29a) (NRSV)

Notice that the lawyer knows the *Torah*, and is able to encapsulate all of the over 600 articulations of *Torah* into the two step format of loving God with your all, and loving the neighbor as one's self. For the lawyer, as it is for many conservatively nurtured church folk, the question is not about my individual relationship responsibilities to God. Rather, perhaps recognizing this lack of love in his own walk with God, the lawyer queries the definition, extent, and challenge of who the "neighbor" may be that the God-related person is required to love.

Jesus responds by telling of one of his most famous of parables—the Good Samaritan (Luke 10:29–37).

Read the Parable of the Good Samaritan

It is important to remember that this parable must have been shocking to Jesus' Jewish listeners at the time. Within the story the obvious "hero" is a hated Samaritan—a member of the break-away Jewish community who worshipped in Shechem rather than in the Temple of Jerusalem. Samaritans were so despised by Jews that they were treated with disrespect, and understood to be so far away from true *Torah* observance as to almost be considered "Gentiles." Yet Jesus makes the Samaritan the one person who responds to the physical wounds of the anonymous "man" who had been accosted by bandits and left for dead. It would also be clear to the original hearers of this Parable that the priest and the Levite who saw the need and chose to "pass by" instead, were simply following the dictates of *Torah* that strictly enforced the code of "clean" and "unclean." If either one of these individuals had even touched this man's half-dead (probably looking dead) body they would have made themselves ritually defiled, and become "unclean." Thereby they would forfeit their ability to serve in the Temple as priest or Levite until elaborate cleansing rituals of purification were performed (Leviticus 21:1–3, 10–11). The Samaritan, on the other hand, fulfilled the entire intent of the "Law and the Prophets" by going beyond rigid *Torah* observance to observance of the entire spirit of *Torah,* which the prophet Micah said was "To act justly and to love mercy and to walk humbly with your God" (Micah 6:8b).

During severe crises—like the mass exodus of survivors of the Hurricane Katrina—all churches joined together to serve the needs of all that bruised and wounded humanity. That is church folks at their best, demonstrating their powerful personal relationship with Jesus Christ with tangible evidence of loving concern for the needy. The Reign of God demands that both sides of God's Church begin to grow toward one another's strengths, rather than condemning each other's weaknesses.

### Discussion Question

Why do churches find it so hard to both love God and neighbors?

The question above insists upon the necessary connection between believing in God and Jesus as the Christ, and exemplifying that belief by living a life that uplifts all humanity—especially outcast and oppressed humanity. I aver that one cannot be a whole and complete Christian who is truly rooted in biblical authority and knowledge if one is not combining the revelation of a personal relationship with Jesus Christ and striving mightily in the name of God against all forces, institutions, ideologies, and practices that negate and oppress other human beings—Christian or not. The simple declaration found in Psalms 9:9: "The LORD is a refuge for the oppressed, a stronghold in times of trouble" is premised on the two previous verses:

> The LORD reigns forever,
> He has established his throne for judgment.
> He shall judge the world in righteousness. He will
> Govern the peoples with justice. (Psalm 9:7–8) (NIV)

While such a strong assertion about God's justice, righteousness, and governing the world, especially by sheltering the oppressed with strengthening power may seem hopelessly naive, out of touch with reality, and romantically idealistic—it nevertheless establishes the connection between believing in the LORD, having relationship with the LORD, and living out a life that is open to serving all human beings and nature. One may notice that even the phrase "the oppressed" can be widened to include more than oppressed human beings. The term oppressed may be related to the whole swath of unjust dealings with fellow human beings, ecological disaster and the violation of the natural world, and oppressed creatures living within nature. Church folk ought to be front-line soldiers in the struggle to gain human agency and responsibility in regard to the dangerous phenomenon of global warming. We ought to be the first champions of animal rights—insisting that all construction and development does not encroach upon the habitats of other living creatures.

For some such claims are, in fact, irrational and needlessly romantic. Such a person is my friend and colleague, Anthony Pinn, who has written a brilliant counterthesis that deserves proper examination as we discuss the fuller ramifications of the term proclamation.

## A Different Gospel

Anthony Pinn's *African American Humanist Principles* is a brilliant declaration of a different, oppositional, and revolutionary African American humanist Gospel. I use the term "gospel" for Pinn's work because he presents it as "good news"—a set of beliefs and life-changing practices that uplift the potential of human beings to responsibly and reasonably take care of the world and transform it. Pinn explains it this way:

> ...human potentiality and creativity must be exalted and both personal fulfillment and social well-being promoted.[11]

Pinn's gospel is distinctively secular humanist, because he negates the need for a God or anything having to do with supernatural explanations:

> Supernatural rationales and explanations for human life are rejected, and religion is understood as being a human construct.[12]

As Islam is established on the so-called Five Pillars, so Pinn, approvingly quoting Charles Lamont's *Humanism as Philosophy*, notes that humanism is built on the "three secure pillars: reason, science, and democracy."[13]

Pinn is interested in giving humanism a distinctively African American locus and focus of concern. He notes that the African American Humanist Declaration of 1990 outlined several "concerns" of which he agrees. The specifically African American humanist points in the Declaration uplifts

- Fight against racism in every form;
- Incorporate an Afrocentric outlook into a broader world perspective;
- Develop eupraxophy, which is "wisdom and good conduct through living" in the African American community by using scientific and rational methods of inquiry;
- Solve many of the problems that confront African Americans through education and self-reliance, thereby affirming that autonomy and freedom of choice are basic human rights;
- Develop self-help groups and engage in any humane and rational activity designed to develop the African American community.[14]

Pinn even uses a biblical figure—that of Nimrod—to speak of the fundamental aims of his gospel. He reinterprets the infamous leader of the Tower of Babel into a symbolic hero that "...suggests that once one breaks preoccupation with supernaturalism and the unfounded cosmic issues it dictates, human beings confront the possibility (although not always realized as existentialists have shown us) of nurturing creativity and potential in transforming ways."[15] Thus African American humanists are encouraged to turn away from being "children of God" toward being, instead, "the children of Nimrod." As the children of Nimrod, Pinn offers Five Principles that orient both African American humanist beliefs and practices:

1. Understanding of humanity as fully (and solely) accountable and responsible for the human condition and the correction of humanity's plight;
2. Suspicion toward or rejection of supernatural explanations and claims, combines with an understanding of humanity as an evolving part of the natural environment as opposed to being a created being. This can involve disbelief in God(s);
3. An appreciation for African American cultural production and a perception of traditional forms of black religiosity as having cultural importance as opposed to any type of "cosmic" authority;
4. A commitment to individual and societal transformation;

5. A controlled optimism that recognizes both human potential and human destructive activities.[16]

Pinn arrives at his secular African American gospel after having renounced being an ordained minister in the African Methodist Episcopal church. He briefly outlines his intellectual and faith journey in a persuasive, tightly organized mini-autobiography.[17] Pinn's move away from faith and the pulpit were precipitated by some profound questions of which many Black Church folk may share:

> "No cross, no crown." This troubled me. If God loves black folk and wants what is best for them, why do they continue to suffer disproportionately in the United States? I couldn't reconcile my Christian beliefs with societal conditions.[18]

Pinn's faith broke apart on the unforgiving cross of what scholars call theodicy—the questioning of the existence of evil and wrong if a good, powerful, and loving God exists. Pinn could not, in all honesty and openness, reconcile belief in a God of power and love with the powerlessness and unloving existence of the oppression of Black folk.

When one reads Pinn's gospel, filled with a sense of his profoundly anti-God religiosity, one can appreciate his deep questions while still disagreeing with his conclusions. Such is my reading. The following Christian gospel points attempt to "answer" Pinn from a biblical perspective:

(1) Human beings do have much to be accountable to and responsible for regarding the present conditions of racism, powerlessness, oppression, and hatred that have dogged the steps of African Americans and others. Nevertheless a biblically based faith would insist upon the realistic evaluation of the human condition provided in the Bible. This biblical realism offers the insight that no human being has the power to redeem either themselves or others (Roman 3:23). Further, the Bible condemns over and over again those who proclaim their faith in God and Jesus, yet continue to oppress the poor (Isaiah 1–3; Amos 5; Matthew 25:31–46 to name a few prominent verses). While faith in God has often been used as escapism from the problems of the world, one look at Harriet Tubman, Sojourner Truth, Mary McLeod Bethune, Bishop Henry Turner, Marcus Garvey, and Martin Luther King would quickly reveal how African American leaders have tapped into the liberating power of the Bible to transform many (though certainly not all) of the brutal conditions facing Black folk here in the United States. Dr. Martin Luther King used Amos 5:24: "But let justice roll down as waters, and righteousness as a mighty stream" (KJV) as one his favorite biblical verses to

energize the freedom protests and civil rights demonstrations of millions of Black Americans (and all other groups as well).

(2) No one likes to say "the devil made me do it" because it is a supernatural explanation, often, for irresponsible and evil behavior. When either wonderful events or terrible events occur, many people attribute them to an all-powerful "sovereign" God. Since I am not the first person to attempt to provide a supernatural explanation of creation, I turn to St. Anselm for aid. For Anselm God "is that than which nothing greater can be conceived."[19] This terse phrase takes into account both our inability to comprehensively and thoroughly grasp what "God" is, and our restless imagination's quest to try to "answer" the God question. When Job encountered God he did so in a mysterious "whirlwind" (Job 40:6); while Moses experienced God calling him to service in the puzzle of a "burning bush." Isaiah 55:8–11 notes:

> For my thoughts are not your thoughts, neither are your ways my ways. As the heavens are higher than the earth, so are my ways higher than your ways and my thoughts than your thoughts. As the rain and snow come down from heaven and do not return to it without watering the earth and making it bud and flourish, so that it yields seed for the sower, and bread for the eater, so is my word that goes forth from my mouth: It will not return to me empty but will accomplish what I desire and achieve the purpose for which I sent it. (NIV)

Isaiah spoke these words to an exiled, downtrodden Hebrew nation; a nation that was captive to the global superpower of its time—Babylon. Through the prophet's speech God was letting the Hebrews know that God was still alive and well, even though their present circumstances were difficult to bear. It is always hard to believe that God is alive, or even that there is a God when times are rough. The Bible answers suffering with the affirmation of God's presence to enable both the capacity to "go through" the persecution, and the encouragement to transform injustice into justice.

The question of human beings being part of an evolving process is answered in the Bible not by Creationism, but by reading in both the Genesis 1 and Genesis 2–3 accounts of creation that the "Adam," or "earth-creature" has been invariably tied to the created environment because his body consists of the dust of the earth—Adamah. Arguments about whether evolutionary theory is "right" or the Bible stories fail to see their fundamental similarity—that humans are the most god-like, and evolved of all of God's (Nature's?) creation. The Bible is a book providing religious answers to the nature of the cosmos, science provides the best naturalistic answer to the origins of life—they are looking at two separate and distinctive issues. Thus one can be a "good Christian" while recognizing the strengths (and the weaknesses) of the evolutionary theory.

(3) Church folk will always discern the "hand of God" as relevant to African American cultural production. Pinn makes the question either one believes in appreciating Black culture, or one subtly rejects it if one believes in the "cosmic authority" of Black religions. Even as Black Christians and Black Moslems fight over the nature of Who formed their distinctive churches and mosques, they both agree that God (Allah) is the ongoing power that holds their faith communities together. One, after all, can appreciate "Black religiosity" without being an atheist!

(4) The letter of James provides the biblical response to Pinn's ideal of "individual and societal transformation." It encourages believers to be "doers of the word, and not merely hearers who deceive themselves" (James 1:22) (NRSV). James proclaims that "Religion that is pure and undefiled before God, the Father, is this; to care for orphans and widows in their distress, and to keep oneself unstained by the world" (James 1:27) (NRSV). James encourages so-called faithful Christians to not merely have compassion for the oppressed (the orphans and widows), but to actively "care for them." Later on in the letter James puts it even more bluntly, "In the same way, faith by itself, without being accompanied by action, is dead." (James 2:17). As was stated above, the gospel enables individual and societal transformation. Thus I would join Pinn in condemning "mouth religion"—any kind of church folk that profess belief in Jesus Christ who do nothing to change the world around them.

It is important to also note that Black preachers recognize that proclamation involves follow-through. As one preacher puts it, "You just can't hear the Word and say "That's good." You've got to receive it and put it into practice."[20]

(5) The "controlled optimism" of Pinn's humanism may be agreed with, but from a biblical realist position of recognizing the inner spiritual motivations that make the human being have a dual potential—for good and evil. "The heart is deceitful above all things" (Jeremiah 17:9) indicates a definite wariness of our human potential. The heart can deceive us so that we do not do what we say or believe; or meaning what we say—especially when we're angry and want to hurt another's feelings. Sometimes we do what we believe is right, but it turns out terribly wrong for all concerned—like an adulterous affair that damages the souls of all involved. At the same time Psalm 8:4–6 states the following positive things about human beings:

> What are human beings that you are mindful of them, mortals that you care for them? Yet you have made them a little lower than God, and crowned them with glory and honor. You have given them dominion over all the works of your hands; you have put all things under their feet. (NRSV)

The Gospel is based upon biblical realism. Biblical realism insists that while we are created beings from a loving God, and are established in the created order "a little lower than angels," we nevertheless are sinners whose hearts are deceptive beyond all reasoning. Because we are created by God we have stamped within our very souls the imprint of Divinity—the image of God (Genesis 1:26–27). With all of these positive aspects, the entire Bible itself is filled with the most inglorious, sinners we can be, deceitful, with the most evil deeds imaginable! We have a hope that through the power of the Holy Spirit we can develop the "fruits of the Spirit"—"love joy, peace, patience, kindness, goodness, faithfulness gentleness, and self-control" (Galatians 5:23). Thus we may be optimistic church folk, not dwelling on what horrible deeds we might do, but rather, on what an optimistic detiny God through Jesus Christ has set in store for us.

Pinn's "Different Gospel" appeals to the rational mind because of its cogency and brilliance. Yet it cannot "save" us—make us whole, complete, and spiritually mature. The potential of human beings for good cannot erase our other concrete and spiritual tendencies toward violence, grief, and misery, no matter how idealistic our goals may be in the end. Biblical realism, the gospel, the good news of Jesus Christ is that we are empowered by God. Like Pinn, we are "controlled optimists," but we believe that God is the one who is in control, not mere human beings.

Proclamation is the initiation of a process, the first step. This first step is a projection that comes from the preacher moving out to the hearers. The Word is carried out on vocal waves from the preacher's inspired voice to the listener's ears, and it is received, rejected, or temporarily housed but lost after a while because there is no proper follow-through. There are three various biblical descriptions of this moment in the famous Parable of the Sower (Matthew 13:1–23; Mark 4:1–20; Luke 8:4–15).

> Read all three versions of the Parable of the Sower. Notice the differences as well as the similarities. Which version do you like the best, and why?

## Overabundance: A Proclamation Principle

Proclamation is, by its very nature, overabundant because it must be. Like a farmer sowing seed, the proclaimed Word must be sent out at a rate many times more than will be received and acted upon. This is what the Parable of the Sower confirms.

> Read the three versions of the Parable of the Sower from Mark, Matthew, and Luke—Mark 4:1–22; Matthew 13:1–23; Luke 8:4–15.

Besides being another comparison of the Kingdom of God to seed, the Parable of the Sower confirms that the seed, which is the Word of God, is so overabundant by nature that it may suffer loss, damage, or harm yet it inevitably flourishes. God expects that this overabundantly sown Word will suffer from various complicating conditions. For some the Word will not last in their lives because it will be taken away by satanic opposition, or sown in persons too shallow to withstand persecution and trouble; or choked by the thorns and weeds of earthly concerns, and the rapacious drive to acquire material wealth (Mark 4:13–19). God is ever sowing more seeds of the Kingdom than will be reaped.

Isaiah 55:10–11 confirms this theological principle of overabundance by comparing God's spread of the Word to rain and snow:

> As the rain and the snow come down from heaven, and does not return to it without watering the earth and making it bud and flourish, so that it yields seed for the sower and bread for the eater, so is my word that goes out from my mouth: It will not return to me empty, but will accomplish what I desire, and achieve the purpose for which I sent it. (NIV)

We all recognize that it takes countless drops of rain and flakes of snow for the earth to be sufficiently "watered." By comparison, the proclamation of the Word of God must be received in countless ways, places, and types to actually accomplish the watering of our souls. It is a proclamation that is not limited to any one kind of preaching, teaching, or medium. It can be high-tech or low-tech because its inner energy and drive is what motivates nurture and establishes the transformation of our lives.

## Three Pillars

Thus proclamation stands on three solid pillars: (1) the objective standard of the kerygma (the Gospel message of the Kingdom of God); (2) the subjective testimony of individuals who have personally received

God's Word that flourishes into transformed lives; and (3) the trans subjective experience of sharing the Word with others—incarnated as both individuals attaining a personal relationship with God through Jesus Christ, and following through with community actions that transform what is wrong in societies, politics, economics, and ecology. These three pillars work and act together. They are inseparable in beauty and function. These three pillars complete a divine architecture that is the *kerygma*—the proclaimed Word that announces the presence of the Reign of God.

## Final Questions

1. What does the kerygma of Jesus Christ mean to you personally?
2. Contrast Pinn's humanism with biblical realism. What is your answer?
3. In what ways can our churches proclaim the Word in ways that represent the Three Pillars more fully?

# 5

# Empowered Witness

In chapter 5 the specific aspect of liberation in the biblical theology of *Bible Witness in Black* Churches expresses itself as "empowered witness." Liberation theology has reminded us that God speaks to us in words and acts that deliver us from social, economic, and political bondage. This deliverance is part of a twofold action in which God acts to both "set the captives free" on the one hand, and "strengthen His people" with the other hand. Thus deliverance and empowerment are the left and right hands of genuine liberation. *In Bible Witness in Black Churches* we want to articulate the side of liberation theology that arises specifically from a biblically centered theology, and that is empowerment. Before we spin forth the implications of what a biblical theology of empowerment can look like, we need to deal with a grassroots issue.

> Whe'evuh two or mo' is gathered... de's trouble!

The above statement was a quote from the lips of the father of Gospel music, Thomas Dorsey, complaining about his lifelong friend Sallie Martin who was in a "friendly feud" with another woman while they were taping the historic documentary "Say Amen! Somebody." One could apply the same logic to any kind of socio-political commentary, opinions, or debates within the sacred confines of a church. Wrangling over the "right" side to be on politically has always been a monumental task for all churches, and has even caused mainline churches to sideline the entire political process as inappropriate to the context of worship experience. Traditional African American Churches, and church folk; however, not only expect biblical-informed socio-political reflection; but look forward to their pastors being actively involved in the social justice movements of their communities. This division of expectations arises from the long history of segregation that has not been erased or even alleviated that much by civil rights movement opportunities. In fact, African American, Latino, Native American, and poor Urban White preachers must be social activists for their communities because the social justice needs require pastors whose biblical commitments walk the dirty streets *and* the pulpits at the same time, seven days a week, and provide more than weekly sermons for the already saved and sanctified.

The Bible, for such activist women and men, is an action-packed shield of faith. It is that Holy Sword one picks up to wield with authority when the daggers of doubt and the profanities of violence threaten to destroy everything good and decent.

Black women, in particular, have been a prophetic source of "trouble" for the all-male dominated power bloc of Black Churches. Figures from Sojourner Truth and Harriet Tubman on down to contemporary womanist leaders like Jacquelyn Grant Emilie Townes, Cheryl Gilkes, and Delores Williams have been redefining, and re-gifting Black Churches. This is especially true when we look at how Black Churches have understood their mission as places of God's empowerment here on the earth.

Empowerment for Black Christian women, historically, has included the political poetry of "coming to voice" according to Black feminist Anna Julia Cooper in A *Singing Something* back at the turn of the twentieth century.[1] Then, as even today, this meant affirming the imago dei as the concrete basis for African Americans knowing that we are Children of God. While Black male preachers from Richard Allen to Martin Luther King, Jr., have also extolled the supremacy of "Black manhood" being tied to the universal "manhood" and "brotherhood" guaranteed in Genesis 1:26–27, most seem to have forgotten the second clause of the biblical creation of humankind "...male and female God created them." In this way Black males have participated in a sexist reading of the Bible in much the same way as did their white brothers, even as they did not read in racial terms.

If it is true that the Bible has always been, and ever shall be the most secure basis for African American liberation theology because its witness starts from the theological assertion that all human beings are created in the imago dei—image of God, then *Bible Witness in Black Churches* must be about the business of creating a freedom space for females and males to use the Bible together. This means that gender apartheid—reading Scripture one way for men, and another way for women—must end. This means that no social or political policies, economic downturns, recessions, or technological depressions can hold back or oppress the progress of African Americans or any people as long as they continue to trust the source of their fundamental dignity. Only God can provide us with our true dignity, and that dignity comes from being created in God's image, male and female.

### Study and Discussion Questions

1. What does the Bible teach in Genesis 1:26–27, and Galatians 3:26–29 about the equal status of both female and male human beings in relationship to God? How do we reconcile these Scriptures with Genesis 3:16, Ephesians 5:21–33 that seem to directly infer a relationship of dominance of the male over the female? Remember, one of the most persuasive and satisfying "answers" to the question lies in comparing and linking together both of the two questions, drawing theological resources from the Old and New Testaments!
2. Has God created men and women to be partners or complements? In other words, has God created us to be two virtually equal and similar, interacting members versus two very different members who "complete" each other?

## A Different Reading of Liberation...

For the longest time liberation theology has made a fundamental methodological error. Correcting the immodest, pseudo-objectivity of previous European and American male theologies, whose so-called objectivity blinded their fundamentally imperialist assumptions, the host of liberationists views like Black, feminist, and Latin American believed that their theology had to begin in locus communitatis—in the place of the specific community. The strength of such an approach was that it provided a much needed voice to those whose thoughts about God and Church did not easily fit into the highly ordered, dry, and abstract universal categories of much of what passed for "theology" at the time. It was exciting, energizing, and spoke with a prophetic urgency.

What could be wrong with being prophetic and injecting some relevance into theology? The problem was, and still is, the displacement of the Bible as central to the creation of theology. If the community is the creator of theology, then what role does the Bible play? Is the Bible simply an exalted moral book of "do's and don'ts?" What is the proper role for the Word of God if the Bible is most often referred to (as it often has been in many liberation theologies) as the object of negative criticism rather than as most church folk (including oppressed church folk!) think of it as "holy" and "the Word of God?" Liberation theologians displaced the centrality of the Bible and threatened to replace it with the very real situational crises of their communities.

Matters are far worse, however, than the above paragraph implies. Many liberation theologians speak of the Bible most often in the cadence and tone of their "mainstream" biblical training. By "mainstream" I mean liberal white, and radically historical-critical. All of these terms, for the church folk reading this, mean that the Bible is read from the viewpoint of "What in this book can be criticized and analyzed as we would any other human book?" Now as any of us knows, church folk do not view the Bible as "any other book!" So when liberation theologians begin their "critical analyses" of biblical passages that they take to be "problematic," "antiliberating," or passages that really "should be erased from the canon...," they automatically turn off church folk! No wonder liberation theology is so unpopular. No wonder most intelligent church folk do not know what "liberation" has to do with the Church, or Jesus Christ! This is not simply a matter of "style," or "presentational skills," so that one could hold onto a faith-less or unfaithful belief stance while sounding like T.D. Jakes! That would make all of us "Jack-Leg Scholars!" Whether liberation scholars like it or not, their biblical stance is as rooted in objective, abstractions as the dry-sounding, universalizing stuff that they so eloquently debunked 20 years ago. As the proverb goes, "You cannot tear down the master's house with the master's tools."

## Faith-Filled Scholarship

My turn toward a more evangelical trust in God, a more personal faith in Jesus as Christ, and a more charismatic experience of the gift of the Holy Spirit revealed to me the ways in which I participated in a "mainstream" biblically critical approach to liberation theology. I do not wish to give examples of others because the point is to move beyond being critical of the Bible to a constructive view of faith in God's usage of the Bible as we create liberating theologies. What I experienced was a kind of personal epiphany about the role of faith in the construction of theology.

If God is truly "in charge" of all that we say or do, and the Bible is a central, authoritative library of witnesses to the Church's struggle to be faithful to that same God, then the Bible may be considered trustworthy of being included initially in any theological construction. What this implies is that one can be certain that if one begins with the Bible's witness, one is beginning with God's intended set of priorities.

Now what in the world does this mean? Does it mean that we merely open up the Bible, and by some sense of spiritual "magic" God begins to "speak" to us? Not at all. Neither does it mean that everyone's theology will look the same, sound the same, and be the same. Rather, it implies that we begin with a trust of the Bible—from Genesis 1:1 all the way to the ending in Revelation 22:21—to provide us with all the adequate fundamental theological information that we need. We "trust the Bible" because we have trust in the creative, constructive Author of the authors of the Bible. Thus we do not idolize the Book, but we trust God to operate in that Book once again, and not merely in our projection of our arrogant, critical approaches designed to debunk and discredit the Book.

What is this "theological information" that a "faithful biblical scholar" is going to "get," that someone not so "faithful" might miss?

If one does a kind of quick bird's eye survey of the overall shape of the Bible, starting with Genesis, Chapter 1, we find out several things both about human beings *and* God. First, we discover

- God is that which has existed from "the beginning" (*bureshith*); even before the delineation of what we know of as time;
- God is that which creates (*bara*) all that is from this "beginning," in successive periods of time the first chapter of Genesis calls "days." Thus the first title we have of God is God is the Creator. Furthermore, this creation that God creates is not neutral, or abstract, but God gives it value in each progressively complex stage, calling each step of creation the powerful moral word good (*Tov*).
- At the height of God's creative "week"—the sixth "day"—God creates humankind. God, whose name is plural—*Elohim*—creates male and female in God's "image" (*tselem*) and "likeness." Hence is established the potent theological dictum that human beings—male and female, of all shapes, ethnicities, colors, and backgrounds, are created *Imago Dei*—in the Image of God. This theological piece of information tells a great deal about ourselves—that we have a Godly and God-granted dignity and value that no power, no trouble, nothing, or nobody else can take away from us, ever. It also tells us something about God, that God exists as something of a "Community" of "Persons"—and that the one God is also "Many" in

some unique and indescribable fashion—or at least in some way that human words cannot fit. This "Many-ness" of God gives value to male-ness *and* female-ness, because *both* are part of what it means to have God-likeness.

• On the seventh "day" God "rests"—instituting the notion of *Shabbat*. Sabbath—rest—means that all activity, even God-like, creative, loving, positive extensive, constructive work requires a moment of recreation. If the God who created the entire universe required of God-self a "day" of rest, so we must institute times for recreation, recharging our physical, emotional, mental, and spiritual lives in order to function fully in our God-likeness. As we shall see later, to not do so is to encourage that negative side of the spiritual realm that we have come to call "sin."

• In Genesis Chapters two and three we have a second creation narrative that focuses on the particular story of the first male "Adam" the one shaped from the dust of the earth (*Adamah*) and his companion made from his "rib," *Evvah*—Eve—"mother of all living." While we are not told how evil comes to be, we are told about a *Nachash* or Serpent, who is the most crafty and cunning creature made by God (Genesis 3:1). This Serpent tempts Eve while Adam simply allows the event to occur while he stands beside her doing nothing! Adam is the one who is specifically forbidden from eating of the fruit from the "tree of knowledge of good and evil" (Genesis 2:16–17); yet he stands by and allows both Eve and the Serpent to misquote God's command (Carefully read Genesis 3:1–6).

• *Arar* or a curse is the specific consequence of Adam and Eve's disobedience, and the Serpent's lies and manipulation. All three are cursed because God's command is overthrown as a lie. My students love the Black folk saying, "The Devil is a Lie!" when rebuking someone for trying to twist the truth, or for someone trying to lie outright. I think that this saying, "The Devil is a Lie!" comes directly from these verses, because if this is where we first meet the Devil, or Satan, in the guise of a Serpent—as many traditional biblical scholars believe, then his lie introduces the sinful proposition that God is a Liar, and Adam and Eve "fall" for it.

• What then is Sin? Sin, when we first meet it here in the Bible, is accusing God of something that is not true, believing the lie, and acting on the assumptions of that lie. Notice that sin is personal and social, both. It was not just Eve's problem, but Adam bore responsibility for allowing things to get out of hand in the first place—not to mention the fact that they were both "under the influence" of a powerful Tempter who seemed to know more than they did about God and the "forbidden fruit." Sinners do not like to sin by themselves, and the Devil enjoys company, too. That is part of the reason why deep wrongs are so hard to convert into rights. Finally, committing sin always changes one's circumstances, as was the case with Adam and Eve, when God drove them permanently out of their beautiful safe haven of the "Garden of Eden" into the cold cruel world (Read Genesis 3:22–24).

• The problem of Sin gets worse in the ensuing chapters following Adam and Eve; as well as the deepening of God's response of love theologians call mercy. Genesis 4:1–8 tells the story of brothers Cain and Abel (Carefully read Genesis 4:1–8; and then verses 9–16 to see how the story ends). The Hebrew word *Chatta* for "sin" appears in verse 7 as a malicious figure ready to pounce on, and take advantage of Cain's angry self. Cain begins with anger at God (verse 5) for not "regarding" his sacrifice; while being pleased with his brother Abel's. *Chatta* wins over Cain, and he kills Abel. This is not an accidental act of passionate outrage; but rather, Cain's act is one of carefully planned, coldly executed murder. As with his parents, Cain is cursed, and the consequences are painful. Notice that as God showed mercy to the First Parents by not killing them, but driving them out of Eden God now shows mercy even to a murderer. God does not destroy Cain as direct punishment for killing Abel, but places him under an *arar* of permanent exile, and then places a "mark" or a "sign" of identification that provides protection in verse 15. Just as Adam and Eve are not destroyed, but spared to live out a new kind of much more harsh life, so Cain is not killed, but spared to live a life under the judgment of his cursed exile and "Sign."

## Study Questions

1. What are the sinful actions that you have taken for which there have been consequences that you now wish you would not have to face? Make this a Ritual of Purification by having members of the class write down their "secret sins" on a sheet of paper to be burned in a proper receptacle. Say prayers over the receptacle and then physically remove the "sins" by burning them. This ritual of burning the "sins" can be viewed as a Ritual of Cleansing—as a way of watching how God "burns away through the Holy Spirit the sins from which we desire liberation. Remember that the "sins" are both personal and social.
2. Notice how God's judgment and mercy are enacted in the stories of Noah (Genesis 6–10); and Jacob, his brother Esau, Leah, and Rachel (Genesis 25:19–34; 27–36).

• Joseph's Story is a parable of God's faithfulness throughout any and all human jealousy, hatred, betrayal, lies, and adversity. Despite everything negative that Joseph must endure, such as the murderous rage and schemes of his brothers (Genesis 37); or the false accusations of Potiphar's wife that leads to his imprisonment (Genesis 39); or even the broken promises of freedom from Pharaoh's cupbearer (Genesis 40:1–23). At the end of the story, after Joseph has redeemed his brothers by providing for them food and shelter because of his exalted office as second in power to Pharaoh, and has reconciled with them despite their fears of being punished for their past wrongdoing, Jospeh is able to say "Even though you intended to do harm to me, God intended it for good, in order to preserve a numerous people, as he is doing today" (Genesis 50:20 NRSV). This statement recognizes several theological doctrines. First, it reveals God's Providence—that God is able to utilize all events—good and bad—in an overall sovereign plan for our good, growth, and flourishing. Second, this verse recognizes forgiveness—a divine gift of being able to set aside past wrongs because of the goodness and love that God places in one's heart for that person; and not because of what they deserve. Forgiveness is a gift of God, not something possible on the human plane of healthy psychological interaction and well-being. Indeed, genuine forgiveness is a gift of the next theological doctrine—Faith. The Bible provides the most enduring definition of faith in Hebrews 11:1: "Now faith is the assurance of things hoped for, the conviction of things not seen" (NRSV).

• All of these theological dicta and dogma: the timelessness, utter creativity, power, and wonder of God; humans being created in God's image; the curse of sin, the complicity of the human heart in acts of hatred, murder, and betrayal; the response of mercy from God; the Providence of God, and the miracle of forgiveness because of the power of faith are revealed in human community. They flourish and grow strong in the connections (and mis-connections) between people. They are both in the beauty and power of faith and forgiveness, and in the ugliness of sinful hatred, and even murder. Genesis suggests a connection between what we conceive in our hearts (the *Lev*) and what we eventually do, and that there is a connection between our inner spiritual life and our outward actions. This has important implications for a biblical theology of liberation. For a theology of liberation to be biblical, it needs to look in a critical way at the soul condition of those who are committing acts of wrong-doing on a social-political-economic level. The Bible does not, indeed, cannot separate things out into neat little categories of what is personal, and then what is social. Things are just too connected together for a genuinely biblical theology of liberation. All of these theological assumptions flow from a critical examination of Genesis.

• Exodus makes it clear, beyond the shadow of any doubt, that God is directly invested in overturning oppressive, exploitive social systems that grind the joy of life out of these creatures created in God's Image. Exodus condemns the overall destructive view of oppressive powers who use socio-political policies of killing babies as a way of controlling unwanted populations. The condemnation is unambiguous when we read about Pharaoh's orders to kill all the male Hebrew babies, and find ourselves applauding the resistance activities and shrewd "truth" of the Hebrew midwives, who refuse to carry out Pharaoh's orders (Read the first chapter of Exodus).

• Moses, for many Black Church folk, is somebody who has been "raised in the Big House, but didn't forget his roots!" (Read Exodus 2:1–15). Moses, while raised in Pharaoh's house, must have identified in some way with his oppressed brothers and sisters, because he could not stand seeing an Egyptian beat a Hebrew, and killed him. Thinking that this act would make the Hebrews trust him, Moses found out in verses 13–14 that once one has the clothing, accent, style, and ways of the "Big House," it is very hard for most folks who live in "the Fields" to trust you! Fearful that he has been discovered (a fear that turns out to be grounded in fact), Moses flees. What interests me about this chapter is that it suggests that Moses may have had the desire to be a "liberator" early on; and even was willing to take the worldly path—the way of violence to prove his worth. There are indications of this within the text in Exodus 2:13, after Moses has killed and buried the oppressing Egyptian, he sees two Hebrews fighting one another. He intervenes by making himself a judge—"speaking to the one who was wrong." (NRSV); or "said to the offender" (NASB). The word for "One who was wrong, offender" in Hebrew is *rasha*—which is a complex word that has to do with "moral wrong, bad, wicked, unrighteous...lawlessness, injustice. It denotes the kind of life which is antithetical to the character of God and draws statements of indictment and judgment."[2] So Moses is judging the actions of one of the Hebrews as being unrighteous and unjust; to which the Hebrew replies, "Who put you in the place of a prince (*Sar* in Hebrew—usually a non-Israelite political leader) or a judge (*Shaphat* a very important Hebrew word)? It is particularly the recognition that Moses is elevating himself to the office of a *Shaphat* that is significant for a liberationist understanding of identifying Moses' premature attempt at being a liberator was rejected by Hebrews themselves. A *Shaphat* is

> one who judges, who decides, gives equity, is an arbitrator. The term was used especially of heroic leaders of the Israelites who delivered their people from the oppression of neighboring nations between the time of Joshua and Samuel. They governed them in peace as supreme magistrates (Judges 2:16; 18; 26:1; Isaiah 1:17; Jeremiah 5:28);...Shaphat means to hear a case and render a decision...This was the process by which law and order were maintained during the period of the judges. However, later, the people clamored for a king to fulfill the same function (I Samuel 8:6–18). They wanted (what they considered) more permanence and stability. They spurned the rather simple, direct method of combining legislative, executive, and judicial decisions in wise, patriarchal (and matriarchal) seniors.[3]

• God's Will—What is significant is that Moses requires a "Burning Bush Experience" to become an effective liberator who can lead oppressed Hebrews. God had not empowered him to be a liberator, while he still lived in the "Big House" of Pharaoh, so he was acting outside of God's will. When he killed the Egyptian, he believed that he did so for the "right reasons." He wound up fleeing to the desert region of Midian where he could be seasoned by becoming a sojourner, or what we would call a legal alien, or immigrant. He took a rather demeaning job for a prince of Egypt—becoming a shepherd. So Exodus 2 is an excellent example of how one can act for good reasons in the wrong way, at the wrong time, and get the wrong results. In order to do the right thing, at the right time in the way and receive the blessed results intended one must walk in God's will. Moses also was tempered in a positive vein by becoming a family man: getting married to *Zipporah*, daughter of *Jethro*, who was a priest; and fathering a son—*Gershom*—a Hebrew name for "stranger." The Bible does not tell us how many years Moses dwelt in Midian as a shepherd, reclaiming his Hebrew roots apparently also under the tutelage of his father-in-law Jethro, but we do know that God heard (*Shama* in this case the word implies to hear and answer) the cries and groans of the oppressed (*nuahqah*) Hebrews. God hears and responds. No matter how long it takes, God is working out a solution. There is a particular kind of groaning and crying out that the oppressed make—so particular that the Hebrew language has its own word for that particularity. God is sensitive to that condition, and we know this because the Bible tells us.

### Study Question

Use a Strong's Concordance to find out other places in the Bible where God responds to the "groans" of the oppressed, exploited, fatherless, and widowed people. This is the usual "list" of those in biblical times who were at the bottom of the socio-political and economic pyramid structure of ancient feudal societies.

• The story of the Liberation of the Hebrews—from the "Burning Bush" mission call in Exodus 3; through the Plagues (Chapters 7–11); the Passover of the Angel of Death (*Pesach*) (Chapters 12–13:1–16); to the dividing of the Re(e)d Sea[4] and the drowning of an enraged Pharaoh's "horses and chariots" (Chapter 14).

• God's liberator name is YHWH. Back in the "Burning Bush" experience Moses asks God to verify Who it is, and by Whose divine authority he will be commanding the Hebrews in Exodus 3:13. At this point God (Elohim) gives perhaps the most enigmatic of all phrases in the Bible *Hayah asher Hayah*. The quick-and-too-easy English translation every Sunday school child learns of this Hebrew mystery phrase is "I am who I am." The dynamism, internal energy, and timeless existentialism of the phrase requires something of a paragraph to truly translate, however. One possible translation of God's NAME could be

> I am the One who exists. I am who I have always been. I am who I am doing, breathing, happening right now. I am who shall become complete and finished in the future. I am everything that everything, everyone, everywhere has and will ever want or need because I have done, am doing, and will do everything that is. I be.

• In Exodus 15 we find the Name YHWH as the God the recently freed slaves have experienced. Biblical scholars and rabbis have long speculated that YHWH—what they call the unpronounceable "divine tetragrammaton"—is really a sacred play on the Divine *Hayah* or "I am" in the earlier section of Exodus. Whatever YHWH, or what contemporary Protestants pronounce as *Yahweh* is seen as a Warrior," (Exodus 3:3) who is a Wonder-Worker (Exodus 3:13).

## Discussion Question

For most Church folks the language of God as Warrior and Wonder-Worker is easy to accept, especially within the context of praise. What happens, however, when we read those Scriptures like the Fall of Jericho in Joshua 6 in which God commands the Hebrews to utterly destroy everything—including children, women, the elderly, and animals! Read the entire section of the Jericho story starting in Joshua 5:13 with Joshua's vision of the "Captain of *Yahweh's* host," until the end of Chapter Six. Thus practice of utterly destroying all living things and saving the silver, gold, and iron is called *Cherem* or what we would call "holy war." In Joshua 7 a person named Achan dies because he disobeys the *Cherem*. Do you believe that we are to spiritualize "holy war in our contemporary world, as a way of finding something positive about the practice of *cherem*, or do you just accept this controversial biblical concept literally? Is *cherem* something that Christians are to leave behind in the "Old Testament" since we are now supposed to be living under the grace of the "New Testament," as some have resolved the issue? If that is so, then how do we pick and choose which parts of the Old Testament we like, and continue to practice, and which parts we do not like, and refuse to continue to practice? Isn't it the case that Christians simply follow along with what "feels right," instead of really having a solid, understandable, and spiritually sound biblical principle for why they choose to follow certain Old Testament practices, and abandon others? *Bible Witness in Black Churches* insists that we begin to prayerfully think about why we do what we do with the Word of God!

• The Decalogue or Ten Commandments are the heart of the Law or *Torah*, the Divine Instruction given to the Hebrews. These are God's unconditional words to the newly liberated slaves concerning their proper understanding, relationship, worship, and lifestyle as the people of *Yahweh*; and their proper relationship to one another because of their being called the people of *Yahweh*. The 10 Commands are written up initially in Exodus 20:1–21; and are repeated in the Book of the second law or Deuteronomy 5:6–21. These 10 Commands, or 10 "Words" are divided into 2 Tables—the first (Exodus 20:2–11) specify the following: (1) Divine self-revelation (the holy Name Yahweh) as connected to the act of being liberated from the state of social-political-economic enslavement (verses 2–3); (2) *Yahweh* is due spiritual worship rather than obeisance to images made by human hands (verses 4–6); (3) *Yahweh's* name is not to be misused, abused, or made profane in any way (verse 7); and (4) Structuring time so that every seventh day of the week is set aside for *Sabbath* or rest, recreation, and worship (verses 8–11). The second Table deals with social relationships—honoring father and mother (verse 12); not committing murder (verse 13); avoiding adultery (verse 14); prohibiting stealing (verse 15 ); condemning false witness against one's neighbor and lying (verse 16); and condemning *khamad*—coveting, lusting after, untoward desire" that leads to jealousy, resentment, and even hatred toward one's neighbor (verse 17). It is interesting that most of us do not read the 10 Commandments as a liberation document, but it is the core of all holy law from which the Bible enables us to recognize what is proper, spiritually inspired, and holy behavior toward one another; and what is not. We ought to note that when we look at the 10 Commands as a core document we see that a biblical understanding initiates with unconditional prohibitions (what Bible scholars call apodictic laws.[5] To put it more plainly, *Yahweh* bases our freedom on unconditionally revealed law that is expected to be obeyed. There is really not a great deal of wiggle room for discussion, debate, and open-mouthed wonder about what God really meant, is there?

## Discussion Questions

1. Discuss how breaking each of the last five Commandments (Exodus 20:12–17) violates the community, disrupts righteousness, and thereby contributes to injustice.
2. Explain the word "covet" in terms that you understand. What are the material things, objects, or people you have coveted? Is it possible to positively covet something?

• *The Torah* is usually simply called the first five books of the Bible—*The Pentateuch*—Genesis, Exodus, Leviticus, Numbers, and Deuteronomy by predominantly Protestant Christians. For our purposes, however, it is better to focus on certain passages of *Torah* like The Mosaic Covenant (Exodus 20:1–24, 8); the Holiness Code (Leviticus 17:1–26, 46); and the Law Book (Deuteronomy 12:1–26, 15).

Take the time out to read all three sections of Scripture carefully.

Notice that all three sections of the *Torah* regulate *mishpat* that broadly translates into the English word justice. Actually the word is one of those amazingly rich ancient Hebrew words used 400 times in the Hebrew Bible. If we take Exodus 23:6, "You shall not pervert the justice due to your needy brother in his dispute," we can elaborate the layers of meaning enfolded in the word we simply translate "justice." The root word of *mishpat* is the word *shaphat* that we spoke of earlier in this chapter. It speaks about "the one who judges, arbitrates a case, etc." *Mishpat* most fundamentally means "a verdict (favorable or unfavorable), a sentence, a formal decree, justice, right, privilege, place of judgment, cause, suit, crime, law, rule, ordinance;...what is due." Significantly for *Bible Witness*, *mishpat* is part of the character and an attribute of God (Isaiah 30:18), loved by God (Psalm 37:28), and to be emulated by God's people (Psalm 37:30; Proverbs 12:5; 21:15; 29:4; Micah 3:1; 6:8). Thus, while many liberation theologies—from Black to Latin America to Feminist—rightfully uplift the issue of justice; the Bible itself is a paramount witness to the importance of *mishpat* (justice) as a central characteristic of the Torah-observant society.

The Book of Leviticus divides up the Torah-observant life into three broad categories: clean, unclean, and holy. It is a difficult book for modern readers because it deals with such highly personal issues as vile physical diseases (leprosy 13:1–14:57); genital discharges (15:1–33); proper and improper foods (11:1–47); and even childbirth "purification rites" (12:1–8). The three categories are ritually and ceremonially established, and not just moral-spiritual statements. The notions of being clean or *tahor* "pure, innocent, righteous, to be purified, cleansed"[6] hinges on unclean being its opposite—*tame'*—"impure, polluted, defiled."[7] While certainly the *Torah*-observant Hebrew yearns to live the life of being *tahor* (clean), the ultimate aim is actually to be *qadosh* or holy. While being clean is something that is ritually established through obedience to certain ceremonial behaviors, being *qadosh* is a relationship with God, a relationship of service and separation from the rest of the world in order to dedicate one's energies to deeper, more profound service to *Yahweh*. To be *qadosh* literally means to be separate; to be distinct from that which is profane, unholy, and indistinct.[8]

## All of Israel Was Called to Be Holy—Individually *and* Collectively:

> The LORD spoke to Moses, saying: "Speak to all the congregation of the people of Israel and say to them: You shall be holy, for I the LORD your God, am holy." (Leviticus 19:1–2) (NRSV)

In Leviticus, within the context of living a life of holiness, flow the commands of obedience to *mishpat* and *tseddeq*—righteousness. *Tseddeq* has to do with truth done without partiality, equity, straightness, honesty, rectitude.. As in Leviticus 19:35–36 wherein the LORD enjoins the Hebrew observer of *Torah* to demonstrate holiness in the economic sphere of weights, balances, and money:

> You shall not cheat in measuring length, weight, or quantity.
> You shall have honest/*just* balances, honest weights, and honest epah;
> And an honest hin: I am the LORD, your God, who brought you out of the land of Egypt. (NRSV)

Church folks know where I am going. One cannot hope to think one's way to righteous honesty, or just equity. It requires that internal transformation of the heart, the infusion of the Holy Spirit. A biblical theology of liberation insists that all the right intentions for liberation cannot actually change any of the concrete unjust economic and socio-political inequities that plague us until we are changed It is not so much a matter of everybody agreeing about every aspect of the Bible, all the time—as if that were even possible! Rather, it is uplifting the revolutionary possibility that reading the Bible as it is encourages all of us to embrace the LORD as the holy God who commands us to live lives of justice, equity, honesty, and righteousness. Further, this command is not merely a personal suggestion, but is imparted as cry for continual renewal of that which is good in our societies, criticism of what has become unjust, unrighteous, and polluted in our world; and transformation of evil into that which is holy and good because of our relationship to the Holy One. A biblical liberation theology is a transformation theology, a theology that calls for the conversion of both individuals and communities.

## Study Questions

1. In Leviticus 25 we read about the concepts of a Sabbatical and Jubilee year. What do these terms mean? How do you think we could institute these ideas in our modern postagricultural society?
2. What is the connection between giving the land "rest" and freeing people from their debts?

• The Law Book of Deuteronomy (Deuteronomy 12:1–26:15) is an elaboration of the Deuteronomist's retelling of the Ten Commandments (5:6–21).

In this way the Law Book has profound links to the Book of the Covenant in Exodus 20:22–23:19, and echoes its concerns. The Law Book elaborates with greater detail every nuance of each Commandment than does the teaching in Exodus or Leviticus.

### Discussion Question

Read and discuss Deuteronomy 13 in light of the first two Commandments that it implies have been broken. Do you think that the *cherem*, or "ban" (absolute destruction of everything) commanded is too harsh? Why or why not? What is the point of this section of Scripture?

• In Deuteronomy 16:18–20 again we find specific reference to the paramount importance of justice and righteousness. In fact, verse 20 reads, "Justice, and only justice, shall you pursue, that you may live, and possess the land that the LORD, your God is giving you." (NASB). The English word "justice" is the Hebrew word tseddeq—which as we stated before means "not deviating from a standard of fairness, righteous conduct, uprightness, doing the right thing..."[9] In *Bible Witness* we need to remember that being just means that we do right, honest, and just actions because our hearts have been made righteous and just, by a Just and Righteous God.

## Sanctity of Marriage and Family

In the last decade of the twentieth century and the first decade of the twenty-first century the institution of family and marriage has become one of the most contentious fronts in the religious cultural war between liberal and conservative viewpoints. For their part, liberals and those on the so-called left end of the socio-political spectrum have encouraged the relaxing of traditional definitions of "family," as that of consisting of the married father, mother, and child. They have advocated for society to accept the minority of homosexual persons—lesbian and gay individuals—as having the same conjugal rights (formal long-term and legally binding relationship rights) as are traditionally understood as "marriage." Strongly reacting to these ideals, conservative religious persons and politicians have successfully rallied public opinion in large states like California and Texas to legally recognize only traditional marriages between a man and a woman. In *Bible Witness* we need to find a way to view what a sanctified marriage looks like utilizing biblical resources, and not appealing merely to the contentious rabble of both polarized ideologies.

Genesis 1:26–27 is a potent place to begin with because it establishes that both the male and the female are created in God's image—*imago Dei*. From the starting point of the *imago dei* the empowering witness moves to uplift the sanctity of marriage and family. The sanctity of family is founded on the presupposition that the members of the family are created in the *imago dei*. Why is family made sanctified by being made in the *imago Dei*? God created us to be a community, not alone. God did not create Adam to be complete in his "Adam-ness." In fact, in Genesis 2, the entire point of the creation of the "Woman" is that she is the *ezer*—or what in Hebrew means the fit helper, companion. Marriage is that state in which both partners are partners—wherein we cry unto each other as Adam cried when he first beheld Eve in all of her perfection, glory, and beauty, "Bone of my bone, and flesh of my flesh..." (Genesis 2:23a). Marriage is sanctified because within it nothing and nobody is closer to the married partner than each other. The very first "marriage," therefore, is found in Genesis 2 as the creation of the Woman from out of Adam's rib—symbolically the creation of companionship and help for the male from the depths of his physical, emotional, and spiritual being. Thus marriage is sanctified because it is an act of holy creation, not a legal recognition, or a political act.

Developing the next step in this view of marriage as holy creation, we see that marriage's purpose is that of creative fellowship. God created Adam and Eve for each other for four reasons: (1) (Genesis 2:20) companionship and fellowship—because Adam did not have suitable companions alone in the Garden of Eden; (2) (Genesis 1:28a); (2) blessing—God would provide the earth with a unique blessing through these unique creatures; (3) (Genesis 1:28); (3) To reproduce—they would have children "be fruitful and multiply, and fill the earth"; and finally (4) (Genesis 1:28) to have dominion that means they would take care of God's creation standing in the place of God, ruling over it as God's stewards.

Africans living in North America for over 300 years never had their marriages recognized as "holy," "sanctified," or worthy of legal, religious, or social honor. Husbands and wives, and children were ripped from each other's arms regularly, at the slave master's whim, for his profit, or even because of his emotional state at the time. If he wished to punish one of the slaves involved because of disobedience he would separate that slave from his or her family intentionally. So slaves learned to improvise "family," and spread out the responsibility of "mothering" and "fathering" to caring females and loving males who made up the community at hand. Whoever "adopted" you became an "Uncle" or an "Auntie," and the closer ones were even called "Ma" and "Pa" because sometimes it was almost impossible to know who was one's biological parents in such a destabilized setting. With such a centuries-long memory still clinging collectively to our churches and to our communities, it is not surprising that Black Church folks tend to be social and religious conservatives, strongly uplifting the "one man–one woman" ideal of marriage, and traditional constructions of family. We strongly defend what was stolen from us for so long.

At the same time, however, we practically recognize in our drug overrun, inner-city, poor neighborhoods in particular, that the older nontraditional structures of raising a family are still intact—with some new lethal twists. Some young fatherless men are turning to older gang leaders for older male mentor leadership—to the detriment of the entire social fabric. Some young females are demanding that aunts, grandmothers, great-grandmothers, best friends, and other women raise their children while they wander down the perilous alleyways of drug addiction, often engaging in a horrific turn to prostitution in order to gain the finances that addiction demands.

Rather than using the all-too-familiar biblical references to marriage and family used in political references as ways to put down gays and lesbians, I believe that the mainstream of Christian tradition must address that breakdown of poor, inner-city families. I prefer to use the Bible in that way. I am saying that the Bible provides a powerfully positive witness to the sanctity of marriage and family; that this sanctity is rooted in our shared *imago dei*, and all Christians (whether liberals or conservatives) ought to affirm the family as space of unity rather than division in Christianity. Furthermore, this family space that unifies rather than divides us is a liberating bulwark that defends us against the destructive satanic influences of drug addiction, teenage pregnancy, and social destruction.

An empowering witness in *Bible Witness in Black Churches* means that Black church folks are intentionally taught to reclaim that thick, religious-cultural heritage of resistance nurtured in Black churches from slavery times. It is a strategy of Christian resistance and liberation that Gayraud Wilmore articulates in *Black Religion and Radicalism*.[10] This tradition radically differentiated the theological presuppositions of African American slaves from those of their European American masters, emphasizing the liberation themes found in the biblical figures of Moses and the entire Exodus narrative of slaves being freed from bondage; Daniel in the lion's den; Joshua's victory marches; identification with Jesus as a cosufferer with all those who suffer injustice;[11] and all instances of the outpouring of the Holy Spirit where physical manifestations of Spirit-possession, dancing, and praise predominated. This form of Christianity was radically opposed to that of the doctrinal Protestantism of white slave masters that stressed adherence to formal doctrines; rigid liturgies; and supported the status quo that legitimated slavery.

How could these largely unlettered slaves read the Bible as being an empowering source of liberation at the very same time that their masters were reading the Bible as the text justifying the institution of slavery? According to biblical scholars like Wimbush, Smith, Bailey, and others, it had to do with their biblical hermeneutic of resistance. They chose to read Exodus, Judges, and Daniel as normative biblical passages, rather than those sections of the Pauline Epistles that gave overt sanction to slavery. What is important about their resistance to oppression, in my mind, is that they read the Bible with a hermeneutic of radical identification with the situation of oppression, resistance to that oppression, and ways in which the injustice could be endured or overcome, or transformed. They choose to identify with Moses, Joshua, Hagar, Esther, and Daniel as representatives of God's will in opposition to that of Pharaoh and Philemon (whom they might have seen as a "sell-out").

Rather than embracing the "Jesus so meek, so mild" of the slave masters' hymnody and spirituality, African American slaves developed a split-level view of Jesus. At one level Jesus was the One who Suffered for all human beings, especially those who suffered unjustly—like the slaves themselves. Thus Jesus was in the unique position of being empowering through His unique position of existential understanding. We find African American slaves reading the Passion Narratives through the lens of their own torture experiences—lynching, whippings, being silenced—as we listen to their Spirituals. "Were You There?"

> Were you there when they crucified my Lord?
> Were you there when they crucified my Lord?
> Oh, sometimes it causes me to tremble, tremble, tremble?
>
> Were you there when they crucified my Lord?
> Were you there when they nailed Him to the tree?...
> Were you there when He hung His head and died?...
> Were you there when He rose up from the tomb?...

Even more graphic is the Spiritual "I know it was the Blood":

> I know it was the Blood, I know it was the Blood
> I know it was the Blood for me

One day when I was lost He died upon a cross
And I know it was the Blood for me

They whipped Him all night long, they whipped Him all night long
They whipped Him all night long for me
One day when I was lost, He died upon a cross
And they whipped Him all night long for me

He never said a mumblin' word, He never said a mumblin' word
He never said a mumblin' word for me
One day when I was lost, He died upon a cross
And He never said a mumblin' word for me.

Well He's coming back again, He's coming back again,
He's coming back again for me.

One day when I was lost, He died upon a cross
And He's coming back again for me.

In both of these Spirituals we have a compact theological and musical rendering of the Passion from the vantage point of African American slaves. We cannot look at them and see specific verses found in Matthew 26–28, Mark 14–16, Luke 22–24, or even John 18–20. Yet the Bible is present, wrapped in the experience of African American slavery.

At the higher level of the split-level view of Jesus was the Final Absolute Judge of the World Jesus. This is the Jesus we find in the Judgment Scene separating the "sheep" from the "goats" based on how individuals treated the needy of the world—the hungry, thirsty, naked, and imprisoned. Jesus insists that as one treats these outcasts of society so one treats Him! So both the "sheep" and the "goats" were simply acting out of who they were spiritually—either generous, Spirit-filled and compassionate, or judgmental, narrow-minded, and pitiless.

Read Matthew 25:31–46. Discuss in what ways it is easy to be a "goat," and difficult to be a "sheep."

In the Spiritual "Ride on, King Jesus" we see the slaves celebrating the victorious power and liberating freedom of this Final Absolute Judge Jesus. The lyrics reveal a familiarity with what Bible scholars call the *eschatological* or "end-times" naming of Jesus that arise in Isaiah, and particularly the book of Revelation. The joyous melody, rhythm, and potent harmony of this Spiritual added to the liberative urgency of its message:

Ride on, King Jesus
No man can-a hinder Me!
Ride on, King Jesus, Ride
No man can-a hinder Me!
For He is King of Kings,
He is Lord of Lords
Jesus Christ, the First and Last
No Man works like Him
King Jesus rides in de middle of the air,
No man works like Him
And calls His saints from everywhere
No man works like Him

While the slaves were blessed that Jesus could suffer with them, they were more blessed that, at the end of all things, Jesus would ultimately Judge all the wrongdoers of the world. The evils that tore their bodies and their spirits would find ultimate justice. Jesus would make things right, "by-an'-by when the Morning comes." As such, Jesus, the Final Absolute Judge provided even the most miserable slave with a magical spiritual ingredient more potent than any drug, the blessing of hope. With hope to stabilize the dashed dreams, and worn-out bodies of African American slaves, their lives took on a meaning beyond the span of their earthly existence. With hope they could envision a day when "Freedom" would be a living and vibrant reality for their children, or children's children. They were empowered to look into the future with a determination, joy, trust, and faith enlivened by the stuff of hope—a living substance that was able to ward off the ever-present demons of despair and death.

# 6

# Proverbs: Mother Wit and Da Streetz

The Book of Proverbs provides a wealth of wisdom resources for all peoples, especially oppressed Black folk. Proverbs, like much of the rest of the Bible, is a part of the common vernacular of the African American community. A recent study on the Bible and African Americans revealed that "the Bible permeates African American life and culture." In fact, the presence of the Bible is so "pervasive" that it is embedded in our "music, art, street conversations, sales, and fortune telling."[1] Such research into the social effect of the Bible on the African American community is significant because it gives weight to the inference that African American church folks appreciate the theocentric insistence of Proverbs 1:7: "The fear of the LORD is the beginning of knowledge: but fools despise wisdom and instruction" (KJV). Furthermore, the Book of Proverbs establishes God's wisdom in the received wisdom of the human family, passed down by a father and mother. Thus only the "fool" despises the instruction of one's father and mother, for it is in hearing, receiving, and applying the proverbial insights of one's elders that one lives a virtuous life. Proverbs insists that the virtuous life reflects the life of a person who is walking in fellowship with God. Thus is wisdom's Circle made complete—wisdom comes from God to one's elders, who pass it down through the generations of families, who are called to follow wisdom's instructions in order to live a virtuous life, and by doing so, turn the attention of everyone not to themselves, but to God.

What is biblical "wisdom" as found in the Book of Proverbs? It is distilled in over 3,000 short "observations" on the conditions of life.[2] These sayings, or what in Hebrew are called *mashal* that root the good and right in life on a God-centered, and God-ordered existence; and evil in a life that is not focused on God. Rather than focusing on *Torah*, or the Law of Moses specifically, the Proverbs focus on the commandments or *mitzvah* of the father who is instructing his children:

> Listen, children, to a father's instruction,
> And be attentive, that you may gain insight;
> For I give you good precepts:
> Do not forsake my teaching.
> When I was a son with my father,
> Tender, and my mother's favorite,
> He taught me, and said to me,
> "Let your heart hold fast my words;
> Keep my *commandments* [*mitzvah*], and live.

"Keeping," or obeying continuously the *mitzvah* that the father has taught—as his father once taught him, is the way of wisdom. It is said to be synonymous with life itself. Stephen Harris notes that it is also akin to a concern with bringing one's daily walk, or life the presence of divine order, rather than its willful absence.[3]

A life lived in *chokmah* (Hebrew for "wisdom") or *Sophia* (Greek for "wisdom"), is a virtuous life. To be virtuous, in the biblical sense, is to live in righteousness (which is following the commandments of *Torah* even as it is distilled in the *mashal* of instructing fathers), and thus one receives the blessings of *Yahweh*. Righteousness, in the fullest Hebrew sense of the term, does not mean self-righteousness or pride, but joyful obedience to God's *Torah*, a walking the paths of uprightness.[4]

In *Bible Witness* the work of *chokmah* in the Black churches (in particular) may be contextualized into the broader contemporary milieu with a metaphor taken from the medical profession. It is a rather shocking, certainly hard metaphor, however apt or suited for our purposes. *Chokmah* helps us identify injustice as the spreading of a gangrene on the soul, character, and fabric of our society. Likewise, *Chokmah* teaches us that to check the unstoppable and potential fatal spread of gangrene, sometimes one is forced to use the extreme measure of applying the measured use of maggots! Developing a critical social analytic that is at the same time earthy, and extends a biblical vocabulary that is "proverbial" suggests that Divine wisdom can act as maggots do—who by their eating, cleanse the spiritual gangrene that infects our body politic. The symbolism comes from witnessing actual experiences during hospitalizations in my life. After many total hip replacement surgeries, and a devastating car accident that completely destroyed my automobile, I was in an enormous amount of physical pain. The searing, burning sensation in my legs felt like someone was trying to tear them off. Multiple surgeries were required. During that period I was exposed to many persons whose conditions were far worse, prognosis far more grim, prospects far more gruesome and piteous than I could even imagine. One gentleman even become so infected in one of his feet that his toes had begun to rot—a condition called gangrene. Gangrene is an ages-old miserable experience, most often caused from the trauma of wounds in battle. Cases occasionally appear in our modern, more-or-less sterile environment known as hospitals, and surprisingly enough, the most ancient "cure" is still being used—the controlled application of living maggots to literally eat away the dead tissue [!] We modern people cringe at the thought of both gangrene and maggots, but both still exist and have a role and place even in our highly technological world. Injustice, exploitation, discrimination, abuse, and violence are also ancient evils that have plagued humanity since before we were able to record their devastating effects; and we require *chokmah*'s scouring, eating, and cleansing power to aid us in the healing of our spiritual, emotional, political, economic, and societal evils.

What do these two ugly terms mean to me in relationship to the Bible, Black Theology, and *Bible Witness in Black Churches* ? They refer to the theological-ethical, and political "state of the world" that we inhabit right now, and to how we as Christians must address what is wrong. My family lost a first cousin, Andre Fletcher, in the tragic collapse of the World Trade Center Tower on September 9, 2001. He died because he was a firefighter, turning off gas valves in the subbasement of building number one. Little did we know that President George W. Bush would use the 9/11 tragedy as a springboard for unleashing policies of militaristic strategies that have led to obvious ploys for American global domination. When your own family has suffered a loss then the "need" for revenge can sometimes loom large in one's mind, and so the war in Afghanistan seemed like a "just war." The military "adventure" in Iraq, however, was presented as part of a "war on terror," and as a sure means for the elimination of "weapons of mass destruction." These weapons were placing the United States in "clear and present danger"—a phrase quoted by Tom Clancy used by presidents when a national emergency is declared *only* at the presidential level. There was a dramatic quick-strike campaign, a growing

Sunni and Shi'ite Iraqi insurgency, and the immeasurable rage of surrounding Arab countries organized into a guerrilla campaign that has drained the lifeblood of American troops, the spirit of the American people, and destroyed the credibility of an American president. Now, instead of being seen as fighting terrorism, the United States is seen (perhaps truthfully) as being "imperialist," grubbing for oil, and as capable of doing anything in order to achieve world domination. The Iraqi war was waged against the express wishes of almost all of our traditional allies except Great Britain. Further, after the major shooting stopped no weapons of mass destruction were found, no "clear and present danger" was established, and it has become abundantly clear that the Iraqi action itself has contributed to anti-American terrorism recruiting throughout the globe! By any such accounting, these policies are themselves rotten, they fester on the body-politic, and threaten to overthrow the entire future of the country.

Lest I describe the gangrene of our times in terms too politically "left," it is important to remember that our country also faces an equally disturbing trend that seems bent on erasing any vestiges of public Christian participation. For example, a generation ago school prayer was banned, then came the slow but steady erasure of creche scenes, as well as Christian Christmas songs during the Christmas season. Now, ostensibly no religion is to be spoken about at public schools, except in practice children hear about Wicca, witchcraft, Hinduism, Islam, Judaism, and practically any other religion except Christianity. It is, in fact, Christianity that is not to be taught, or mentioned in public. Christianity has been labeled, de facto, and de jure, as "religion" in the public sphere. Since Christianity has been labeled as "religion" legally, and groups like the ACLU (American Civil Liberties Union) have taken an unabashedly anti-Christian bias in their lawsuits, then openly espoused views of Christian belief and practice itself in contemporary United States are at risk.

This anti-Christian religious scene is complicated further by a collapse of personal ethics. Throughout the media, sexual escapades, exposes, and infidelities are trumpeted as entertainment in a steady, daily diet of gladiator-style, confrontational television shows. Jerry Springer, Ricki Lake, and Howard Stern have become media legends on the bared bodies, and exposed lives of embarrassed individuals who literally brawl with their betrayers in front of millions to the delight of jeering fans. Drawing out persons into lewd confessions of the basest sort debases the morality of the body-politic. To do so for ratings and entertainment creates a kind of immoral savagery that unhinges moral civilization itself. It is as if we are watching the dawn of a New Age of the Heathen, a New Dark Age (although I dislike the association of "dark" with evil and wrongness). The irony is that the rise of such a New Age of Heathenism (what scholars have called "postmodernism"), comes on the heels of the growing maturation of the so-called High-Tech Age. Thus we live in an era shot through with moral irony and spiritual paradox, nay, spiritual devastation. Such irony and paradox slips away from those interested in simply objectively describing the "signs of the times" by dressing the crisis up in sophisticated philosophical terms like "deconstruction" and "post-structuralism."[5]

The irony and paradox of the New Age of the Heathen cannot be truly discerned without the guidance of a biblically informed conscience, a conscience guided by principles found in the book of Proverbs. Proverbs understands itself to be a spiritual formation ground in which trust or *Batach* permeates the *Lev*, or "heart," and the trusting heart is able to discern good and evil far more accurately than the *Biynah* or "understanding."

> *Trust* in the LORD with all your *heart*, and lean not on your own *understanding.* (Proverbs 3:5) (NIV)

When we dig into the words "trust," "heart," and "understanding" we get a rich theology of the wisdom-informed conscience. The word "trust," or *Batach* fundamentally means to attach oneself, to rely on, to trust in, to confide in, to feel safe, to be secure, and even to be careless. The NASB *Key Word Study Bible* informs us that it is a word used 181 times in the Hebrew Bible; some 50 times in the Psalms alone. "The word expresses the sense of well-being which results from knowing that 'the rug won't be pulled out from under you.' "[6] Thus the father instructs the child through the media of proverbs in order for the child to gain a sense of *Batach* in *Yahweh.* Such trust enables the child to gain complete confidence, faith, and assurance and reliability in the ongoing ability of *Yahweh* to be there to handle every situation.

Trust is the necessary precondition that Proverbs sets up, but the location of trust is the "heart," or the *Lev.* While *Lev* often is used with its correlated word *Levav* for the physical organ that pumps blood known as the heart, the biblical authors used this some 850 times in the Hebrew Bible to represent the heart as the center and totality of our inner, human, immaterial nature. Some persons have understood the Hebrew usage of *Lev* to be close to our modern usage of the word "soul." Theologically, the *Lev* is the dwelling place of both "wisdom and understanding" (Proverbs 16:23) and our emotional life. The NASB *Study Bible* notes that it is the seat of our "deepest , innermost feelings," and the "whole spectrum of human emotions." What is vital to remember about the *Lev*, as the seat of our emotional life is that it also controls human will. Thus the "heart," while a romantic emotional and sentimental concept for contemporary persons, is a complex and rich term for a person willing to take on the biblical worldview. To *trust* God with my whole *heart* means that I am placing and attaching myself with complete and utter confidence in God. This trust in the *heart* means that my spiritual confidence and rest dwells securely within the center of my innermost being; in my will, my emotions, and in the place where wisdom and understanding have the opportunity to operate within my choices, decisions, and actions.

Proverbs 3:5 directs our moral life to be rooted in trust, and to dwell in the heart rather than in a place that it calls rather ambiguously the "understanding." What is this "understanding?" *Biynah* means insight, intelligence, prudence, and skill. It derives from the verb *Biyn* that has to do with discerning, perceiving, paying attention, instructing, teaching to attend; and that morally refers to ethical discernment of good and evil. While Proverbs 28:5 notes that the seekers of the LORD have *Biyn*; and Psalm 119:34 enjoins us to pray for it—nevertheless this early verse in Proverbs 3:5 warns us that misplaced trust in *Biynah*, rather than trust that is seated in Yahweh alone and grounded in one's heart, is insufficient for a complete life. The verse tells us not to "lean" or *Sha'an* on *Biynah*.

The term *Sha'an* has a fascinating history. It means "to support oneself, to lean against." It is an idiom that arose from "lean upon someone's hand" as was the custom of kings when they made public appearances! It is used as an antonym of the proper ideal of biblical trust, opposing the weakness of trusting in anything human versus the power and confidence we gain in relying upon God.

## Study Questions

1. Search the Book of Proverbs to find out how many times the reader is warned to curb or control their tongue, lips, or mouth.
2. Discuss the reasons why you believe that the Bible spends so much time and space discussing our speech and controlling what we think and say?

3. Proverbs 15:4 and 16:24 make a specific connection between pleasant and sweet words with the healing of the body—or "bones." What is the connection?
4. Find and read the proverbs that warn us to avoid contact with violent persons. Why shouldn't a gentle and peace-loving person have more influence over a violent person than is apparently true in the opposite direction, as the Bible directly implies?

## Da Streetz

At such a juncture in this conversation many would suppose that I might bring up rap music as one of the "bad guys" we need to roundly condemn. For many reasons I resist that temptation, primarily because those Baby-Boomers such as myself tend to not be familiar enough with the Rap music scene to state anything about Rap with any credibility.

For urban and poor African Americans, rappers have described the condition of our communities from the perspective of "Da Streetz." It is from that vantage point, that gritty viewpoint that *Bible Witness in Black Churches* makes its plea for the Mother Wit of Proverbs to take its stand.

Proverbs has contributed to the store of Mother Wit resident in Black communities. In the hip-hop generation, Mother Wit has passed on through the medium of rap music. I will briefly examine the Mother Wit and scriptural references and allusions in secular rappers like Kanye West, Nas, 50cents, and Puff Daddy. Christians have slowly, over the past decade, developed their own version of Gospel Rap that is taking root in Black churches. It can be heard in Da Streetz-informed lyrics of Cross Movement, or L.G. Wise, T. Bone, Rough Riders, Christsyde, and several other excellent Gospel rappers. Gospel rappers are reaching out to Da Streetz in proverbial wisdom.

First, it is important to differentiate Gospel Rap from commercial Rap that most persons hear blared from their radios every day. The music industry has capitalized on the most desperately inexperienced, young teenagers whose raging hormones can think of nothing and describe nothing in their lyrics but the most raw and vulgar form of sexual conquest, contact, and bravado. For such music there can be Streetz wisdom gained, gleaned, or garnished.

Rap music seems to fall into various categories, and commercial secular artists often cross-over, and mix two or more categories into one CD in order to increase the sales values of their "product."

Building on the categories of Anthony Pinn, I loosely organize Rap into the following general types based on their lyrical content:

A. Gutter Trash—dance music—Lil' John; Ying Yang Twins, 50cents.
B. Avant-Garde—pushing the boundaries—Missy Eliot, Busta Rhymes.
C. Bubble Gum—innocuous—Snoop Dogg; L.L. Cool J., Will Smith.
D. Message—Social justice critique—Ice Cube, Nas, Jay Z.
E. Gospel—Cross Movement, T Bone, L.G. Wise.

Of interest to any contemporary student of Gospel Rap is the emergence of the commercial Rapper Kanye West with his hit song, "Jesus Walks" While his album, "College Dropout" might be loosely categorized as containing mostly Message music, its level of profanity certainly would eliminate it from consideration as a Gospel rap album! Nevertheless Kanye West unabashedly expresses his desire for Jesus to "walk with me" over and over again in the hit song "Jesus Walks." Such a cross-over into the realm of Christian faith by a primarily secular artist is not surprising, even as it was a bold move on his part.

L.G. Wise takes on the crude, exploitive, and overtly sexual aspects of the secular Rap industry as his way of spreading Streetz wisdom. He notes that supporting a music industry that ignores the plight of people who are dying from casual violence on city streets, encouraging casual sex that leads to fatherless households, and glorifying the drug culture as being a "P- I- M-P!" needs to be condemned as a "Burn Baby Burn" ethos that leads urban African Americans to a living Hell on earth. Such Gospel Rap understands itself as calling for a spiritual change that combines personal salvation with a revolutionary social justice message whose ultimate aim is to "save the children" across the country from imprisonment, drugs, and the death of Da Streetz. The album "Me vs. the Industry" is filled with positive and uplifting "shout-outs" (greetings) to "All the Shorties on the Block, All the Thugs toting Rocks…the World is Yours!"

L.G. Wise places the choice as very clear in one very danceable number—"Live or Die." The verses catalogue all of the various temptations and vices available to an average person on city streets, but they are not glorified as being the proper choices. The refrain "Live or Die" is punctuated by the thought "…because the way that you live is the way that you die." While such a simple thought might seem obvious, it reveals the obvious proverbial insight about reaping what one sows.

How is this "proverbial," or an example of biblical wisdom? If one reads the Book of Proverbs with a sensitive eye and a willing spirit, the similarity becomes apparent immediately. God offers human beings a stark choice that may be stated simply, but is not simplistic. We may choose to do the right things continually, and to reap the benefits of that kind of behavior; or choose the wrong or evil things of life, and pay the consequences of those choices. Choices lead to actions, and actions lead invariably to consequences. Wisdom ethics flows from a *connection*, not, a disconnection with God's express desires and commands.

For some this kind of plain talking might seem just too insulting, or too facile for their level of intellectual sophistication. If so, then let these next words say the same thing. Charles Scobie sums it up nicely when he states that the Wisdom tradition of the Bible lays the foundation for the creation of a potent "theology of responsibility" in which Spirit-endowed human beings prayerfully cooperate with one another, are accountable to one another, and take responsibility for the results of our ethical choices.[7] Some church folk grow up under the "Amazing Grace" theology that emphasizes the utter wretchedness and fallenness of human nature. While such a theology points us to God's amazing grace, they can also overemphasize our inability to do anything good or worthwhile for ourselves or toward other people. After all goes the kind of twist in the wretchedness theological logic. "If I am so wretched and evil, then I might as well keep on being sinful until God decides to pour out 'His grace' and make me good!" The Proverbs, by contrast, remind me that I need to do something to be righteous and good even as I live in the watchful presence of God's grace.

Proverbs call us to do many things in the work of living in *righteousness*. Perhaps first among those things is to control what we say. Wisdom's depth or lack is revealed through the mouth. Proverbs 13:3 places the problem in terms of the mouth being guarded or wide open: "The one who guards his mouth preserves his life. The one who opens wide his lips comes to ruin" (NASB). Proverbs 21:23 has a slight variant on the same idea, "The one who guards his mouth and his tongue, guards his soul from troubles" (NASB). The Hebrew word for "mouth" is *Peh*, it occurs some 500 times in the Hebrew Bible most frequently in the Psalms and Proverbs. When referring to "...the mouth of the LORD" it means that something is the very last, authoritative word on the matter. When referring to human beings, the *Peh* is an "extreme manifestation of an individual's character and disposition, whether for good or for bad."[8] The ancient Hebrews thought of the "lips," or the *Saphah*, as the "key organ of speech" that could be understood as the "gates of honesty or deception." Thus *Saphah*, the lips, was the place from which all kinds of language and speech could flow—from flattery, to lies, healing to violence.

What brings together the "heart" or *Lev* with the other three aspects of speech (the mouth—*Peh*, the lips—*Saphah*, and the tongue—*Lashon*) is the emphasis on formation of righteous character because of the established relationship with *Yahweh*. Proverbs 16:1 restates the insights of Proverbs 3:5, but it does so in a very self-critical manner:

> To humankind belong the plans of the *heart* (*Lev*)
> But from the LORD comes the reply of the *tongue* (*Lashon*) (NIV)

Gospel Rappers believe that "heart" and "lips" cannot be separated in a biblical worldview, or that the "mouth" and "tongue" do not have a central place in the uplifting of the Gospel message of Jesus as Christ. Church folk have always tended to find it difficult to accept the "radicals" of their generation, so that Andrae Crouch and the Hawkins Brothers of the 1960s were viewed as introducing a "crossover" sound into holy places that was utterly unacceptable to many holy folk of that time. Now rappers whose commitment to proclaiming the Gospel with the fire of a Tupac Shakur or a 50 cent (but without their secular taint) are finding it very difficult to be taken seriously in many quarters.

One Gospel Rap group named Christsyde has a CD entitled "Who Dat?" that is filled with one danceable tune after another. It is quite clear that the underlying theme of the entire CD is that one can "Boogie for Jesus," moving one's body while listening to Scriptures about Christ dying for one's sins, meditating about the utter goodness and absolute ricbes of Jesus' love. It is a strong and radical philosophy, because it insists that young people can move their bodies in celebration while mouthing the words of salvation. Taking their musical cues from the "West-side" musical tradition of Ice Cube and Snoop Dogg, their music has a strong dose of heavy synthesized bass; George Clinton-Parliament/Funkadelic type influenced musical borrowings. One particularly important funky chorus that reinforces the notion of Godly wisdom is rooted in a relationship with Jesus Christ combined with spiritual combat with Satan goes as follows:

> It's God's Way or no Way
> We're breaking that Devil with this Gospel Funk
> Shaking that Devil on with this Gospel Funk.

Another important and influential Gospel Rap group, Cross Movement, not only creates their own CDs, but has sponsored an entire "school" of young artists coming up beside them. In their 2004 hit CD "Holy Culture" Cross Movement insisted on the notion that holy words from the Word of Jesus could transform hip-hop culture into Holy Culture. The entire album was built upon this transforming theological theme, a theme that they stretched beyond the traditional evangelical boundaries of personal salvation to the need to clean the streets of drugs, to encourage urban females to understand themselves as more than sexual objects, to encourage young street males to aspire to lives beyond the pimp lifestyle, drug hustling, and its attendant violence.

Cross Movement takes the theme of transformation to a higher level in their most recent CD rendering "Higher Definition." In this CD the notion of transformation is stretched into the notion of redefinition. In the theme song the Chorus calls for Gospel rap to do the following:

> Re-define City
> Re-define verse
> Re-define him
> Re-define her
> Re-define "pimp"...
> Re-define "church"....

The task of redefining is the next logical step to an insistence upon transforming Hip-Hop Culture into Holy Culture. What makes it interesting for wisdom thinking is that it incorporates a self-critical, prophetic element that is unafraid to redefine the parameters of "church" while it transforms the most scandalous ("pimp") elements of masculinity. Such prophetic criticism expands the boundaries of a narrow definition of what "wisdom" can mean for contemporary church folk as they seek to reach Da Streetz for Jesus Christ.

By insisting that gaining a personal relationship with Jesus Christ has a strong cleansing effect on the worst corruption of Da Streetz, Cross Movement incorporates elements of the most radical Message Rap traditional Rap music with the evangelical fervor of Gospel Rap. Such cross-fertilization of Gospel Rap demonstrates a growing maturation of Gospel Rap—something it has needed since its humble beginnings as a recorded music in the early 1990s. In those days the poor recording quality, insistence upon a watered-down presentation of Scriptures, repeated over and over again, with little or no critical social analysis left many supportive persons begging for more even as we saw the need for a Rap style of Gospel presentation.

One of the earliest Gospel Rappers, but certainly not the earliest, was T-Bone. T-Bone is a Latino brother coming from East L.A. Calling himself a "Streetz Preacha," T-Bone's music has always incorporated elements of popular Rap with Scriptural content. T-Bone is a reformed Gang member whose testimonial of personal conversion and transformation has formed the core of his entire Gospel Rap ministry from the early 1990s throughout the last several years. T-Bone's Rap-songs are filled with urban stories of persons whose lives are object lessons to be avoided as one moves toward a closer relationship to Jesus Christ.

### Discussion Question

Many well-meaning and highly valued religious leaders throughout the years have never been very progressive in their acceptance various changing musical trends and styles in Gospel music. Do you think that Church leaders ought to keep out of the business of telling young people what particular type of music is "truly Christian" or not?

## Mother Wit

Contemporary Gospel music appeals to the hip-hop tastes of a new generation of church folk. From Kirk Franklin's early "Shout," to the "Personal Jesus" of Tonex, or even the offerings of J. Moss, Karen Clark Sheard, and her daughter Kiki Sheard. There is an entire new generation of very popular Gospel artists who are bringing a new "radical sound" to the Church, that is dating the sound of my generation of Edwin, Tremaine, and Walter Hawkins; Shirley Caesar; and Andrae Crouch. That is the way that Gospel music has been since the time that a blues-playing, brothel piano player named Thomas Dorsey began to scandalize "good church folk" with his version of "gospel music" in the 1940s! What all of these popular musical songs have in common is their usage of spiritual Mother Wit to convey messages of comfort, wisdom, and hope in times of trouble and despair.

What is "Mother Wit?" Every ethnicity and culture has their own name for it. The dominant culture calls it "common sense." In East Texas many of the good ole boys and gals I have grown fond of seem to call it "horse sense." In my limited experience African American folk call the transgenerational passing down of proverbial maxims, sayings, and aphorisms "mother wit." It is not confined to mothers, grandmothers, aunts, or female elders, but may come from respected and revered male elders as well. Mother Wit is a universal inheritance; however, and may be passed onto one from the lips of a passing stranger on the street who bears no familial relationship. For example, if one does something that is particularly thoughtless or cruel to someone else out on the streets (at least in a traditional Black neighborhood), it is not surprising if someone will "signify" (say something to their neighbor in a voice loud enough for the person spoken about to clearly tell that they are being addressed indirectly!) "Ooh, chile, they better watch out, cause what goes around comes around." Here not only is the proverb of "reaping what you sow" given its African American cultural "twist," but it is also immediately applied as a direct social criticism to impolite or rude behavior.

Through the medium of signification I remember my home church folk applied many disciplinary injunctions toward me when I was a child within the sacred walls of my home Baptist church. Proverbial wisdom is often rooted in remembering what one has been taught as right and wrong by one's parents. When I would talk too loudly, respond rudely to a question by an adult, or be caught fighting in the hallways of the church I remember the rejoinder, "I know your parents did not raise you that way." Even the hint of having my parents being told about my behavior as being subpar was always an effective form of bringing me—and other children—back "in line."

Mother Wit is inferential. It points to a world of meaning, experience, and expectations with an economy of words. Such usage of inference disguises an enormous amount of social power, but the few words that are deployed within the sayings of Mother Wit are effective because they "work." Thus they are mother witticisms, because they are foundational. They give birth to an entire world of intended meaning.

## Study Questions

1. Name one or two "Mother Wit" phrases you remember that helped shape your childhood, and that continue to affect you today.
2. With the breakdown of traditional neighborhoods, the kind of "It takes a village to raise a child" ethos has been severely curtailed in many areas. Has Mother Wit been curtailed and limited as well?

## Wisdom and Work

While Genesis 1 most assuredly has God blessing work for six "days," while sanctifying rest and recreation for a day of *Sabbath* renewal, most church folks (and everyone else for that matter!) tend to look at work as part of the "curse" of the Fall! More specifically, we tend to view all of the various forms of work available to us as part of the punishment placed on Adam in Genesis 3:17–19 because of his disobedience to God's will, lack of taking responsibility for what happened between the Serpent, Eve, and himself; and finally, for his blaming of Eve for the disaster.

> Read Genesis 3 and take especial care to notice what each character says. Remember to read which kind of tree and fruit the LORD specifically forbids in Genesis 2:16–17 to Adam. Look up the different meanings of the word "toil" in Genesis 3:17.

The Book of Proverbs even uses the organized, busy life of ants as an example from God's good creation of how we ought to emulate the positive effects of diligent planning and daily, communal work in Proverbs 6:6–11. Altogether, when we gather together these verses, along with Proverbs 10:4; 13:4; and 24:30–34, we find one underlying moral "lesson" that repeats itself in various ways as an overarching theme that is stated outright in Proverbs 10:4: "Lazy hands make a man poor, but diligent hands bring wealth." The interpretation of these words does not literally equate laziness with all poverty, nor diligent work with every wealthy person, however. We ought to interpret the words "poor" and "wealth" with a sense of freedom; so that the verse may be understood as saying laziness and sloth impoverishes both our life and financial status, while in contrast hard work and diligence enriches our material and spiritual lives. Not all of us can be "rich" in the standard of worldly accumulation of material assets and value; as a matter of fact, the Book of Proverbs specifically condemns riches gained by illicit, unjust means:

> Ill-gotten gotten gains do not profit,
> but righteousness delivers from death (Proverbs 10:4) (NASB)
> Treasures gained from wickedness do not profit,
> but righteousness delivers from death (Proverbs delivers from death)
> (Proverbs 10:2 NRSV)

Likewise, Proverbs 11:4 reveals how trusting is one's wealth in times of trouble can lead to death:

> Riches do not profit in the day of wrath,
> but righteousness delivers from death (NASB), (NRSV)

The aim in both of these verses is not "riches," or "treasures," but is the feminine version of the word "righteousness" (*tsedaqah*) that we spoke of in the last chapter. *Tsedaqah* means justness, rightness, rectitude, justice (divine and human), mercy, midness, moderation, and prosperity. It implies both "fairness," and "right relationship" between God and human" and "human beings with each other."[9]

The contrast is between the slothful lazy person called a sluggard; and the steady, stable, and diligent worker called wise. The one refuses to discipline his or her self enough to do the daily tasks necessary to fulfill their craving for the things they desire (see Proverbs 13:4). The wise person is willing to schedule his or her tasks, accomplish the goals that have been set by the plan; and willing to rise early in the morning to do what is necessary.

### Study Question

1. Find all of the verses in the Book of Proverbs that condemn slothfulness while praising hard work.
2. Doing a word search, look up other places in the Bible where hard work is valued positively, and sloth is condemned (i.e., Ecclesiastes).

Without hard work and diligence Proverbs teaches us that we shall most assuredly be "poor" in every sense of the word! Yet ultimately hard work cannot make one rich, and here prosperity Gospels fail to hear the Word properly. Proverbs reminds us the true prosperity, in the end, is a Blessing from God:

> It is the blessing of the LORD that makes rich
> And God [He] adds no sorrow with it. (Proverbs 10:22) (NASB)

The word for "blessing" here is a variation of the standard word *barakah*, and it is *berekah. Berekah* means reservior and was the watering place for camels. So the verse literally means, "Out of the reservior of the LORD comes the resources that make us wealthy, and from that place God adds no worries and no sorrow." What a potent verse that we often never hear from those preaching a Gospel of Prosperity. Money, wealth, and finances come out of God's place of abundance, and from that place we have no worries, and no sorrows because we know that it is not our wealth, but wisdom teaches us that since it came from God's overabundance, it really belongs to God! It is not ours to "Name and Claim," but ours to be thankful for whenever we experience any experience of its abundance and overflow. But it is not merely given to us, we receive its blessings more and more through diligence and hard work.

### Study Question

Can you find any more verses in Proverbs (or any other parts of the Bible) that equate hard work with the Blessings of God?

# 7

# Vision

African Americans, like all Americans, require a new spiritual vision that is positive and life-affirming. *Bible Witness in Black Churches* is rooted in a biblical, theological hope that springs from an appreciation of what the Bible teaches us about human nature, and God's vision. The book ends with an analysis of one of the Bible's most systematically theological books, Romans; and a framework for interpreting the first three chapters of one of the Bible's most obscure texts—the visions of the seven churches in the Apocalypse of the Book of Revelation.

While the Epistle to the Romans is Paul's most complicated contribution to the Christian Gospel, it also presents the complex texture of a biblical vision of humanity standing in relationship to God through Jesus Christ. In Romans certain important theological principles are established:

1. Universality of human sin and grace—Justification (Romans 1–5);
2. Sanctification—Conflict of *Sarx* and *Nomos* (Flesh and Law) (Romans 6–7);
3. Glorification—Triumph of *Pneumatikos* (Spirit) (Romans 8);
4. God's Sovereign Mystery-Israel (Romans 9–11);
5. The Life of *Pneumnatikos* in Community (Romans 12–14).

Since the Book of Romans has been extensively written about by some of the greatest minds—from Anders Nygren to Karl Barth—I recognize that my listing of five theological principles must seem oversimplified by comparison. Nevertheless one can argue that their presence provides the overarching theological movement of the Epistle as we look more intensively into each particular chapter of Romans.

Biblical scholars agree that the book of Romans was written by the Apostle Paul between 57 and 58 CE. Its audience was the multiple house churches present in the city of Rome. Of interest to us is that this epistle is addressed to a church that Paul neither founded nor had visited. Further, it presents itself as a theological sermon, not merely a letter. In fact some scholars believe that Paul may have written it to be a circular letter, to be read by several churches as it dealt with controversial topics that had divided other churches.[1]

Read all of Romans Chapter 1, focus now on Romans 1:14–17

## Universality of Sin and Grace

The Epistle to the Romans begins with an affirmation of the *Kerygma*—the Gospel message. Paul is convicted to be an apostle to both Jews and Gentiles, to "Greeks and non-Greeks, both to the wise and the foolish" (Roman 1:14). For Paul the Gospel is the power, the *dunamis* of God for the salvation, the *soteria* of all peoples, Jew and Gentile alike. Thus the reader is informed of God's vision through Jesus Christ as the setting by which the complicated and (for beginners!) difficult to understand condemnation of human nature is cast. Yet, in Paul's vision, God does not begin with critical, destructive analysis; but rather, by presenting the "plan." Before any analysis there is the radiant affirmation proclaiming a detailed *kerygma* as being dynamically capable and inherently powerful (*Dunamis*); and capable of providing rescue and deliverance (*Soteria*) to all humanity. What is so important about this positive beginning? It reveals to us that *vision*, when truly rooted in a Godly pattern, presents the heart of God's positive plan first, before any indications of why the vision has been presented. The lesson is clear for us church folks—we cannot "save souls" or "transform the world" unless we are clear in our own minds and hearts about the powerful *kerygma* of salvation. Too often church folk and church leaders are too involved in decrying what they do not like, too wrapped up in the following passages about sinners rather than presenting what in its own context is a carefully presented, overarching positive vision.

## Doctrine of Justification

The salvation (*soteria*) of God is not the only aspect of God's gospel revealed in Romans 1:16–17. Paul tantalizes the careful reader by introducing, in a nutshell, and fleshing out for the next few chapters of Romans—the doctrine of justification. Simply, justification is being made right in God's eyes:

> For in the Gospel a righteousness from God is *revealed*, a
> righteousness that is by *faith* from first to last,
> just as it is written, "The righteous will live by faith."

The righteousness of God is one of the most important qualities of the Gospel because it is the first mention of what becomes a theme in this section of Romans 1–5. Righteousness, or *dikaiosyne* in Greek, is derived from *dike*, which means "just, righteous, and upright. *Dikaiosyne*," a tongue-twister for sure, is said to "fulfill the claims of *Dike*, which in the case of the believer is a fulfillment of God's claim." Thus righteousness is "conformity to the claims of higher authority and stands as the opposite of *anomia*—lawlessness."[2] Righteousness is something God grants us—a gift. It is not something we do, or which we earn. It is something God grants us—the state of being made right in God's presence. *Dikaiosyne* is therefore one of the most important words for us to remember as we go forward in our exegesis and theology of Romans.

*Dikaiosyne* characterizes God's nature and activity, "particularly in relationship to God's covenant with Israel." It occurs some eight times in the epistle of Romans—(1:17; 3:5, 21, 22, 25, 26, and twice in 10:3).[3]

God is said to reveal this righteousness from God. The verb reveal is *apokalypto*, which, as we said before, means "to remove a veil or covering, exposing to open view that which before was hidden." So God unveils (in the *Kerygma*) what has been previously hidden and covered up—the righteousness of God—to us in this gospel that is God's power to save us.

Finally, quoting Habakkuk 2:4, Paul notes that the *righteous* will live by *faith*. The word used here for "righteous" is *dikaioo* that is also derived from the word *dike*. Since *dike* is important for *dikiaosyne* and *dikaioo*, perhaps we need to look at it first. Let's unpack the word *dike*—"righteous" just a little more than was revealed in the above paragraph. *Dike* is another one of the important, complex terms that Paul uses. It means

> "Justice, judgment, penal sentence, retribution, vengeance." In Classical Greek, *dike*...was the name of the daughter of Zeus and

> Themis, whose task was the rendering of judicial sentence (deciding who is right) among men. Early on meant a state of mind, an attitude, a mode or manner of action, later a tradition, custom, rule, or standard. It denoted the right treatment of something, or the right conduct for a situation. The standard of rule expressed what was proper, befitting, appropriate, or due. Each situation and object were seen as having due [to] them a certain kind of treatment which called for a specific standard conduct...a due measure of treatment. The measure or standard was based upon the character, function, and purpose of a given object, an harmony and congruity what action was necessary to maintain its character, perform its function, and fulfill its purpose in order to achieve harmony and congruity. It expressed the standard of conduct expected by society...*Dike* was used for the judicial sentence and meant penal justice, just retribution, vengeance...in the NT it is used with this meaning, to render justice.[4]
>
> Since *dikaioo* derives from *dike*, its meaning is also somewhat long-winded: Right, justice, Just, righteous, upright...conformable to the right, pertaining to right, that which is just, which is expected by the one who sets the rules and regulations whereby man must live, whether that is society or God...conformity in his behavior can fully meet the expectations of God in his life...The heathen say, "My right is my duty." On the other hand, the Christian says, "My duty [to God and others] is my right."

How is God's righteousness established within us if we cannot gain it by ourselves? Paul answers this question by noting that it is by a spiritual mechanism—the gift of faith—that God's righteousness becomes both a possibility and reality for us. Not only is God revealing through the *kerygma* the "righteousness of God by faith from first to last," but also that "the righteous will live by faith."[5] What is "faith?" It is *pistis*, the other important word in the doctrine of justification because it is the driving force that activates, motivates, and maintains within human beings the righteousness of God living in our hearts and affecting our hearts. *Pistis* means "trust, belief. Subjectively, firm persuasion, conviction, belief in the truth, reality, or faithfulness of something—Objectively, that which is believed, doctrine, the received articles of faith...the immediate instrument of preservation, dependent upon and made to work by the power of God..."[6] Faith, like righteousness, cannot and does not motivate or activate itself, according to Christian belief. Rather, faith is that which is created and sustained by God's power acting within us. Not only that, faith is that which "secures our salvation."[7] It is the power operating within the *dunamis*—the dynamic energy—of the Gospel message and lifestyle.

## The State of "Natural," Unrighteous Humanity

What makes the next section (Romans 1:18–32) so jarring to us is that Paul goes right for the heart of humanity's "problem." Further, God is presented as wrathful and angry about this "problem." Why is God presented through the phrase, "The wrath of God is being revealed from heaven...?" Why is God revealed as Divine anger toward us? Is God a God of wrath and anger because of something that we have done? What did we do wrong?

Fundamentally, the phrase "the wrath" of God is presented as *orge*—which means, (literally "to strive for, desire". It is used in the New Testament as "fury, anger...angry state of mind"). According to the *Key Word Study Bible NIV* the phrase is used "...to indicate a rational calculated anger...as opposed to *thymos* which means unreasoning, emotional, outburst of anger."[8] Anders Nygren puts it as God's "holy displeasure with sin." He goes on to state that this "wrath" is not unimportant, because it reveals God's active view of humanity standing against God's will for all of us:

> As long as God is God, He cannot behold with indifference that His creation is destroyed and His holy will trodden underfoot. Therefore He meets sin with His mighty and annihilating reaction.[9]

Paul's God is not standing by and passively accepting that human beings actively stand against all which represents godliness. In fact human beings are first presented as being guided by "godlessness and wickedness." "Godlessness" comes from the Greek word *asebeia*—which literally means "impious, irreverent, disrespectful. Impiety, irreverence, lack of respect for or fear of God."[10] The word "wickedness" derives from the Greek word *adikia*, meaning "no, not *dike* (justice), injustice, unrighteousness, wrongdoing, misdeed, impropriety, fault. In classical Greece, *dike* originally meant a state of mind, an attitude, a mode or manner of action; later a tradition, custom, rule, or standard. It denoted the right treatment of something, or right conduct for a situation. The standard or rule expressed what was proper, befitting, appropriate, or due. In legal sense *dike* referred to law, justice, what is established as right conduct, the proper, and lawfully established as right conduct, which leads to the due treatment of persons or things. *Adikia*, then, is "the failure to discharge one's duties toward others (people or things), the failure to abide by the lawful standard of appropriate conduct...a disregard for order, convention, harmony and beauty..."[11] This long and complicated definition of *adikia* could actually, and simply stated, be unrighteous. Human beings are actively irreverent, showing a lack of respect for God, and unrighteous.

It is always a risky venture to tell Black folks that God was and/or is "angry" with them. A few Black preachers elaborated an angry God back in slavery times, but it was not a common sermonic theme. What was more common was the theme of Blacks being placed by the "Providence of God" into the hands of an "unrighteous nation" in order for God to "train" Blacks in a holy "work." This "work" was the "civilizing and evangelizing the land whence they were torn...preserving them under the severest trials and afflictions."[12]

Romans 1:18 states that not only are we impious, irreverent, and unrighteous, but we are also human beings "who suppress the truth by their wickedness" (NIV). We "suppress" or *Katecho*—to detain, hinder, delay"[13] the "truth" of God. "Truth" is a big word when we relate it to God. It is *Aletheia*—meaning "reality fact...opposite of falsehood, error, or wrong. Theologically absolute truth, ultimate truth, transcendent truth, divinely revealed truth. Truth here refers to the reality of things in their relation to God."[14] So human beings actively suppress what they know to be the absolute Truth, and divinely revealed truth of God being God, and we humans being in a relationship with God.

Why are these three concepts combined to describe humanity? To put it in a somewhat clumsy fashion, why are the *asebeia*, *adikia*, and *katecho* of *aletheia* so heinous to God? Verse 19 answers our question by noting that all these things are particularly wrong "since what may be known about God is *plain* to them, because God has made it *plain*." God has made it *phaneros*, "to shine, make to shine, cause to appear, apparent, manifest...in the sense of being public, open."[15] God's truth, justice, and righteousness, according to Paul, are public, open, and apparent to all of us.

So now the question arises, "How can this truth, justice, and righteousness of God be so apparent to us, since God is not visible to us in the ordinary sense of the word?" Verse 20 answers this question:

> For since the creation of the world God's invisible qualities—his eternal power and divine nature—have been clearly seen, being understood from what has been made, so that men are without excuse. (NIV)

We can discern that there is a God who has ordered all the "world"—the *kosmos* in Greek that means "the created world or material universe…(usually the earth as contrasted to the heavens)," as well as "humanity, the people, the people of the earth."[16] So we can "know" God by looking around and seeing all of creation as we ought.

Human beings have consciously turned away from God according Romans 1:21:

> For although they *knew* God, they neither *glorified* him as God nor gave thanks to him, but their thinking became futile and their foolish hearts were darkened. Although they claimed to be wise, they became fools and exchanged the glory of the immortal God for images made to look like mortal man and birds and animals and reptiles. (NIV)

There is something so fundamentally Jewish about this verse. It discerns rebellion from Yahweh as being the root cause of human beings creating idolatry—the worship of created things rather than the worship of the true and living God. Here we see Paul, the educated Pharisee turned Christian preacher-theologian, at his best. As a person raised in the monotheistic language of being a Hebrew, Paul creates Christian theology on his former firm foundation of Hebrew theology.

Verses 21–23 notes that human beings have known God. The Greek word for knew is *ginosko. Ginosko* means "to know, to come to know, experience…to perceive, observe, be aware of…"; they knew God "simply suggests that they could not avoid the perception of God."[17] Having known God, human beings, rather, have neither "glorified" nor given thanks to that Being from which we have clearly perceived in creation. We have not "glorified—*doxazo*"—recognize, honor, praise. Derived from *doze*, the verb depicts action involving the recognition or bestowal of that quality or property that is manifestly excellent and highly impressive"[18]— the clearly revealed God.

The result of all of these negative qualities of the unrighteous, God is said to "give them over in the *sinful desires* of their hearts to *sexual impurity* for the *degrading of their bodies with one another*." (verse 24). God's action is harsh, with dire consequences for humanity. God releases humanity from the bonds of created humanity to being bound to the bonds of sexual impurity. Instead of having righteousness by faith, we become slaves to our *akarthartos*—unclean, filthy, dirty—desires. God releases us to our *epithymia*—to desire greatly…sexual;

desire, cupidity, libido...the unleashing and directing of it [our passions or pathos] toward certain objects." *Epithymia* is the opposite of Godly love; *agape Epithymia* is lust—an almost uncontrollable urge, a desire that demands satisfaction in our bodies. Many have used the word for the sexual desire necessary for reproduction. Thus it is not necessarily bad, but Paul qualifies just what kind of *epithymia* he is referring to. When God has released us from the possibilities of *agape*—divine, unconditional love that springs from God—we fall into a form of *Epithymia* that degrades us. What does it mean to degrade us? What is degraded *epithymia*? Degraded *epithymia* is lust that is twisted, distorted desire, but God does not just turn us over to *Epithymia*, God also abandons us as well to a "depraved mind to do what ought not to be done." Because of these things, God has given sinful humanity over to shameful lusts (verse 26).

> Carefully read verses 26–27; then read 28–32. What example does Paul use to indicate *epithymia*? What are the qualities of a depraved mind? Do you agree with Paul's example of *epithymia*, or do you believe that such a life is "normal" and "natural?" Why do you believe as you do? Notice that while Paul seems to single out a particular form of sexuality, his usage of depraved mind seems to include everyone.
>
> Next, read Romans 2:1–4 and 12–16.

This portion of scripture has often been singled out as the Scripture upon which one can condemn homosexuals biblically. Paul is to blame for this perception, because for him "natural relations" meant heterosexual ones.[19] Anything outside of such "natural relations" Paul viewed as worthy of being condemned as sin. Further, it is clear from his usage that he believed that others probably agreed with him. I cannot go along with such interpretations because they use the Bible as a bludgeon, and not as a document of potent love and forgiving grace.

While some may be tempted to judge the homosexual with harshness by using Romans verses 26–27 as a condemnation of an entire group of human beings, notice that Paul states that nobody has any right to pass judgment on others "you who pass judgment do the same things" (Romans 2:1). I believe that Paul rewords Jesus' Sermon on the Mount injunction found in Matthew 7:1–2: "Do not judge, or you will be judged, For in the same way you judge others you will be judged, and with the measure you use, it will be measured to you."

With every sermon that condemns the homosexual we are judged by God as well for our adulterous, angry, stealing, and covetous hearts and actions. Since many Black churches use this Scripture to focus on homosexual "sin," I believe that we need to remember that there is no room for judgment. Paul wants us to preach that with the standard, intensity, and measure we hold others to, so we too will be judged.

Notice how Romans 2:16–32 uplifts the fact that God judges each of us according to what we do with the *kerygma* and *Torah* that we have. If someone has never been acquainted with either, they are considered to know God's law in accordance with their following the "law for themselves... since they show that the requirements of the *law* are written in their hearts." For Paul the all-present, everlasting, and eternal God has created all human beings in God's image (Genesis 1:26–27), and thus we have the basic "Law" the fundamental *Nomos*—"law, principle, rule... the divine Law given by Moses as well as law in general"[20] is engraved by God in our hearts. Paul wants the Jewish and Gentile Christians of Rome to know that everyone, Jew and Gentile, is to be measured by what they do—whether under the dictates of *Nomos* and the *kerygma*, or having never heard it.

> Finish reading all of Chapters 2 and 3. Notice the "shift" that occurs in Romans 3:21. What happens from there to the end of the chapter?

No one can attain or deserve the righteousness of God. No one is "righteous" by all the good deeds that they can think up and do. Being "righteous" is not a human action but a divine gift through the death and resurrection of Jesus Christ. All human beings have sinned, *hamartano*—derived from *hamartia*—which means "to miss the mark, one who keeps missing the mark in his relationship to God,... failing to meet an objective, or fulfill an obligation."[21] Sin is the condition of being human, no more and no less.

Paul returns in this section of Scripture (verses 21–25) to proclaiming the righteousness of God that Paul clearly states comes "through faith in Jesus Christ to all who believe" (Romans 3:22). In the style of posing opposites to one another typical of Paul, we feel the "questions" Paul both asks, and answers with an unconditional affirmation. Have all sinned? Yes Paul affirms unconditionally. Are all capable of being "justified freely by God's grace through the redemption that came by Christ Jesus" (Romans 3:24)? Paul says, "Yes" once again. Indeed this call for faith in Christ Jesus is as universal an affirmation of our human condition with Jesus as the previous universal condemnation of humanity without Jesus . Paul holds a "No" to human sin in one hand, and a "Yes" from God because of God's justifying power. We are made "right"—"justified" by God, not by the *Torah* of Hebrew faith, nor the works and actions of the Gentiles. Neither is enough to do what Jesus did by dying on a Cross, and rising to eternal life. "God presented him as a sacrifice of atonement through faith in his blood" (Romans 3:25). In Romans 4:25 Paul says the same idea more specifically, "He was delivered over to death for our sins and was raised to life for our justification." To be "justified" in Greek stems from the word *dikaioo*—"to declare righteous, acquit; to demonstrate or show to be just or rightness, to exercise righteousness."[22] *Dikaioo* is related to the noun *dike* as well.

> [All are] justified freely by his *grace* through the *redemption* that came by Jesus Christ. (Romans 3:24)

The motivating intent of justification is the action of redemption that brings about the state of Atonement. These three words, then—justification, redemption, and atonement—describe what Paul means in the doctrine of Justification. In Romans 3:24 Paul uses the Greek word *apolytrosis* to speak of the word translated "redemption." *Apolytrosis* also means "to release on payment of ransom, ransom, liberation, manumission, the freeing of a slave through payment of ransom."[23] Through the loving gift, or grace (*charis*) of Jesus dying on a Cross for our sins, He has freed us from being slaves to sin. Jesus has liberated us from the condition of sin to the spiritual state of Atonement with God. Atonement, *hilasterion* in Greek, means to "propitiate, to expiate, merciful," and refers back to the "mercy seat" found on "the lid of the atonement cover of the ark of the covenant made of pure gold, on or before which the high priest was to sprinkle the blood of the expiatory sacrifices on the Day of Atonement (*Yom Kippur*)."[24] Thus, literally, *hilasterion* refers to a place of conciliation—the place where God meets humanity. Through the sacrifice of Jesus' blood we are brought back to a place of conciliation—one-ness—with God. Therefore, by the actions of being crucified, and resurrection what Jesus Christ accomplished makes right our standing; such actions accomplish all the requirements of our atonement with God, making it secure.

This part of Romans has ever been its most densely packed theological conundrum. It is clear that Paul presupposes that we are all sinners before God. Why does Paul lump all human beings into one word? What really is "sin?" Is it something that I am born with, like a genetic inheritance from my parents, who got it from their parents, and so on? Is it just that no matter how "good" we try to be, or how right and just our actions may be, we cannot measure up to the perfection and righteousness of God? Isn't it disturbing that if Paul is merely speaking of our finitude, our mortality, that he uses such a loaded word as "sin?" Isn't it in some ways unfair? These questions are fair, reasonable, and relevant to our reading and theological analysis. Let us answer these questions by looking at how Paul treats the phrase "righteousness by faith" in the example of Abraham in Chapter 4, and then uses Adam and Christ as two examples of humanity as symbols of the condition of all human beings.

> Read Romans 4, paying close attention to all the phrases referring to the words "faith," "believe," and the phrase "credited to..." Romans 4:3 is the key question that Paul elaborates into a theological argument.

Paul uses Abraham as the quintessential example of faith, turning to Abraham more times in his writings than any one except Jesus Himself.[25] Quoting Genesis 15:6, "Abraham *believed* God, and it was *credited to him* as righteousness," we not only have his central question, but the key words used in this chapter. Abraham *believed* God's promise to him—"believed" being the verb of the word *pistis* (Faith) *pisteuo*. *Pisteuo* means "to have faith, trust, to be persuaded in the truthfulness or reality of."[26] *Credited* in Greek is *logizomai*—a term derived from the famous word *Logos*. It means "to reckon, impute, number...to put together with one's mind; to count..."[27] Thus the passage may be translated, "Abraham was persuaded in the truthfulness and reality of God, and it was counted and reckoned toward him by God as righteousness."

Paul uses Abraham as an example of the contrasting results of either our "works" toward God, or our "faith" and "belief" in God (verses 4–6). He notes that "works...are not credited to him [us human beings] as a *gift* but as an *obligation*. God cannot be brought under the constrictions of "obligation" to us, because our salvation is a "gift" from God. A "gift" is "grace, a benefit, favor...causes joy, pleasure, that which creates delight in the recipient or observer"[28] in Greek—*charis*. When one is working toward salvation one cannot receive the pleasure, the joy, or delight that comes from believing in God's grace. Works toward righteousness implies that we are attempting to place God under an "obligation" to save and justify us! Righteousness is a grace, a gift; not of the same order as "obligation"—*Opheilema*—"to owe, debt, that which is owed, which is strictly due."[29] The gift of God—our justification—is attained through trust (*pisteuo*) rather than works.

Paul notes that it is neither circumcision nor the *Torah* that enables us to receive the gift of justification. Rather, it is receiving the "promise"—*epangelia*—"a legal term denoting a summons or promise to do or give something...the thing promised, a gift graciously given, not a pledge secured by negotiation."[30]

Read Romans 4:9–15.

The promise of God—that Abraham's heirs would be as numerous as the stars of the heavens—Paul sees as a grace guaranteed "to all Abraham's offspring," to the Jew and the Gentile who have "the faith of Abraham" (4:16–17). Here Paul begins his long and extensive reinterpretation of both the strength of "the law" and of how it also brings about God's "wrath." Paul uses a hyperbole—exaggeration—to demonstrate how important faith is, in contradistinction to observance of law only (verses 14–15). This sounds very condemning of the Jewish *Torah* and all those who follow it. That is not Paul's point; however, because he is trying to establish the supremacy of trusting in the gift of God—our justification through faith. The point is that Abraham is the father of all who have faith, the "father of many nations," and not merely the father of Jews only.

Did you understand this last section? Reread and discuss each term carefully, allowing for the different translations to effect different interpretations. Afterward, continue reading by focusing on Romans 4:18–25.

For Paul faith is so important that it establishes the sacred quality of hope. Hope—*Elpis* in Greek—means "expectation, prospect. Subjectively, the inner, psychological sense of hope; confidence, eager anticipation,...longing, or aspiration of the heart."[31] Hope enabled Abraham, although he was so old that he was "as good as dead—since he was about a hundred years old—and that Sarah's womb was also dead" (4:19) did not waver in faith, but rather was "strengthened in his faith and gave glory to God" (4:20). Hope enabled Abraham to be completely and absolutely persuaded that "God had the power to do what he [God] promised" (4:21). Such a faith is that toward which we also ought to aspire, in Paul's mind. For church folks, we must exercise hope that God will be God, and that God can do all that God promises to do, despite whether we "see" the results or not. Such is the long view, the future perspective of hope.

Read Romans 5.

Romans 5 completes the first section of Romans with a paean of praise to the glories of grace the believer experiences through all human conditions. Justification creates a righteousness that is not merely "forensic" or the legal term concerning an objective and ethical state standing at a distance from the heart. Justification is also eschatological—an orientation of hope toward God's future judgment as affecting our present walk with the LORD.[32] Thus justification has the eschatological quality known as hope. Hope enables a proper orientation to both the present ethical and spiritual reality of righteousness, and the future judgment of God.[33]

Black Churches have been centers of eschatological hope. From the ceaseless moans and cries of African slaves longing for the day of their release from hard bondage to contemporary church folks demanding an end to DWB (Driving While Black), and its corrosive social effects. Hope has been, and ever shall be, one of the fundamenta of Black Churches experience.

Thus Christians can rejoice even in the midst of persecution and sufferings. This was a timely note to first-century Roman Christians whose lives were harried with the turmoil of government-inspired and Emperor-directed persecution toward their religious beliefs:

> Not only so, but we also rejoice in our sufferings, because we know that suffering produces perseverance, perseverance character, and character hope. And hope does not disappoint us, because God has poured out his love into our hearts by the Holy Spirit whom he has given us. (Romans 5:3–5) (NIV)

## Adam and Christ

God has justified us through Jesus Christ by the sending of God's Son, so that we, the children of Adam, are given the overflowing gift of grace and life from the second Adam—Jesus Christ. Romans 5:12–21 elaborates the two "men" who determine our spiritual inheritance. On one side is "Adam," through whom sin has entered the world

(Romans 5:18), and who brought death, and condemnation (3:15–18). "Christ," on the other hand, through his death brings overflowing grace, life, and release from the sure judgment of God against Adam's "trespass" (Romans 5:15, 17). While "Adam" created a reign of death "from the time of Adam to the time of Moses"; Jesus Christ brings into being a new age, the age of grace:

> But the gift is not like the trespass. For if many died by the trespass of the one man, how much more did God's grace and the gift that came by the grace of one man, Jesus Christ, overflow to the many! Again, the gift of God is not like the result of one man's sin; the judgment followed one sin and brought condemnation but the gift followed many trespasses and brought justification. For if, by the trespass of the one man, death reigned through one man, how much more will those who receive God's abundant provision of grace and of his gift of righteousness reign in life, through the one man, Jesus Christ. (Romans 5:15–17) (NIV)

Through the justifying work of Jesus Christ the influence and power of grace absolutely cancels the power of sin. Paul again turns to the role of the Law to see how it increases the intensity and awareness of sin. Yet, despite the power of sin, Paul also uplifts the power of Christ to cancel sin's power. This is a theme that Paul continues as he speaks about sanctification in the next section:

> The law was added so that the trespass might increase. But where sin increased grace, grace increased all the more, so that just as sin reigned in death, so also grace might reign through righteousness to bring eternal life through Jesus Christ our Lord. (Romans 5:20–21)

## Sanctification: Conflict of *Sarx* (Flesh) and *Nomos* (Law)

Romans 6 and 7 flesh out how the Christian is obligated to move toward righteous living, and away from misinterpretations of the concept of righteousness by faith in such a way that cancels out ethical living. Righteousness by faith may be misinterpreted by twisting one's interpretation of the "increase of grace" as license to a way of life that leads to *anomie*—lawlessness. Just because our righteousness by faith has been a gift of grace from God, and we had nothing to do with its establishment, Paul does not want Christians to believe that they can continue sinning in order for grace to "increase" as well!

Paul counters living lawlessly (*anomie*) by offering a more apt contrast—the difference between "death" and "life." He notes that because one is "dead to sin" one is created to be "alive in Christ." Paul uses the ritual of baptism as a symbolic journey of death and resurrection to life. Thus baptism itself is a ritual enactment of our death to sin, and rising up out of the waters of baptism as living the new life in Christ:

> What shall we say then? Shall we go on sinning so that grace may increase? By no means! We died to sin; how can we live in it any longer? Or don't you know that all of us who were baptized into Christ Jesus were baptized into his death? We were, therefore buried with him through baptism into death in order that, just as Christ was raised from the dead through the glory of the Father, we too may live a new life. (Romans 6:1–4)

Believers not only have "died with Christ," ritually in baptism, but are actually "dead to sin" insofar as they now live a justified life. Paul fervently insists that baptism unites believers to Christ in both His death and His resurrection (Romans 6:5–7).

Moving on, Paul intensifies the difference between being "dead to sin" and "alive in Christ" by insisting that we are always enslaved by either sin's demands or enslaved to righteousness of God (Romans 6:15–18):

> What then? Shall we sin because we are not under law but under grace? *By no means!* Don't you know that when you offer yourselves to someone to obey him as slaves you are slaves to the one you obey—whether you are slaves to sin, which leads to death, or to obedience, which leads to righteousness? But thanks be to God that, though you used to be slaves to sin, you wholeheartedly obeyed the form of teaching to which you were entrusted. You have been set free from sin and have become slaves to righteousness. (NIV)

In contemporary U.S. society we do not think about slavery except as something that used to be an evil practice that afflicted American history. Black Church folks react strongly to any language that suggests that we are "slaves" to anything! The pain and destructive legacy of our centuries-long servitude in bondage is still far too close for this imagery of slavery to be embraced very closely. Yet it gives one pause to consider that what Paul is really saying is that whatever impulses we obey we become enslaved to by the force of habit. If we obey the impulse and choice to disobey, then we are slaves to sin. If we obey the impulses and actions of righteousness, then we are God's slaves. A slave must obey the master, so this verse really helps us to focus on who is the master of our lives—God or sin?

Paul moves on to indicate that he recognizes that such analogies of baptism into death, rising to life, and slavery are but "humans terms" because of our weakness in our "natural selves" (Romans 6:19). The Greek word for "natural selves" is the famous word *Sarx*. The *Sarx* is literally the "flesh of a living creature." Symbolically, however, the Bible uses the term *sarx* to refer to the "infirmity of human nature (Hebrew 5:7); the corrupt nature of man subject to filthy appetites and passions."[34] Paul recognizes that the Christian begins where all others remain—as *sarx*—the weak spirituality of a corrupt nature that follows the impulses of its passions and appetites. Sanctification begins where we are, not some ideal, abstraction. Paul extends the slavery analogy in verses 19–23.

> Read Romans 6:19–23. Be careful to note how slavery to sin leads to "impurity and ever-increasing wickedness," whereas slavery to God's righteousness leads to "holiness" (verse 19).

Paul draws out the contrast of *sarx*—the weakened natural selves that are enslaved to "*impurity* (*akatharsia*) and *ever-increasing wickedness*, (*anomie*)" with the "*righteousness* (*dikaiosyne*) that leads to *holiness* (*hagiasmus*)." Instead of being enslaved to the "uncleanness, filth...moral uncleanness, lewdness, sexual immorality, and fornication"[35] that is *akatharsia*, plus the lawlessness, and wickedness of *anomie*, we are freed to live a life of righteousness and *hagiasmos*—"to sanctify, make holy, treat as holy." According to James R. Edwards of the NRSV, *hagiasmos* may be understood as the sanctification that translates into "the ethical transformation that results from the saving grace of God once sinners (5:8) and enemies (5:10) have been reconciled and granted righteousness for sanctification."[36] *Hagiasmos* is associated in English parlance with the word "saved." Hence becoming righteous and holy presents sanctification as being and acting like one who is "saved." Church folks like to talk about being "saved," but do we really know what that means? It means being a slave to righteousness to use Paul's words.

Paul uses the language of freedom to explain why his rhetoric of enslavement is so important. We have been freed from enslavement to sin. "When you were slaves to sin, you were free from the control of righteousness...But now that you have been set *free* (*eleutheros*) from sin, and have become slaves to God, the benefit you reap leads to holiness, and the result *is eternal life* (*aionos zoe*). While we believed ourselves to be 'free' from the fetters and bonds of obedience to God's ways, we were actually slaves to sin. Instead, through sanctification we become the inheritors of *aionos zoe*, or 'eternal, everlasting, ageless, perpetual life."[37] We are freed from "the wages of sin" that is *death* (*thanatos*)—"to die, death, natural and spiritual death, eternal death...which implies everlasting punishment"[38]) to enjoy the benefits of a sanctified life. By laying out these contrasts Paul makes clear just what the exact benefits of sanctification are.

Romans 7 is one of the most famous chapters in Romans because it speaks about the conflict within Christians between knowing sin and recognizing it as being wrong, and doing what is right. So doing, Paul presents a thick description of the moral and spiritual dilemma of the unspiritual, or carnal Christian. Sanctification is that process of becoming more holy—more like God. To live a sanctified life, however, is impossible for a carnal Christian because that person remains living under the influence of the *Sarx*—the antispiritual, natural nature of human beings.

Read Romans 7:7–25. Pay close attention to verses 14–17

In verse14 Paul recognizes the Law as being "spiritual" but himself as being "unspiritual." To be "unspiritual" in Greek is *sarkinos* or "fleshly, of the body." This *sarkinos*-being is "sold as a slave to sin." The *sarkinos* human being is a Christian who knows what to do that is right, but does not have the power to do the right thing that they want to do.

> I do not understand what I do. For what I want to
> do I do not do, but what I hate I do. (Romans 7:15) (NIV)

Since he recognizes that what he is doing is wrong, Paul insists that he recognizes the Law as being good, since the Law informs him of his sinfulness. Yet Paul believes that sin has so distorted this consciousness as to having "taken advantage" of the law, and then using one's awareness of what is right and wrong against one's self. "For I have the desire to do what is good, but I cannot carry it out" (verse 18b).

This moral dilemma is, at the same time, a spiritual dilemma. It is unbearable because of the frustration of not being able to do what one knows is the right choice and action:

> For what I do is not the good I want to do; no, the evil I do not want to do—this I keep on doing. No if I do what I do not want to do. It is no longer I who do it, but it is sin living in me that does it. (Romans 7:19–20)

Paul lays the blame on "another law at work in the members of my body" that is "waging war against the law of my mind" (Romans 7:23) This "another law" is sin, and is so potent that Paul believes it is "…making a prisoner of the law of sin at work within my members" (7:23b). Paul cries out in anguish, "What a wretched man I am! Who will rescue me from this body of death?" (7:24). Yet and still he can give praise even though he is frustrated. "Thanks be to God—through Jesus Christ our Lord" (verse 25). Paul recognizes that in his "mind" (the *nous* that is "the seat of emotions and affections, a way of thinking and feeling, attitude, and moral inclination"[39]) he is a "slave to God's law, but in my *sinful nature* (*sarx*) a slave to the law of sin" (verse 25b). According to the *Key Study Bible* Paul likes to contrast the *nous* with the *sarx* since the *nous* is the place where God's law resides as represented particularly in the conscience.[40] The old expression "mind over matter" comes to mind, yet Paul says that the "matter" or *sarx* can have control over our "mind" even as the mind seeks to control the flesh. Paul is reminding us that even though God's law may be within us, we can still be enslaved to sin because we need more than a mind stayed on Christ. Sanctification involves recognizing this cycle of desire and failure, and how we need something more than mere desire to become holy. How do we overcome this quandary? How are we to be rescued from this cycle of moral and spiritual failure, even as we seek to do what is good and right? Holiness is not a wish, it cannot be accomplished without an intervention of God's Holy Spirit.

## Glorification: The Triumph of *Pneuma* over *Sarx*

Romans 8 "answers" the dilemma of Romans 7. Paul sees the way out of the anxious dilemma of being influenced by the *Sarx* by the Christian spirit being set free to be filled with the *Pneuma*—the Holy Spirit.

Read Romans 8:1–17. Notice the contrast between the "law of sin and death" and "the law of the Spirit of life" (8:2)

In Romans 8 Paul demonstrates how the frustration of sanctification is having a "mind set on the *flesh* (*sarx*)", rather than having a "mind set on the *Spirit* (*Pneuma*)" (Roman 8:6). The *sarx*-driven mind leads to frustration and "death"; whereas the mind that is filled and guided by the Pneuma is enabled to experience "*life* (*zoe*) and *peace* (*eirene*)" (8:6). *Zoe* is a Greek word meaning "the principle of life in the spirit and soul" as distinguished from "*bios* which is physical life." *Zoe* is the nobler word, expressing all of the highest and best which Christ is, and which He gives to the saints."[41] The Holy Spirit grants us the most noble, exalted, and blessed form of life that there is. Not only *zoe*, but *eirene* —which means "peace, rest, the opposite of strife, denoting the absence or end of strife... a state of untroubled, undisturbed well-being."[42] With the *eirene* of the Holy Spirit living in us, we live life to its fullest in a state of untroubled, undisturbed blessedness. Now let's not misunderstand this state as being a kind of Christian "high!" It is an active state of being able to cope with whatever comes in our lives, whether trouble or good times.

How can we live in such a blessed state? Paul makes it clear that the *Sarx* has no place in truly sanctified Christians:

> However, you are not in the flesh but in the Spirit, if indeed the Spirit *dwells* in you. But if anyone does not have the Spirit of Christ, he does not belong to him. (8:9) (NASB)

Paul uplifts the indwelling of the *Pneuma* in our lives. The Spirit "dwells"—*oikeo* in Greek—meaning "to inhabit, to dwell or cohabit"[43] within the "house" of our bodies, minds, spirits, and soul. In other words, God's *Pneuma* cohabits within our bodies and spirits. The indwelling of the Spirit is key for Paul, because it endows the Spirit-filled Christian with (1) no condemnation because of the depredations of the *Sarx* and sin (8:1–3); (2) a "walk" with God (8:4–5); (3) "life and peace" (8:6); (4) an end of hostility to God, and proper subjection to God's will (8:7); and (5) an ability to please God (8:8–9).

Glorification is the result of our sanctification. It is the proper fulfillment of a sanctified life. One cannot be glorified if one is not sanctified—filled with the indwelling presence and direction of the *Pneuma*. When one is "in Christ" and "in the Spirit," then one is led to *ago* in Greek, 'to lead, to lead along, to bring, carry, remove... translated to bring, to lead gently and without violence…'[44]] by the Spirit of God" (8:14). Paul states that such that are "led by the Spirit" may be called "children of God" (8:14b). As God's Children, we are granted freedom from the "spirit of slavery" that possesses, determines, and undermines all others. In fact, for Paul, we are God's Children because we have been granted "a spirit of *adoption* (*huiosthesia*—"receiving into the relationship of a child, a son…filial relationship..denotes the adoption as it regards the future"[45]). Being adopted into God's family with Israel, Christians are given the privilege of crying out to God "*Abba*, father!" or "Daddy, Daddy!" Such are the intimate words that come from being led by the *Pneuma*. We are God's children, God's sons and daughters, and intimately bound to God alone. Sin, and all of its effects, are being "put to death" within us.

Read Romans 8:12–17.

Take care to notice how Paul lists a progression of intimacy that leads to glorification. The progression moves us from slavery to sin to the status of adopted sons and daughters (8:12–15). Then Paul uplifts the rights of children of God to become "*heirs* also and *fellow heirs* with Christ, if indeed we *suffer with* Him in order that we may also *be glorified with Him*." (8:17). An "heir" in Greek is *kieronomia* refers to the one who gains an inheritance; while "fellow heirs" are *sugkieronomos* refers to "an heir, one who has a lot or who is allotted something. One who participates in the same lot, a joint heir. Refers to a personal equality based on equality of possession."[46] Isn't this wonderful? Scripture states that we are called to become children of God—sons and daughters who are also the heirs of God's promises, power, and future glory with our Elder Brother, Jesus Christ. Yet the new status we are offered is not free of a painful duty and a rugged obligation. We are called to the highly exalted status of adopted Children of God because we willingly "suffer with" (*Sumpascho*—to suffer together with, related to "sympathy") the same sufferings that our Elder Heir, Jesus, suffered. If we willingly suffer as Jesus Christ was made to suffer, Romans 8:17 promises that we will be "glorified together with Him." This is a "hard saying." It holds out a promise and then, seemingly, makes it impossible for us to attain. After all, how many of us are really willing to suffer unto death, be tortured, and willingly experience such physically destructive pain as Jesus of Nazareth? Certainly the history of most Black Churches is replete with such sufferings. But is that what this passage is really asking?

Perhaps it is asking us to have both a willing spirit to go through anything for our faith, including suffering for what we believe. The Roman Christians that Paul wrote to were suffering lethal persecution from the Roman Emperor, and the Gentiles of Rome. They certainly understood what it meant to "suffer with Christ," because everyday they had to cope with their Christianity in ways that could end their lives. We here in North America live in a land of "more-or-less" religious tolerance, so we do not fear suffering unto death as did the Roman Christians of Paul's day. Yet this "word" leaps out at us, challenging church folk to "get real" with their faith, and stop playing around with Jesus Christ as a Sunday-only experience.

This "hard saying" calls us to be glorified with Him—*sundoxaco*—which means bringing together the words sun "together" with *doxazo*—"to glorify, or "to glorify together." Let us examine the rich word *doxazo* in order to unveil the mystery of the term "be glorified..." *Doxazo* means

> To recognize, honor, praise, invest with dignity, give anyone esteem, or honor by putting him into an honorable position... When Christ is said to be glorified, it means simply that His innate glory is brought to light, made manifest.

Paul considers "... the *sufferings* (pathema—"afflictions... sufferings of the saints because of Christ"[47]) of this present time are not worthy to be compared with the *glory* (*doxa*—commanding appearance, recognition..embraces all that is excellent in the divine nature"[48]) that is to be revealed to us." What a testimony of Paul's faithfulness to his calling as an apostle, especially when we consider that he wrote this letter while being under the restraints of imprisonment!

Read Romans 8:17–27.

Notice in this passage how Paul connects all of creation to the future manifestation of our glorification. Creation waits for us, the children of God, to be "revealed" (*apokalypsis*—to reveal, uncover, revelation, unveiling, disclosure[49]). This *apokalypsis* of us has spiritual and eternal consequences for "creation" because it was subjected to the "frustration" (*matelotes*—"vanity, futility, meaninglessness, worthlessness... the absence of true purpose and meaning"[50]) of paying the price for Adam's sin. Thus the true purpose of creation, for itself as well as for us, is in a period of "frustration" even as both we and creation live in a "hope that the creation will be liberated from its bondage to decay and brought into the glorious *freedom* (*eleutheria* "liberty, latitude, privilege, autonomy, independence, generosity"[51]) of the children of God" (8:21).

Although much can be said about the connection of creation's liberation with our sanctification and glorification, verses 22–27 let us know that what we are now experiencing of the outpouring of the Holy Spirit within our hearts and spirits is but the "*first-fruits* (*aparche* meaning "the first ripe fruits... to the gifts of the Holy Spirit as a foretaste of their eternal inheritance"[52]) of the Spirit" (8:23). Thus the riches of our personal and group experiences of the blessings of the gifts of the Holy Spirit in the midst of us in worship is just a "foretaste" of what it will be like on the eternal plane of existence. No matter how well we prophesy, teach, preach, administer, or even speak in tongues—all these are still but a "foretaste" of the full measure that God has set in store for us. One cannot hear this without stepping back in wonder and awe.

> Read Romans 8:28–39. Pay particular attention to Paul's doctrine of glorification in verses 29–30. Then go on and note what a "glorified Christian life" looks like!

In many circles Romans 8:28 is one of the "favorite verses" quoted by church folk to one another, especially in times of trouble and trial. In its context, however, it is even more powerful with regard to how it connects the action of God—using all of our experiences for our good and beneficial purposes. We need to notice the progression initiated in this verse with verses 29–30. Paul points to the spiritual "fact" that God has summoned us, foreknown us, predestined us, called us, and justified us in order to ultimately glorify us. The word "called" in verse 28 is different than the word translated "called" in verse 30. In verse 28 "called" is *kletos*, meaning "invited, welcomed, appointed, summoned."[53] Thus God works together all things for those who have been summoned, invited, and welcomed by God, according to God's *purpose* (*prothesis*—"plan, a setting forth, presentation, an open display of something, purpose, resolve, design"[54]). God has a "design" and a "plan" for our lives no events can ultimately interrupt. Why? Because God has foreknown us. Foreknown is the Greek word *proginosko* from which we have derived the English word prognosticate. It means "to perceive or recognize beforehand... to grant prior acknowledgement or recognition to someone."[55] Like Jeremiah said of himself in Jeremiah 1:5, "Before I formed you in the womb I knew you." God has known all about us, and God has planned and designed our lives. This leads to the difficult word "predestined" that in Greek is *proorizo*—meaning "to determine or decree beforehand, foreordain."[56] The Key Word Study Bible helps us to gain insight how foreknowledge and foreordination operate with one another:

> Foreknowledge and foreordination proceed together. The former emphasizes the exercise of God's wisdom and intelligence in regard to His eternal purpose, and the latter emphasizes the exercise of God's will in regard to it.[57]

We are "predestined to be conformed to the likeness of the Son..."(8:29). This is a general summons, invitation, and welcome for all believers. We are foreordained to be conformed to the likeness of God's Son, Jesus Christ, whom we recognize as the "firstborn of many brothers and sisters" (8:29b).

Paul goes on to list why God's foreknowledge and foreordination is so important to the formation of a glorified life. He says that those who are predestined have been *called* (now another word for "called"—*kaleo*, which means "to call someone in order that he might go somewhere... particularly with a voice... the call of God to the blessings of salvation... associated with the sovereign will of God in human redemption"[58]]. This calling specifies the summons of God that is under the mandate of God's sovereign will.

Those whom God has called, Paul goes on, are also *justified* (*dikaioo* to acquit, made just, righteous, to exercise in righteousness).[59] We are called to do something with what God has gifted us—the making righteous of our lives since we have been acquitted of sin. So often we church folk live beneath our calling, merely going about knowing that we are saved. Being "saved" is not enough for the living out of the word justified. We are summoned to exercise the righteousness God has bestowed upon us.

Justification is not all that God has planned for us, according to Paul. Ultimately we are called and justified in order that we might be *glorified* (*doxazo*—"depicts the action involving the recognition or the bestowal of that quality or property which is manifestly excellent and highly impressive... to exalt to a position of honor or treat with honor, make glorious.")[60] Glorification is often thought of as something in the end of time only. Certainly there is the *eschatological* meaning inherent in the word. But leaving glorification in the future undercuts what Paul meant by the word. We need to remember that Paul believed that Christians were living in the End-Times during his lifetime, in the first century. He believed that Jesus would return at any time (I Corinthians 15); although he was uncertain as to exactly when He would appear. So Paul was expecting the Christians of his time to be gifted with the attainment, rigors, and beauty of glorification. If it is true that sanctification is fulfilled in glorification, then we may read this verse as saying that we are on an upward track toward God—beginning with God's justifying action by sending His Son to die for us; in the sanctifying action of the Holy Spirit dwelling with us and guiding us; and by the unveiling of that which is manifestly excellent in our lives in the action of glorification. God does not want us to be merely sanctified. No. We are called to the spiritual high ground of glorification, even right here, right now.

Secure in the knowledge of our glorification—the action of God in our lives that encompasses justification and sanctification—Paul ends Romans 8 with a rhetorical tour de force about our status as *more than conquerors*. The English phrase "more than conquerors" is the Greek word *hypernikao*—which means "to thoroughly conquer, go beyond conquest."[61] We, church folk, have operating within us the Holy Spirit-power that enables us to thoroughly conquer all and any trials that we face in our lives. By living the exalted and sanctified life of a *Pneumatikos*, and aiming toward the promise of eventual glorification, Paul reminds us that we live in the blessed state of *hypernikao*—being "more than conquerors":

> For I am convinced that neither death nor life, neither angels nor demons, neither the present nor the future, nor any powers, neither height nor depth, nor anything else in all creation, will be able to separate us from the love of God that is in Christ Jesus our Lord. (Romans 8:38–39)

We cannot continue "having church" only in the safe confines of the walls in our clean, holy places. The business of "having church" means getting messy and down "dirty" with the common, ordinary folk who have no contact with the powerful Spirit of God. Having church is more than a temporary spiritual "high" fostered by great singing and preaching—it is a movement of sanctification and glorification of the saints. It is not a "high," but rather, it is a daily exploration and confirmation of the height, depth, and width of God's love operating within the limited confines of our individual lives. Having church is an exaltation of the common, glorification of the lowly, and a summons to live out the deepest meaning of being a *Pneumatikos*. There can be no deeper spiritual challenge with a lifetime of benefits than to explore the living reality of Paul's words in Romans 8:31–39. We are not alone, we are not abandoned. As Romans 8:31b states , "If God is for us, who can be against us?"

## God's Sovereign Mystery—Israel

> Read Romans 9–11. Take care to note how Paul speaks of "the descendents of Abraham" (Romans 9:6–14) and "God's mercy" in the following verses (9:15–18); the idea of a "remnant" (Romans 11:1–6); of Christians being "ingrafted branches" (Roman 11:11–24); and the ultimate hope that Israel will ultimately be "saved" (Romans 11:25–32)

Who are these two chapters really addressing.? Why does Paul "interrupt" his explanation of the glories, privileges, and promise of being a *Pneumatikos?* What is gained by discussing the spiritual role of "Israel" insofar as justification, sanctification, and glorification are concerned? Is Paul an "anti-Semite" in some perverse manner, trying to force Jews to become Christians under the banner of the "sovereignty of God?"

Paul is vexed to the marrow of his soul with what he considers to be the "hardened heart" of Jews. Yet he extends his doctrine of the uttermost reaches of divine grace and election—justification—to Israel—the people he considers to be "his people" and His "race" (Romans 9:3). In his anguish he turns to the doctrine of the sovereignty of God to try to "explain" why Israel as a nation has not believed in Jesus as the Christ and Messiah.

I believe that this whole sequence of theological moves in the Bible ought not be viewed by Christians as condemning of Jews. It ought not be a reason to view Jews as somehow being fundamentally wrong, and perhaps even pernicious. In essence he states that everything that is "wrong" with Israel has to do with its unbelief in Jesus as Christ and its "hardness of heart." Yet Paul sees in Israel a kind of ultimate salvation upon which the salvation of we Christians (the "ingrafted branches") remain incomplete until "Israel" comes to believe as well. The discussion in these two chapters is not to "explain" the unbelief of Jews in Christ to Jews, but is rather a "special exposition on the providence of God."[62] As such it is an explanation of the need for

Christians to find their ultimate salvation as in synch with the ultimate salvation of the Jewish community.

At the same, I truly believe that such an "explanation" is heinous to Jews because it negates the traditions and history of Judaism in the post-Jesus era. I cannot defend its fundamental anti-Jewishness. I choose to see its real purpose as aiding Christians to appreciate the ongoing role that Jews, as Jews, contribute to the larger work of "salvation." Seen in this light, these chapters can be useful to having a less hostile relationship to Jews who remain Jewish.

Because it is a summons to a broader interpretation of the reason for Jews being Jewish, it is not an "interruption" in Paul's thought. Rather, it is a kind of final elaboration of the themes of "grace" and "Law."

In a way, reading this Scriptural section shows both the strength and weakness of a genuinely biblical theology. On the one hand what we find preserved in the Bible is made to serve as a truly sterling, objective "standard" from which all of our doctrinal musings are based. On the other hand, though we "believe" that God is operating in Scriptures, we have these "difficult" sections that appear to negate whole sections of humanity—be it the first chapter of Romans on homosexuals, or Romans 9–11's condemnation of Jews as being hard-hearted. I believe that God's word is carried amidst the "words" of the Bible; yet not in every sentence with the same intensity or level of inspiration. Sometimes, like David stating that he "hates them [God's enemies] with a perfect hatred" (in Psalms 139:21–22), the inspiration of Scripture arises from understanding what the authors of a text are wrestling to articulate. This cannot and does not "excuse" Scripture; but it may aid us in our quest to develop a compassionate, just, and spiritually enlivening biblical theology. As Clarice Martin, Black womanist New Testament scholar, has taught us, the Bible must be interpreted not only from a "hermeneutics of truth" (what is the truth-value of the contents of the message), but also from the vantage point of a "hermeneutics of effects" (what are the socio-political and cultural effects that a Scripture has upon the hearers and practitioners).[63] Reading Scripture from a "hermeneutics of truth" deals with questions of the universality and place of meaning in a text; while a "hermeneutics of effects" wrestles with "questions of cultural value, social relevance, and ethics."[64] While Christians may or may not view Romans 9 as "the truth," Jews can only view such a Scripture as contributing to an overall negative viewing of all Jews by non-Jews. That is an "effect" of this Scripture, no matter how much one might consider sugar-coating it to mean. Paul's argument, whether he means it to be or not, contributes to an anti-Jewish "underside" of Christian Scriptures.

## The Life of *Pneumatikos* in Community

Read Romans 12–14.

The last section of Romans we shall deal with reveals Paul's commands to Christian *pneumatikoi* as they live both in the Christian community, and the larger secular society. We shall present a rigorous exegesis of the first two verses of Romans 12, and then use them as the root and basis for the rest of the chapter.

Romans 12:1 has Paul in his gentle but firm commanding tone. He *urges* (*parakaleo* "to call to one's side…Used of every kind of calling to a person which is meant to produce a particular effect…").[65] the brothers and sisters of the Roman church to present your bodies as *living* (zao "to be alive, warm")[66] and *holy* (*hagios* meaning "holy, set apart, sanctified, consecrated, devotion to the service of Deity, sharing in God's purity and abstaining from earth's defilement".)[67] This leads to *sacrifice* (*thusia*—"the act of sacrifice or offering").[68] The act of sacrificing our bodies is "….*acceptable* (*euarestos*—"pleasing, agreeable…well-pleasing")[69] to God, which is *spiritual* (*logikos* meaning several things—"reasonable, pertaining to reason." In Romans 12:1 the reasonable service or worship is to be understood as that service to God that implies intelligent meditation or reflection without heathen practices)[70] Spoken of as *service* (*latria*—"divine service, to worship")[71] of worship. Christians who are Spirit-filled and Spirit-led are urged to offer up their very bodies as living, breathing, and consecrated offerings to God. Dedicating our bodies in this way pleases God very much because in such actions we give an intelligent meditation and reasonable act of divine worship. Devotion to God is an intelligent choice, not a coercion of a tyrannical Deity, demanding that we give ourselves up. God is well-pleased by our willingness, the willingness of the "spiritual," the *pneumatikoi*, to offer their very bodies, indeed, their entire lives to service.

Romans 12:2 expands the idea of reasonable divine service. "And do not be *conformed*" (*suschematizo*—a complicated compound word meaning "to fashion according to external form, to conform…do not fall in with the external and fleeting fashions of this age nor be yourselves fashioned to them, but undergo a deep, inner change [*metamophousthe*] by the qualitative renewing [*anakainosei*] of your mind as the Spirit of God alone can work in you.")[72] to this world. Condemning conformation to the things of this present, external reality, Paul urges another path, "... but be *transformed* (*metamorphoo*—change of form...In Romans 12:2 and II Corinthians 3:18 the idea of transformation refers to an invisible process in Christians that takes place or begins to take place already during their life in this age".)[73] How is this transformation to be effected? By the *renewing* (*anakainossis* that which is "qualitatively new." Therefore, Paul urges a "renewing or renovation of one's self in God, which makes a person different than in the past."][74] *of the mind.* This renewal is of our *mind* (*nous*—a rich Greek word used to mean "the organ of mental perception and apprehension, the organ of conscious life; the organ of consciousness preceding actions or recognizing and judging them..."].[75] This renewed mind enables an important discernment, "that you may prove what is the *will* (*thelema*—"the result of the will." Will, not to be conceived as demand, but as an expression of inclination of pleasure towards that which is liked, that which pleases and creates joy when it denotes God's will. It signifies His gracious disposition toward something...to designate what God Himself[!] does of His own good pleasure...Nowhere, however, is it a name for the commands of God as such, whether in any particular case or in general. Rather, it designates what occurs or should be done by others as the object of God's good pleasure in the carrying out of the divine purpose or the accomplishment of what He would have. That which God purposes, or has purposed, what He regards or does as good")[76] To discern God's will is to recognize "...that which is *good* (*agathos*—"good and benevolent, profitable, useful")[77] and *acceptable* (*euarestos* cf. above), and *perfect* (*teleois*—"to complete, goal, purpose...image." To be "perfect" is to be "Adult, full grown, of fully-completed growth as contrasted with infancy and childhood").[78] The transformed Christian is not to follow the fleeting external things of this age—the drive for success, material possessions, quick-and-easy love relationships—but is urged to constantly renovate her/his mind *in order to prove* to ourselves and others what is God's good pleasure, plan, and purpose. So doing, we wind up both discerning and accomplishing that which is benevolent, useful, agreeable, well-pleasing, and act as fully mature, adult *pneumatikoi.*

These first verses of Romans 12 have been one of my favorite biblical passages. As a young preteen and teenager I was always frustrated with church folk for not even trying to "renew" their minds! The pastor would turn to these verses often, pushing the folk to "get right" with Jesus. In my young reading of this passage I interpreted the verses as saying that a truly genuine and vital Christian faith was one of exciting transformation. I still believe in that meaning for these verses.

However fully we try to enact God's perfect will on this earth, we cannot accomplish it alone. Christians were not meant to try to live out the rigors of the Christian life without the spiritual succor, aid, and empowerment provided in the fellowship of the *ekklesia*—the Church. Thus verses 3–21 articulate Paul's vision of the one Body—*Soma* of Christ that is the *ekklesia*. It is an abbreviated version of what Paul has also described in I Corinthians, Chapters 12–14.

> Read Romans 12:3–21 paying close attention to the ethical commands for life in the Body of Christ.

This section begins with a warning—for no one to "think of himself more highly than he ought to think, but to think so as to have sound judgment as God has allotted to each a measure of faith" (verse 3). No one gets all the gifts of the Holy Spirit, no matter how powerful a *Pneumatikos* they are. We are many "members" of the "one body in Christ" (verses 4–5); thus we belong together, many members functioning in one accord. When one possesses the surging power of the *Pneuma* flowing through one's body, one can fall into the trap of spiritual pride, of thinking of yourself as more highly qualified, more spiritually empowered than anybody else. Paul wants us to judge ourselves with this fact in mind, that we are to recognize that each one has only been given a "measure of *faith* (*pistis*, which in this case means "belief, in general it implies such a knowledge of, assent to, and confidence in certain divine truths . . . Fidelity, faithfulness").[79]

We are called to be faithful in our particular service to the *Soma*. Paul delineates those areas of faithfulness as "gifts" (Charism in Greek)—from prophecy (verse 6) to service, exhortation, teaching, to being liberal givers and merciful (verses 7–8). Importantly for us Paul reiterates what he did in I Corinthians 13, making *Agape* (divine love) the central characteristic of all the *pneumatikoi*.

> Let love be without hypocrisy. Abhor what is evil; cling to what is good. (Verse 9)

> Read the rest of Romans 12 keeping the command of following *Agape* in mind. Read the text out loud.

Paul ends Romans 12 with an echo of Romans 8, with an injunction to be an overcomer—"Do not be overcome by evil, but overcome evil with good" (verse 21). Those who overcome evil with good are those who remember that nothing can separate them from the *Agape* of God. Overcomers are *pneumatikoi* who do more than believe that the Holy Spirit is with them and in them; they are practitioners of the Word.

Read Romans 13:1–7 and notice Paul's view of government and authority.

Notice that Paul's view of the *Ekklesia* is quite activist in the sense that a true *Soma* of Jesus Christ is busy doing something positive in this world. It serves and gives liberally, it is merciful. The *ekklesia* is supposed to be the living embodiment of Jesus Christ's care and compassion for the world—spiritually and physically. Such an activist vision of the church can seem to be somewhat mollified, and perhaps even negated by the first verse of Romans 13. Here Paul calls every *pneumatikoi* to be "in subjection to the governing authorities." To be *in subjection to* in Greek stems from the word *hupotasso* that means "to place in an orderly fashion, to order, submission, dependent position….the verb does not immediately carry with it the idea of obedience or compulsion."[80] Paul enjoins the Spiritual to place themselves in a dependent position to "the governing *authorities* (taken from the word *exousia* that means "executive power…also justified, rightly supra-ordinated power, ability, permission").[81] Paul "goes conservative" here because he was addressing Roman Christians who sat at the very feet of the Emperor of the Roman Empire. He was, in fact, ordering Christians not to be revolutionaries. He did not want them dying deliberately for any cause that had to do with the overthrow of the Empire. After all, Roman Christians were dying just because they were considered traitors to the divine-cult of the Emperor—by refusing to treat the Emperor as if he were God God's Self! Christians were already viewed as a "threat" to order by Romans. The question is not whether or not we take part in political action, but that we have proper deference to the rightly ordered power of those who govern over us. The rightly ordered power of the Emperor, for Paul, was the power that is ordained to maintain order. It is of great importance that we note that Paul does not say "have faith in governing authorities," or even "believe in governing authorities." No, Paul enjoins. Christians to give the Empire what it is *due* (*opheile* meaning "a debt which must be paid, obligation, a service which one owes anyone").[82] He called specifically for the simplest forms of recognition of the divinely ordained power of the Empire—pay taxes, give customary respect, fear, and honor (verses 6–7).

So does Paul negate Romans 12 in the first part of Romans 13? A part of me thinks that Paul sold-out, gave in to outside pressures, caved in to an overriding concern for the ongoing life of the Roman church. Yet another part of me agrees with Paul that a small, dedicated group of the Spiritual must keep a "low profile" when one is in the heart of the enemy's main territory. I believe that the ecclesial powers that canonized the Epistle to Romans recognized the revolutionary potential of Romans 12, so they deliberately emphasized the ordering and politically submissive principles that Paul expressed in Romans 13. Paul can be seen as trying to maintain some kind of unspoken balance between being spiritually political and spiritually conforming to the powers-that-be.

Christians are to owe nothing to anyone at all except the rigors of *Agape* (verse 8). Dr. Martin Luther King, Jr., put into practice what the power of *Agape* can accomplish within a political framework that oppresses some and unjustly rewards others. To owe *Agape* is not a passive acceptance of wrong, it is the active pursuit of that which builds up, heals, mends, and renders good what has been evil. Dr. King, our modern prophet, showed us that *Agape* has political consequences, but that it works within the current system to transform it, it does not seek to overthrow it. *Agape's* power is the power of transformation, a power that does not "resist" authority, but also does not simply ignore its toxic excesses. Such power is fragile yet potent because it depends upon the *conscience* (*syneidesis*—"to be one's own witness; one's own consciousness coming forward as a witness..it denotes an abiding consciousness whose nature it is to bear witness to the subject regarding his own conduct in the moral sense").[83] Conscience is that internal witness that judges our actions right or wrong. Dr. King taught us that one cannot transform an unjust and oppressive political system unless one has appealed to the conscience of those in authority. A change of conscience is a change in consciousness. It is relearning what is right or wrong. Paul wanted the Roman Christians to be preoccupied with *Agape*, not political action. In our time we have seen that being preoccupied with *Agape* has important political implications in regard to race relations. Christian political action is *Agape* action, depending on God to use our actions to transform that which is not right.

Read Romans 14 and notice how all of the chapter is based on the dictates of conscience regarding how we treat one another as mature *pneumatikoi.* Mature Christians set aside judging one another's particular foibles (eating certain foods, or observing special days) for the sake of not putting a "stumbling block in one another's way" (vs. 13). Paul is interested in building the *kingdom* (*Basileia* rule or reign) of God, which is "righteousness and peace and joy in the Holy Spirit" (verse 17).

The thick theological and ethical textures of the Epistle to the Romans can lose us if we do not keep in mind the theme of vision. Black churches, like all of the Church, need a richer and more humane vision to keep inspiring our Christian efforts. Christian work is spiritual labor that breaks out into loving action. The love of God is "spread abroad" in our hearts, yet if it remains only in our individual hearts, and not in our practical everyday actions, then we have failed to live as successful *pneumatikoi.* It is time to grow up church folk, and move from bended-knee prayers to a lifestyle of worshipful service.

## Musings on Revelation—Apocalypsis and the Church.

In order to keep the focus on a biblical exposition vision, *Bible Witness in Black Churches* confines its articulation of the Apocalypse of the Revelation to the letters addressed to the seven churches.

Read Revelations 1:17–3:22.

These letters contain that which might be called an eschatological vision. John is a visionary, and crafts his prophetic speech in letters that describe their critique of each individual church in this sense. Since space is limited we briefly note that John encouraged the various churches to be faithful in the following ways:

1. Maintain one's original, zealous love of Jesus (Letter to Ephesus, Revelation 2:4–5);
2. Maintain that faithfulness which leads to the eschatological "crown of life" (Letter to Smyrna, Revelation 2:8–11);
3. Maintain faithfulness to sound teaching and practices (Letter to Pergamum Revelation 2:12–20);

4. Renounce false prophetic teaching, and embrace the authentic authority of God (Letter to Thyatira Revelation 2:18–29);
5. Wake up from spiritual death and strengthen what remains (Letter to Sardis, Revelation 3:1–6);
6. Continue Holding fast to the Conquering Word (Letter to Philadelphia, Revelation 3:8–13);
7. Condemnation of Lukewarm Spirituality, Call to be Earnest, and Repent (Letter to Laodicea 3:14–22);

Spend time on each Church letter, carefully exegeting the passage for its important words. Do the Greek translation work. Theologize in accordance with the meticulous, step-by-step procedure that you have learned throughout *Bible Witness in Black Churches*

When we combine the theological richness of Romans and the eschatological vision of Revelation's letters, we gain something of what each one of the letters conclude when they state that believers are meant to be overcomers. As overcomers, African American church folks have been serving God and each other through slavery, Jim Crow, lynching, beatings, good times, hard loving, and low-down dirty blues. Through faithfulness and faithlessness the community still has marched on, and "the ole ship of Zion" still sails every Sunday morning. The Bible has provided an anchor and a guidepost to the faithful, "a rock in a weary land," and a mighty good Word for God's people. Black theology and the Bible need to find a way to speak new words as the Word launches new initiatives in this new century. It is an exciting time to be alive.

# Notes

## Preface

1. "*Literary criticism* tries to discover the significance of the text as we now have it...The task of literary criticism is to examine the texts' final form, searching for ways to identify important themes and thus interpret their meaning. To a great extent, every experienced student is a literary critic, reading not only to acquire information but also to recognize the author's main interests, assumptions, and message." *Understanding the Bible*, Sixth Edition. Stephen Harris (New York: McGraw-Hill, 2003), p.33.

## Introduction

1. I learned this Lutheran "triumvirate" at Harvard Divinity School under Professor Margaret Miles, *History of Christian Thought* course, spring 1983.
2. Cf. Gayraud Wilmore, *Black Religion and Black Radicalism* 3rd edition (Maryknoll: Orbis, 1998).
3. Cf. Proverbs 2:8: "He keepeth the paths of judgment, and preserveth the way of his saints" and in its negative valence Proverbs 2:12–13: "To deliver thee from the way of the evil man...Who leave the paths of uprightness, to walk in the ways of darkness."

## 1 Standing on the Shoulders of Those Gone Before

1. There are numerous other colleagues and friends worthy of mention like Randall Bailey, Allen Callahan, Abraham Smith, Demetrius Williams, Obery Hendricks, Edwina Wright, and many others.
2. Cf. Randall C. Bailey "Academic Biblical Interpretation among African Americans in the United States," in *African Americans and the Bible; Sacred Texts and Social Textures* edited by Vincent Wimbush (New York: Continuum, 2001), p.696.

3. This is the "buzz" on Internet conversation and e-mails for the past three–five years, in fact there is great discouragement and anger at an increase in a return of overt white racism in academia.
4. *Ibid*. p.597.
5. Cf. Bailey "Academic Biblical Interpretation among African Americans in the United States," p.697 and p.708 n.3.
6. *Ibid*.
7. Bailey, p.708 n.12, 13 Cf. *Ibid*. Bailey notes that he gained this knowledge from extensive reference to the scholarly works of James B. Pritchard *Ancient Near Eastern Texts Relating to the Old Testament* 2nd edition (Princeton, NJ: Princeton University Press, 1955); and James Breasted, *Ancient Records of Egypt* (New York: Russell & Russell, 1906, reissued 1962).
8. *Ibid*., p.697, 708 n.3. Robert Bennett, Jr., "Africa and the Biblical Period," *Harvard Theological Review* 64 (1971): 501–524; Charles B. Copher *Black Biblical Studies: An Anthology of Charles B. Copher*, Biblical and Theological Issues on the Black Presence in the Bible (Chicago: Black Light Fellowship, 1993); "The Black Man in the Biblical World," *Journal of the Interdenominational Theological Center* I (1974): 7–16; "The Black Presence in the Old Testament," in *Stony the Road We Trod: African American Biblical Interpretation* edited by Cain Hope Felder (Minneapolis Fortress, 1991), pp.141–162.
9. *Ibid*., p.698. Bailey is exercised about the way in which Molefi Kete Asante's Afrocentrism exemplifies this sort of thing in an uncritical fashion.
10. *Ibid*., p.708 n.5 also cf. Clarice Martin "A Chamberlain's Journey and the Challenge of Interpretation for Liberation," *Semeia* 47(1989): 105–135; "The Function of the Eunuch's Provenance for Acts 1:8c." PhD. Diss., Duke University, 1985.
11. *Ibid*., p.699, 709 n.20 Cf. Abraham Smith's extensive writings, "'Do You Understand What You Are Reading?' A Literary Cri-tical Reading of the Ethiopian (Kushite) Episode (Acts 8:26–40)"; *Journal of the Interdenominational Theological Center* 22 (1994): 48–70; "A Second Step in African Biblical Interpretation: A Generic Reading Analysis of Acts 8:26–40" in *Reading from this Place*, vol. I, *Social Location and Biblical Interpretation in the United States* edited by Fernando F. Segovia and Mary Ann Tolbert (Minneapolis: Fortress, 1995), pp.213–228.
12. *Ibid*., p.709, n.23 Cf. Bailey, "Academic Biblical Interpretation among African Americans in the United States," p.699; and "Beyond Identification, the Use of Africans in Old testament Poetry and Narratives," in Cain Hope Felder, *Stony the Road*, pp.165–184.
13. *Ibid*.
14. *Ibid*., p.709 n.25 699; Brian Blount, "A Socio-Rhetorical Analysis of Simon the Cyrene," *Semeia* 63 (1993): 171–198.; Boykin Saunders, "In Search of a Face for Simon the Cyrene," in *The Recovery of Black Presence: An Interdisciplinary Exploration* edited by Randall C. Bailey and Jacquelyn Grant (Nashville: Abingdon Press, 1995), pp.51–64.
15. *Ibid*., p.699.
16. *Ibid*., p.700.
17. In fact my education at Harvard Divinity School by Paul Hanson revealed archeological digs have shown that the ancient proto-race in Mesopotamia,

the Sumerians, revealed "Negroid features" such as full lips, large flat noses, etc!

18. *Ibid.*, p.700, 709, n.27 Charles B. Copher, "Three Thousand Years of Biblical Interpretation with Reference to Black Peoples," *Journal of the Interdenominational Theological Denominational Center* 13 (2) (Spring 1986): 223–246: idem, in *African American Studies: An Interdisciplinary Anthology* edited by Gayraud Wilmore (Durham NC: Duke University Press, 1989), pp.105–128.
19. *Ibid.*, p.709 n.28.
20. *Ibid.*, p.704, 709 n. 31 Cain Hope Felder, *Troubling Biblical Waters: Race, Class, and Family* (Maryknoll: Orbis, 1989).
21. Bailey, "Bible and African Americans," p.700. Cf. Cain Hope Felder *Stony the Road We Trod*, pp.127–145.
22. *Ibid.*, p.709 n.31 Cf. Cain Hope Felder, "Race, Racism, and the Biblical Narratives," in *Stony the Road We Trod: African American Biblical Interpretation* edited by Cain Hope Felder (Minneapolis: Fortress, 1991), p.128.
23. *Ibid.*, pp.128–129.
24. The expression "Black Chu'ch" or "Chu'ch folks" is the way in which many Black Church people refer to themselves.
25. Bailey, p.701.
26. Bailey, p.702 Vincent Wimbush, "The Bible and African Americans: The Outline of an Interpretive History," in *Stony The Road We Trod*. p.84.
27. *Ibid.*, using Wimbush outside of Bailey's argument.
28. *Ibid.*, pp.84–97.
29. *Ibid.*, p.84.
30. *Ibid.*, p.85.
31. *Ibid.*
32. *Ibid.*, p.86.
33. *Ibid.*
34. *Ibid.*
35. *Ibid.*, p.89.
36. *Ibid.*, p.88.
37. *Ibid.*, p.90.
38. *Ibid.*, p.92.
39. *Ibid.*, pp.92–93.
40. *Ibid.*, p.93.
41. *Ibid.*
42. *Ibid.*
43. *Ibid.*, p.94.
44. *Ibid.*, pp.94–95.
45. *Ibid.*, p.96.
46. *Ibid.*
47. Bailey, p.702, cf. Renita J. Weems "Reading Her Way through the Struggle: African American Women and the Bible" in *Stony the Road,* p.57.
48. *Stony the Road*, p.58.
49. *Ibid.*, p.59.
50. *Ibid.*, p.60.

51. *Ibid.*, p.61.
52. *Ibid.*
53. *Ibid.*, p.61.
54. *Ibid.*, p.63.
55. *Ibid.*, p.64.
56. *Ibid.*, p.63.
57. *Ibid.*, pp.65–69.
58. *Ibid.*, pp.70–71.
59. *Ibid.*, p.76.
60. Bailey, p.703, 710 n.52. I follow Blount's argument beyond Bailey here. Cf. Brian K. Blount *Then the Whisper Put on Flesh: New Testament Ethics in an African American Context* (Maryknoll: Orbis, 2001), p.34.
61. *Ibid.*, p.32.
62. *Ibid.*, p.32.
63. *Ibid.*, p.33, idem. Jacquelyn Grant *White Women's Christ and Black Women's Jesus," Feminist Christology and Womanist Response* (Atlanta: Scholars Press, 1989), p.212.
64. *Ibid.*, p.34.
65. *Ibid.*, p.17.
66. *Ibid.*
67. *Ibid.*, p.50ff.
68. *Ibid.*, p.19, idem. Enrique Dussel. *Philosophy of Liberation* translated by Aquilina Martinez and Christine Morkovsky (Maryknoll: Orbis, 1985), p.193. Dussel has a much more determinative view of space than do any of our authors.
69. *Ibid.*
70. *Ibid.*, p.34
71. *Ibid.*
72. Bailey, 704, 705; p.711 of Renita Weems, et al., p.711 n.72–74 Cf. Clarice Martin, "The *Haustafeln* (Household Codes) in African American Biblical Interpretation: "Free Slaves" and "Subordinate Women" in *Stony the Road*, p.219. *Haustafeln* is the German word for "Household Codes," the strongly patriarchal ordering present in Roman households present in the early church. It ranked family authority down from the highest—Father, Mother, Children, to the lowest—Slaves.
73. *Ibid.*, pp.222–223.
74. *Ibid.*, p.226.
75. *Ibid.*, p.227.
76. *Ibid.*
77. cf. Ronald C. Potter, "The New Black Evangelicals," in *Black Theology: A Documentary History, 1966–1979* ( Maryknoll: Orbis, 1979), p.307.
78. *Ibid.*
79. Cf. William Bentley "Factors in the Origin and Focus of the National Black Evangelical Association," in *Black Theology: A Documentary History*, pp.319–320.
80. Cf. a German biblical scholar's term for "life situation" or originating life community.

81. Karia Bunting is Karen Baker-Fletcher's cousin. Conversation June 26, 2004.
82. Cf. James Cone *A Black Theology of Liberation* p. 31.
83. Cf. James Cone *God of the Oppressed.* (Maryknoll: Orbis, 1997); James Evans, Jr. *We Have Been Believers: An African American Systematic Theology* (Minneapolis: Augsburg Fortress, 1992), p.35.
84. Cf. Dwight Hopkins *Down, Up, and Over: Slave Religion and Black Theology* (Minneapolis: Augsburg Fortress, 2000), pp.120–121.
85. Cone, *Black Theology of Liberation,* p.30.
86. *Ibid.*
87. *Ibid.*, pp.46–47.
88. *Ibid.*, p.69.
89. *Ibid.*
90. *Ibid.*, p.113.
91. James Evans *We Have Been Believers* p.33.
92. *Ibid.*, p.40.
93. *Ibid.*, p.40.
94. *Ibid.*, pp.40–41.
95. *Ibid.*
96. *Ibid.*, pp.42–43.
97. *Ibid.*, p.46, idem. Robert Alter *The Art of Biblical Narrative* (New York: Basic Books, 1981), p.12.
98. Biblical scholar Frank Kermode also discusses this kind of thing in the New Testament in his book called *The Genesis of Secrecy: On the Interpretation of Narrative* (Cambridge, MA: Harvard University Press, 1979), p.xi, 20.
99. *Ibid.*, p.47.
100. *Ibid.*
101. *Ibid.*
102. *Ibid.*
103. *Ibid.*, p.51.
104. *Ibid.*
105. *Ibid.*
106. *Ibid.*, 52.
107. *Ibid.*
108. Cf. Hopkins, *Down, Up, and Over* p.121.
109. *Ibid.*
110. *Ibid.*, idem. Frederick Douglass *The Life and Times of Frederick Douglass* revised edition 1892 (New York: Crowell-Collier, 1962), pp.79–80.
111. *Ibid.*, pp.168–169.
112. Cf. Dwight Hopkins *Introducing Black Theology of Liberation* (Maryknoll: Orbis, 1999), p.42.
113. *Ibid.*, p.22.
114. *Ibid.*, p.23, idem *Down, Up, and Over*, pp.193–195.
115. *Down, Up, and Over*, pp.197–199.
116. *Ibid.*, idem. James W.C. Pennington's "The Fugitive Blacksmith; or Events in the History of James W. C. Pennington, Pastor of a Presbyterian Church, New

York, Formerly a Slave in the State of Maryland, United States," in William Katz ed., *Five Slave Narratives* (New York: Arno Press, 1968), pp.82, 83.

117. *Ibid.*, p.229.
118. *Ibid.*
119. *Ibid.*
120. *Ibid.*
121. Cf. J. Deotis Roberts *Liberation and Reconciliation: A Black Theology revised edition* (Maryknoll: Orbis, 1994), pp.37–40.

# 2 The Word

1. Cf. W.E.B. DuBois *The Souls of Black Folk* (1903).
2. Professor Preston Williams is retired Houghton Professor of Social Change and Ethics at Harvard Divinity School. He was my mentor from 1982 to 1991.
3. Cf. Dale P. Andrew *Practical Theology For Black Churches: Bridging Black Theology and African American Folk Religion* (Louisville, KY: Westminster John Knox Press, 2002), p.20.
4. I use the King James because it is the version in the vast majority of Black Churches. I use it in this chapter because of its poetic intensity while recognizing that sometimes newer translations are more "accurate" in their documentation and translation. Yet I am not "bound" to the KJV, as other chapters will demonstrate by my usage of more contemporary translations.
5. Cf. Warren H. Stewart, Sr. *Interpreting God's Word in Black Preaching* (Valley Forge, PA: Judson Press, 1984), p.14.
6. This phrase is one of the favorite repeated phrases of the Grammy award winning Gospel song "On-Time God" by Dottie Peoples (1998, Malaco Recording).
7. Cf. Cecile Coquet, "My God Is a Time-God: How African American Folk Oratory Speak (of) Time," in *African Americans and the Bible* p. 514; idem; Mircea Eliade, traite d'Histoire des religions (Paris, Payot, [1948] 1959), pp.332–348, Coquet's translation.
8. *Ibid.* p.514.
9. I remember learning about how ancient Jews considered each letter of the Hebrew alphabet to be sacred when I was learning Hebrew at Harvard Divinity School, 1982–1985.
10. Conversation in my in-laws kitchen, Indianapolis, July 17, 2004.
11. Finis Jennings Dake *Dake's Annotated Reference Bible* 6th edition (Lawrenceville, GA: Dake Bible Sales, 1988), p.95.
12. *Ibid.*, p.95. Dake understands exousia as the delegated power of "every man to be saved if he wills" (John 3:16; 6:37; I Timothy 2:4; 2 Peter 3:9; Revelation 22:17).
13. Pastor Michael Jones quoted these statistics from his research on the Internet in his Sunday morning Sermon "Discipline to Study the Word," July 18, 2004 Progressive Baptist Church, Indianapolis, IN.
14. *Ibid.*

15. The term "messianic secret" was coined by the German Bible scholar William Wrede (1901) Modern scholars hold the post-resurrection aspects of Mark (Mark 16; 8–20) is a later emendation added by pious apostles.
16. Cf. Stephen L. Harris *The New Testament: A Student's Introduction* 4th edition (Boston: McGraw-Hill, 2002), pp.213–214.
17. *Ibid.*
18. *Ibid.*, p.219.
19. *Ibid.*
20. The first translation came directly from the Hebrew words, the second from Black preacher's idiom, and the third from the Dake's Bible.
21. footnote #r., Dake's Holy Bible, p.96.
22. I learned this from Prof. Elisabeth Schussler-Fiorenza in the class I took with her, "The Gospel of John" at Harvard Divinity School 1987.
23. Transubstantiation is the traditional Roman Catholic view that the wine and the bread become the body and blood of Jesus Christ, and that we eat and drink them. Consubstantiation is that we participate in the body and blood of Jesus Christ as we drink the wine and bread.—Lutherans, Methodists, etc. The Baptists believe that the Communion is a simple memorial of the Last Supper Jesus celebrated with His disciples, an ordinance He commanded we celebrate until He comes again.
24. Cf. Raymond Brown *An Introduction to the Gospel of John* edited by Francis J. Maloney (New York: Doubleday division of Random House/The Anchor Bible Reference Library, 2003), p.253.
25. *Ibid.* p.252, idem. Oscar Cullman The Christology of the New Testament (London: SCM, 1959), 137.
26. *Ibid.* p.253.
27. *Ibid.* p.255.
28. Cf. These patterns of religion are discussed more fully in Gary E. Kessler *Studying Religion: An Introduction Through Cases* (Boston: McGraw-Hill, 2003), pp.344–348.
29. *Dake Holy Bible* N.T. p.112. Footnote #h first column
30. *Ibid.* Footnote #i first column.
31. Cf. Dake Holy Bible N.T. p.113. John 15:1 footnote #g where Dake produces a very anti-Semitic opposition between the Christian true vine and the false Israel of Is. 5:1–7. I disagree strongly.
32. Brown, *Introduction to Gospel of John*, pp.226–227.

## 3 Translated Witness

1. In fact "hermeneutics" is the related field of *interpretation* that involves both strict linguistic analysis and philosophical training.
2. Some believe that the Jesus Seminar of recent years has many proponents of this belief, because they proclaim an extremely reductionist viewpoint on what can be embraced as the genuine statements of Jesus, versus those that were added on by later editors (whom they call "redactors").

3. Marcus Borg, N.T. Wright *The Meaning of Jesus: Two Visions* (San Francisco: Harper SanFrancisco, 1999).
4. The common tongue (French, German, etc.).
5. The old word for clerics, ordained persons.
6. Margaret Miles stressed this aspect of Calvin's character in both her "History of Christian Thought" and "Calvin" courses that I took at Harvard Divinity School between 1984 and 1987.
7. Spiro Zodhiates and Warren Baker *Key Word Study Bible* (NIV) "Old Testament Lexical Aids" (Chattanooga, TN: AMG, 1996), p.1559.
8. Meaning "belief in one God" such as Judaism, Christianity, and Islam.
9. "Belief in many gods, goddesses, and spirits" as in the religions of Egypt, Mesopotamia, Babylon, as well as modern Hinduism, Voodoo, African Traditional Religions, and traditional religions throughout the world.
10. *Encarta Webster's Dictionary of the English Language: Second Edition* (New York: Bloomsbury, 2004), p.1973.
11. *Ibid.*
12. *Key Word Study Bible*, p.1540 has the following extended quotation which describes the controversy and complexity of translating almah and parthenos: '*Almah.* virgin, maiden, girl. One of the most controversial words in the entire OT because of its use in Isaiah 7:14 and its connection with the virgin birth of Jesus Christ. Almah occurs only nine times. Two are musical notations (1 Chronicles 15:20 and the title of Psalm 46), perhaps referring to young female singers, soprano voices, or others singing in a falsetto voice. The term appears in Genesis 24:43, in reference to Rebekah, who was clearly a virgin (Genesis 24:16). In Exodus 2:8 it is applied to Miriam, who was still living in her father's house, and presumably unmarried; it is probably safe to assume that she was a virgin. The occurrence in Psalm 68:25 does not specify whether the girls were married or unmarried; they were old enough to play tambourines in the solemn religious processions to the Temple. The usage in Proverbs 30:19 may refer to sexual love. There is nothing in the context of the Song of Songs 1:3 that indicates whether or not the maidens were virgins. The term parthenos that was used to translate 'almah in Isaiah 7:14 in the Septuagint, was used of both a virgin and a nonvirgin in the Septuagint and in earlier Classical Greek.
13. *Encarta Webster's Dictionary,* p.1973.
14. *Key Word Study Bible*, p.1510.
15. *Ibid.*
16. Modern day "Ur" is Baghdad, and "Chaldees" is Iraq.
17. *Key Word Study Bible*, p.1549.
18. Definition according to *Webster's,* p.1927.
19. A message from God carrying unwelcome news or judgment *Quest Study Bible* (NIV) revised (Grand Rapids: Zondervan, 2003), p.995 footnote for Isaiah 13:1.
20. *Key Word Study Bible*, p.2124.
21. *Ibid.*, p.1685.
22. *Phone* in biblical Greek, *Ibid.*, p.2124.

23. Cf. Jacques Derrida and Gianni Vattimo eds *Religion: Cultural Memory in the Present* (Stanford, CA: Stanford University Press, 1996); Jacques Derrida, *Acts of Religion* (New York: Routledge, 2002); and John D. Caputo *The Prayers and Tears of Jacques Derrida: Religion Without Religion* (Bloomington, IN: Indiana University Press, 1997).
24. *Acts of Religion* "Des Tours De Babel," pp.108, 118.
25. Here I am using the KJV because Derrida uses it.
26. *Ibid.*, p.116.
27. *Ibid.*, pp.132–133.

# 4 Proclaimed Witness

1. Karia Bunting June 10, 2004 in an extended conversation about the shading of meanings about kerussen.
2. *Key Word Study Bible* (NASB), p.1847.
3. *Key Word Study Bible* (NIV), p.1676.
4. *Ibid.*, p.1648.
5. *Key Word Study Bible* (NIV), p.1598.
6. *Ibid.* pp.1677–1678.
7. *Ibid.* p.1659.
8. *Ibid.* p.1630.
9. Cf. Pastor Gerald Brooks "You are Made for This"—sermon at Grace Outreach Center, Plano, TX, July 30, 2006.
10. Cf. Study notes on Luke 14:15–24 in *Life Application Study Bible: New International Version* (Grand Rapids: Zondervan, 1991), p.2176.
11. Cf. Anthony Pinn *African American Humanist Principles* (New York: Palgrave Macmillan, 2004), p.45.
12. *Ibid.*
13. *Ibid.*, p.45.
14. *Ibid.*, p.38.
15. *Ibid.*, p.6.
16. *Ibid.*, p.7.
17. *Ibid.*, pp.xiii–xxi.
18. *Ibid.* p.xx.
19. Anselm *Proslogion.*
20. Pastor E.L. Brunner, Macedonia Baptist Church, Dallas, Texas Sunday Morning sermon "Putting It Into Practice When You Just Want to Put It Away." June 10, 2004.

# 5 Empowered Witness

1. My spouse, colleague, and most fervent critic, Karen Baker-Fletcher, wrote about Anna Julia Cooper's notion of "coming to voice" in her Harvard Dissertation *A Singing Something* (Minneapolis: Scholar's Press, 1992).

2. *Key Word*, p.1778.
3. *Ibid.*, p.1788.
4. Among biblical scholars there remains a lively debate about whether the phrase Yam Suf means "Red Sea," or "Sea of Reeds." While some more scientifically skeptical scholars use the Sea of Reeds definition to discount the "parting of the waters" incident as a mere *tidal* or weather event; as an evangelical I have no problem with the notion of God acting through the natural agency of "a strong east wind all night..." (Exodus 14:21) to make *either* the Red Sea (traditional interpretation), *or* the Sea of Reeds (contemporary) passable.
5. Apodictic laws are unconditional written in the form "You shall not..." in contrast to case law, or *conditional law*, which "is written with the formula." If you do something, then the punishment will be..."*The New Interpreters Study Bible* New Revised Standard Version With Apocrypha", (Nashville: Abingdon, 2003), p.115.
6. *Key Word*, p.1728.
7. *Key Word*, p.1729.
8. *Key Word*, p.1769–79.
9. *Key Word*, p.1768, 1767.
10. Cf. Gayraud Wilmore *Black Religion and Black Radicalism* 3rd edition (Maryknoll: Orbis, 1998).
11. Anthony Pinn's *Why Lord*? calls into question the adequacy of this view of Jesus and God. We shall explore this Christology later in the chapter.

## 6 Proverbs: Mother Wit and Da Streetz

1. Cf. James M. Shopshire, Ida Rousseau Mukenge, Victoria Erickson, and Hans A. Baer "The Bible and Contemporary African American Culture II," in *African Americans and the Bible: Sacred Texts and Social Textures* edited by Vincent Wimbush (New York: Continuum, 2001), p.73.
2. Stephen L. Harris and Robewrt L. Platzner *The Old testament: Aan Introduction to the Hebrew Bible* (Boston: McGraw-Hill, 2003), p.298.
3. *Ibid.* p.296.
4. Cf. Proverbs 2:8: "He keepeth the paths of judgment, and preserveth the way of his saints" and in its negative valence Proverbs 2:12–13: "To deliver thee from the way of the evil man...Who leave the paths of uprightness, to walk in the ways of darkness."
5. I spent a good deal of my teaching career in the 1990s reading the works of noted deconstructionist philosopher Jacques Derrida, and post-structuralist philosopher of power discourses, Michel Foucault. Both of these philosophers share a vivid anti-Christian bias, even though they provide credible reasons for their intellectual choices. Much theology has grounded itself in their work; however, including my own earlier work!
6. *Key Word* (NASB) p.1714.

7. Charles H.H. Scobie *The Ways of Our God: An Approach to Biblical Theology* (Grand Rapids: William B. Eerdmans), p.756.
8. *Key Word*, p.1764.
9. *Key Word*, p.1768.

## 7 Vision

1. Stephen L. Harris *The New Testament: A Student's Introduction* 4th edition (New York: McGraw-Hill, 2002), p.337.
2. *Key Word* (NIV), p.1608.
3. James R. Edwards *The New Interpreter's Study Bible: New Revised Standard Version with Apochrypha* in the *Excursus: The Righteousness of* God (Nashville: Abingdon Press, 2003), p.2011.
4. *Key Word*, p.1609.
5. Paul quotes from Habakkuk 2:4. In the *New Interpreter's Study Bible* (NRSV) a footnote reads "The quotation of Hab. 2:4 (in v. 17) is perhaps better rendered, 'The one who is justified by faith will live'—that is, God grants life to the one first made right by faith" (p.2010).
6. *Ibid.*, p.1662.
7. *Ibid.*
8. *Key Word* (NIV), p.1656.
9. Anders Nygren *Commentary on Romans* (Philadelphia: Fortress, 1949 sixth printing 1983) , p.98.
10. *Ibid.* p.1595.
11. *Key Word* (NIV), p.1576.
12. Gayraud S. Wilmore ed. *Black Religion and Black Radicalism: An Interpretation of the Religious History of African Americans* 3rd *edition* (Maryknoll: Orbis Books, 1998), p.145.
13. *Ibid.*, p.1640.
14. *Ibid.*, p.1582.
15. *Ibid.*, p.1683.
16. *Ibid.*, p.1642.
17. *Ibid.*, pp.1601–1602.
18. *Ibid.*, p.1611.
19. James Edwards says that this passage talks more about unrepented sin *Study Bible*, p.2011.
20. *Key Word*, p.1654.
21. *Ibid.*, p.1583.
22. *Key Word*, p.1608.
23. *Ibid.*, p.1591.
24. *Ibid.*, p.1634.
25. Footnote on p.2015 *The New Interpreters Study Bible* (NRSV).
26. *Key Word* (NIV), p.1662.
27. *Ibid*, p.1645.
28. *Ibid.*, p.1686.

29. *Ibid.*, p.1657.
30. *Ibid.*, p.1623.
31. *Key Word* (NIV), p.1619.
32. This distinction of "forensic-eschatological" is something beautifully articulated in Rudolf Bultmann's classic *Theology of the New Testament* (New York: Scribners, 1955), pp.270–274.
33. *Ibid.*, pp.271–279.
34. *Key Word* (NIV), p.16.
35. *Ibid.*, p.1580.
36. *The New Interpreter's Study Bible* (NRSV), p.2018.
37. *Key Word* (NIV), p.1580.
38. *Ibid.*, p.1631.
39. *Ibid.*, p.1654.
40. *Ibid.*
41. *Key Word* (NASB), p.1838.
42. *Ibid.*, p.1829.
43. *Ibid.*, p.1859.
44. *Ibid.*, p.1798.
45. *Key Word* (NASB), p.1882.
46. *Ibid.*, p.1877.
47. *Ibid.*, p.1862.
48. *Ibid.*, p.1826.
49. *Ibid.* p.1590.
50. *Ibid.*, p.1649.
51. *Key Word* (NIV), p.1619.
52. *Ibid.*, p.1589.
53. *Ibid.*, p.1641.
54. *Ibid.*, p.1666.
55. *Ibid.*, p.1666.
56. *Ibid.*, p.1667.
57. *Ibid.*, p.1666.
58. *Key Word*, p.1636.
59. *Ibid.*, p.1608.
60. *Ibid.*, p.1611.
61. *Key Word* Greek Dictionary p.2121.
62. UNew Interpreters Study Bible, p.2023.
63. Clarice J. Martin "Black Theodicy and Black Women's Spiritual Autobiography," in *A Troubling in my Soul: Womanist Perspectives on Evil and Suffering* edited by Emilie Townes (Maryknoll: Orbis, 1993), p.25.
64. *Ibid.*
65. *Key Word Study Bible* (NASB), p.1864.
66. *Ibid.*, p.1838.
67. *Ibid.*, p.1797.
68. *Ibid.*, p.1842.
69. *Ibid.*, p.1836.
70. *Ibid.*, p.1851.
71. *Ibid.*, p.1851.

72. *Ibid.*, pp.1878–1879.
73. *Ibid.*, p.1856.
74. *Ibid.*, pp.1804–1805.
75. *Ibid.*, p.1859.
76. *Key Word*, p.1839.
77. *Ibid.*, p.1796.
78. *Ibid.*, p.1880.
79. *Ibid.*, p.1867.
80. *Ibid.*, p.1884.
81. *Ibid.*, p.1833.
82. *Ibid.*, p.1862.
83. *Ibid.*, p.1878.

# Index